My God, Accept My Heart This Day

M. Bridges

My God, accept my heart this day,
  And make it always Thine;
That I from Thee no more may
    stray,
  No more from Thee decline.
Before the Cross of Him,
  Who died, Behold I prostrate fall;
Let ev'ry sin be crucified,
  Let Christ be All in all.
Anoint me with Thy heav'nly grace,
  Adopt me for Thine own,
That I may see Thy glorious Face,
  And worship at Thy throne.

Joe Kotcka

142H

DESIGN COPR. 1955 DEVOTIONAL PUBLISHING CO. LITHO' IN U.S.A.

DE VALERA

AND THE

MARCH OF A NATION

DE VALERA
AND THE
MARCH OF A NATION

MARY C. Coogan BROMAGE

NEW YORK

THE NOONDAY PRESS

TO

A. W. B.

CONTENTS

DE VALERA
AND THE
MARCH OF A NATION

KEY TO ILLUSTRATIONS

1. Eamon de Valera during World War II

2. Springville, Cross Avenue, Blackrock. Home of the de Valera family, 1932

3. Eamon de Valera's mother as a young woman

4. Mrs. Eamon de Valera, about 1932

5. Eamon de Valera at the age of 22

6. At Grosvenor Hotel, London, July, 1921. *Seated, left to right*: Eamon de Valera and Arthur Griffith. *Standing, left to right*: Count Plunkett, Erskine Childers, Laurence O'Neill (Lord Mayor of Dublin), Lily O'Brennan, Dr. R. P. Farnan, Mrs. Farnan, Robert Barton and Kathleen O'Connell

7. Eamon de Valera speaking in Wexford, spring, 1922

8. Commandant Eamon de Valera after surrender to English soldiers, Dublin, April 30, 1916

9. Eamon de Valera released after arrest by Northern Ireland authorities, November, 1924

10. New Irish Cabinet, 1932

11. Eamon de Valera welcomed to Aran Islands, 1947, by islands' oldest inhabitant

12. At 10 Downing Street, London, in September, 1953, Prime Minister Sir Winston Churchill shakes hands with Prime Minister Eamon de Valera. At right is Irish Minister for External Affairs Frank Aiken

1.

7.

8.

9.

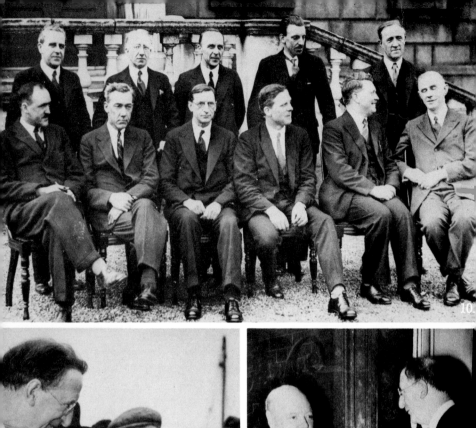

10.

11.

12.

PREFACE

SITTING around a turf blaze at the hearth of one of Ireland's old country houses is conducive to talk, and it was in such a place I thought of writing this book. First there is the drive away from the city of Dublin with the tawny sky set with pearls of sea clouds coming in for the night. Along the road of County Dublin, the skeetering car finds a track between deep meadows and beyond rises the tall, grey, stone chimney.

Within, the talk covers the face of the globe to confound the notion of Ireland's provinciality, and sooner or later words fly over the mention of Eamon de Valera, called Dev.

To honour dead heroes, which for centuries was all that the Irish people could do, is apt to be easier than to obey a living leader. Yet de Valera, within his lifetime, outgrew the legend into which the people would instinctively have turned him as the only commandant to survive the Easter rising of 1916. From gunman to vote-getter proved a hard road for him to find and a harder one to persuade others to follow. In his enormous determination for Ireland, he made the country get up off its knees and raise its head.

Apart from my original commitment of respect in undertaking a life of this man, and ultimately of devotion, the carrying out of it necessitated an eye and ear for fact. Ability to embellish the circumstance with the wish, the very penchant of the Irish mind for myth-making, is what has given us the Ireland portrayed at the Abbey Theatre and the Irishman seen on other stages. In dealing strictly with matters of history, whether national or individual history, my hope is to disclose an Ireland not so apt to be seen on the boards as in the cottage and the town house, the council chamber, university or church. So while imagination has played a part in the tracking down and the selecting of fact, the actual happening, the word written close to the moment and the incontrovertible outcome have been the criteria in my view of this man and the country he made his.

De Valera must be seen not in and of himself as a solitary

figure in the Irish picture, but as a part of the whole national
canvas dating back for centuries, peopled with a host of others,
each—though dominant as an individual—subjected to the historical coloration of rebellion, imprisonment, underground
strategy, and recurrent violence. As one figure placed in the midst
of all this, de Valera works his way toward the centre because of
an intrepidity and a staying power. Not as an old man exercising
hindsight at the middle of the twentieth century, but in 1921 as
a young man just before going on the run, he said in reference to
England, ". . . one of my earliest dreams, next to securing Irish
independence, was that there might be reconciliation between the
people of these two islands. . . ."

On one of Dublin's dark winter afternoons in 1936, the note
delivered at the door of our Merrion Square flat gave us our first
opportunity to call upon the man who was at the time more
legend than elected representative, part villain and part hero in
the Irish mind. He was then at the height of his power, still
invested with revolutionary glory but seated squarely behind
the great, dark desk of the chief executive in Government
Buildings across the Square.

Tall, smiling, informal, he rose to extend a warm hand, almost
as would a professor to university visitors from America. His
talk, beginning with reluctant recollections of his part in Ireland's
fight for freedom, quickening over details of political structure
and strategy, flowed regardless of secretarial prompting as all
light left the sky behind the dark tweed curtains at his office
window. Full of his party's ups and downs at the polls, he let
no word escape him of his personal jeopardy or as to his family,
all of which he seemed bent upon subordinating to the principles
he deemed at work in the national destiny. He did not allow his
person to be singled out for comment. And each time when we
returned to Ireland before and after World War II the man,
though growing older and more burdened, remained unaltered
in mind and thought.

If, through his political family and intimate staff, the members
of which scarcely changed over the years, he guessed he was
talking to a biographer, he gave no quarter in conversation.
Always the cause and not the individual came to his lips. By the
1950s, reminiscences of heroes he had outlived and of vicissitudes
he had surmounted brought light back into his shadowed eyes.

To see where Ireland as a nation and the Irish as a people stand in the twentieth century after seven centuries of struggle led to Eamon de Valera's door inevitably. The legend about him, proliferated by both hate and love, is less compelling than what really transpired as a result of his boyhood dream.

MARY C. BROMAGE.

Ann Arbor,
  Michigan,
    1956.

CHAPTER I

NO SILVER SPOON (1882–1905)

LATE in a lifetime filled with public affairs, Eamon de Valera rose in the Irish parliament to set straight a point about his private life. "My father and mother were married in a Catholic Church on September 19, 1881. I was born in October 1882. I was baptized in a Catholic Church. I was brought up here in a Catholic home. I have lived amongst the Irish people and loved them and loved every blade of grass that grew in this land. I do not care who says, or who tries to pretend that I am not Irish." It was in New York City at the old structure, since burned, of St. Agnes Church on 43rd Street, near Grand Central Station, that he was baptized in December 1882.

Birth and baptism records give his mother's name as Kate. Three years earlier Kate, as Catherine Coll was called, had come to America from Ireland, being then twenty-one years old and the eldest of a widow's four children. The immigrant girl, slight but purposeful of carriage, with an eagerness lighting up her even features, brought with her hopes for the kind of future not attainable at home even for those with the quickest of minds, the strongest of wills, and the liveliest of desires.

The baby's father, Vivion de Valera, four years older than Kate, was listed on his son's birth records as having been born in Spain and as being by occupation an "artist." The surname Valera was that of a high-born Spanish family known to the world at the time chiefly because of Juan de Valera, novelist and diplomat who, as it happened, arrived in the United States as Minister from Spain the year after the baby's birth. Members of the Coll family in Ireland were to link him with the baby's paternal family. Those who heard about Vivion through Kate were to recall him variously as a sculptor, a professor, an actor, a linguist, a doctor, a singer, a raconteur, but always as a gifted, educated and entertaining individual. Some said afterward his name was John Vivion de Valera and that he had come from the Basque region in Spain. Some were under the impression that he had come from South America, others from Cuba where his father

15

was a sugar planter. There were those who called him Portuguese and attributed Jewish blood to him.

Kate and Vivion's son was not baptized until he was over six weeks old. He had been born on October 14, 1882, in the Nursery and Child's Hospital on Lexington Avenue at 51st Street, the first public institution of its kind in New York. A certificate filed with the city at the time listed the baby as George de Valera, but it was not as George that he was baptized. That name was almost though not quite forgotten and never, as a matter of fact, used. The Irish custom of carrying on family names prevailed, for when he was christened it was as Edward or, in the Irish, Eamon, the name of a young uncle who had come to America with Kate. The names the sponsors signed in the church records, Mary Shine and John Hennessey, indicate that they were, like the baby's mother, Irish.

For all the mother's dreams about the new world, trouble soon beset her. Her family in Ireland got the news that Vivion was taken ill and that, in 1885, he died. Though he did not leave financial provision, Kate's grey eyes under high-arching brows conveyed a poise that misfortune did not dispel and she held herself in tightly, shielding her emotions behind an appearance of aloofness, not ready to give up when faced with having to board her child out to go to work.

Her brother Edward was having difficulties as well. In the Connecticut River valley where he found outdoor work on an estate, he was taken ill with malaria. When he decided to return to County Limerick to recuperate, he suggested to his sister that he take his namesake back with him, at least for a visit. Since the steamship lines were waging a price war, the cost of a child's passage would be only a few dollars. Kate knew that her mother would welcome the child; that her younger brother, Patrick, was at home; and that her sister, Annie, still in her teens, could help. As Edward Coll carried the two-and-a-half-year-old boy aboard the eastbound steamship, *City of Chicago*, Kate watched from the pier of the Inman Line one afternoon in April 1885, and then, alone, turned back to the metropolis which had so far fulfilled few of her ambitions, her path and that of her firstborn moving in steadily separating directions. The voyage took ten days; the supply of fresh milk ran out; but when at last the distant Irish coastline was sighted, it seemed to garland the horizon, and as the

man and little boy came on deck to go ashore on the waiting
tender they could see the verdant arms of Queenstown's bay
reaching out to meet them. They were in the old Cove of Cork
where the harbour lay under the terraces of the town rising steeply
behind it.

The Colls lived in County Limerick not many miles north of
Queenstown but well beyond the city of Cork, and a mile or so
beyond the centre of the village of Bruree. Because they occupied
one of the first of the labourers' cottages, they were considered
among the more fortunate local families. These low, rectangular
dwellings were being started by the authorities under the British
in an attempt to meet the demands of Irish farm workers. Only
an acre of land or less went with such a cottage but the rent was
a nominal tenpence a week. The Colls' door, divided across the
middle, opened onto the kitchen which, with its low ceiling and
stone floor, was the heart of the house. Across the far end of the
room was the fireplace used both for cooking and heating, and on
the inner wall were doors to two other rooms. In the corner,
a red light burned under a small shrine on the wall. There was no
running water and "Eddie" was never to forget from his later
boyhood having to carry to the outhouse a paraffin lamp, smoking
in his hand.

"I know something about these cottages," he said years after.
"I was brought up in a labourer's cottage." He soon felt at home
with his grandmother close by him. Not old in her years but with
a face resigned in spite of worries and a figure bent with hard
work, Mrs. Coll—Elizabeth Carroll Coll—wore a black shawl
over her shoulders. For generations, the Colls and the Carrolls
had lived in this part of the country and the child from America
settled into the security of belonging here. The goats and donkeys,
the flocks of sheep and the cows that trudged down the road by
the patch of front garden he learned to like, and when his Uncle
Edward left to go back to Connecticut, the child turned naturally
to his other tall uncle, Patrick. To the Colls' neighbours, who
remembered Kate from her own girlhood, her son had a surname
that sounded strange to their ears, and his pallid complexion
suggested less of his mother than the Spanish father whom they
had never seen. But so completely was Eddie adopted by the parish
priest, by the shopkeepers, and by the other children that it seldom
occurred to them or to him that he had not been born in Bruree.

His early impressions were of the soft, Limerick hills under low-slung clouds. At the cottage fireside he heard the undulating Limerick voices and smelled the astringent fragrance of smoulder-ing turf. With his fingers he could trace in its white dust on the hob while he waited for his stirabout and milk in the morning, for his potatoes and cabbage and fat bacon at dinner-time, or for his tea in the early evening. His grandmother told him stories, using expressions from the disappearing Irish language, and though she died while he was still a boy, those first words he heard from her in Irish he never forgot.

Patrick Coll, like his neighbours, was struggling to make a living, and after he married there were more in the cottage to feed. He managed to rent additional fields on which he kept a half-dozen cows and he became a dairyman. "Few of us," his nephew afterwards said of this time, "were born with silver spoons in our mouths. . . ." Much of the countryside was owned by landlords living in England to whom the tenants paid their rents. The blight upon the potato crop and the famine it had caused at the mid-century had driven thousands across the ocean, and in the village dooryards tearful farewells were still being said as grown sons and daughters left for Queenstown. The Colls knew that all was not milk and honey in America, but there was evidence that Kate and Edward were getting on when they sent for their younger sister Annie.

Though Eddie was living in childhood's detached world of its own, he could not help but hear the demands rising among the farm workers for the "three F's"—fair rent, fixity of tenure and free sale. There was talk of a Land League which the men were joining, and of a great patriot named Charles Stewart Parnell. It was in Cork, not far from Bruree, that Parnell made one of his speeches, declaring in ringing tones that "no man has a right to fix the boundary to the march of a nation." Home rule was the phrase gaining in volume and in eloquence as it was repeated by this "uncrowned King of Ireland." When Parnell, whom the boy never saw for himself, was thrown into Kilmainham Jail up in Dublin by the British, people spoke with a hardening in their voices and the talk Eddie overheard when sent on errands to the butcher's or in the sweet shop or over the scales at the chemist's dispensary was always about Ireland for the Irish. The women in their shawls said less than the men as they lugged their pails and pans of water from the pump on the village street to their sagging doorways, but their faces looked grim.

After home rule was denied by the English and after new coercion acts were imposed, Eddie felt the wave of anger that swept County Limerick. Moderate-minded families like the Colls believed in securing self-government without the use of force. His Uncle Patrick looked for action by the Irish member of Parliament from nearby Mallow who was championing the farm people, William O'Brien. For all that the Parliamentarians like Parnell and O'Brien could say or do, violence flared up early in the 1880s when British officials were murdered in Dublin's Phoenix Park by men called the Irish Invincibles, and when the House of Commons was shaken to its foundations by dynamite explosions. But all that was going on in Dublin and in London seemed far away from Bruree.

Eddie, learning quickly to read and being inclined to stay by himself, was soon living in a world populated by the old heroes in Ireland's story-books, as well as by the new heroes whose names were on all tongues. The square schoolhouse of grey-black stones to which he was sent like the other children in the parish district of Knockmore stood behind a high wall in the centre of a cobbled yard. It lay at the far end of the village where the road sloped away from the shops and post-office and divided, one fork continuing a short distance beyond the school to a towering creamery plant with a wooden water-wheel on the River Maigue. The other fork crossed over the reedy river and wound out of town to join the highway going south to Charleville and Cork. There were two classrooms, one for boys and one for girls, each having its own hearth and long wooden benches with little communication between the two rooms.

For the growing lad, Bruree, rustic and remote from the main road, held traces of the country's history. The name came from *brurigh*, meaning the fort of kings, and in the fields, earthen breastworks could still be seen. The square, stone keep standing across the river from the school on a hill was all that remained of Maigue Castle, built when Norman families held the region. It was crumbling slowly under a weight of ivy and creepers and gave substance to a shadow world into which the boy could transport himself. Irish bards, those wandering artists who had entertained the people with Gaelic poetry and song, had, until the century before, made Bruree a gathering point. The village shoemaker, whose tales Eddie heard in the Irish language about Feargus, Cuchulainn and Fionn, resembled the ancient *seanachaidhe* or story-teller.

As he progressed in school, Eddie cast his own compositions in a vocabulary that, by its grandiloquence, set him apart from his classmates. In arithmetic he could tutor older pupils. In learning about farming he tried to take an interest, marking in the margins of his study books the paragraphs to memorize. When he was fourteen, the age when his schoolmates finished their education and started farmwork, his teacher, and also the priest who knew him well as an altar boy, went to call on Patrick Coll. Both had kept in close touch with the uncle after the boy's grandmother had died. Patrick Coll, aware that his nephew had had all the schooling he could get in Bruree, was not taken by surprise at their report on Eddie's studiousness. On walks together, the boy wanted answers to all kinds of questions. At the meal table, he would prop a book by his plate, Dumas or the tales of William Wallace or Jane Porter's *Scottish Chiefs*. Sent early in the morning to the creamery, he would read as he waited, his feet dangling over the side of the cart, his head in a book until it was his turn to unload the big cans of milk. The other boys would congregate round the warmth of the boiler in the creamery yard to pitch pennies, but Eddie did not join in, only raising his eyes from his page to see who might be winning. But to send him to a school like that run by the Christian Brothers in the town of Charleville, even as a day pupil, meant expense, and there were three other children in the household to consider: Patrick, Elizabeth and Mary Coll. The boy's uncle, at the urging of the priest and teacher, nevertheless drew upon family savings and on November 2, 1896, the name of Edward de Valera was entered on the register of the Christian Brothers.

The Cork-bound train passed just behind the cottage in the morning, and the boy would catch it at the station between the cottage and the centre of the village. In comparison to Bruree, Charleville, just across the border in County Cork, seemed a bustling centre. Back from the main street, in the middle of the town, stood the Christian Brothers' high, angular building, a plain cross at its roof peak. Behind its iron fence, a religious statue faced the street on a pedestal above the paved playground. Lacking the social prestige associated with Jesuit institutions and regarded by some as for working-class children, this teaching order had a reputation for giving a sound foundation and for inculcating a virtuous disposition. The Christian Brothers had published their own Irish grammar and a number of them had played a personal part in the nationalist cause. The Bruree pupil's special interest in mathematics soon asserted itself. French he learned to read but not to speak. In geography he had to recite long lists of imports and exports from countries of which he had never heard before, like Assam. The class would be seated in front of a big map of the world and the boys would try to stump each other, "Where is Christmas Island?" Such questions seemed to him useless. Poetry he did not mind conning by heart, but his other lessons including grammar he did not like to have to get by rote. Though he disliked physical drill and marching, he pitched into sports with vim, having grown up in the enthusiasm of athletic matches in his home parish.

His first Irish history book was O'Sullivan's *Story of Ireland*, in which he read how Red Hugh, a noble Irish youth, was kidnapped and taken to sea, then thrust into Dublin Castle by the old Queen Elizabeth to escape not once but twice; and how, after Red Hugh finally got away on a winter night, his toes were cut off because they were frozen stiff. Edward followed the soldierly virtues of Owen Roe who, like Red Hugh, came from the North of Ireland, the home of as many heroes as the South. Owen Roe after winning glory in Flanders came home to do battle for Ulster against England, his men armed with long-shafted pikes.

For the boy from Bruree, the new school was at first a strain and he watched the clock for the hour until he could head for home. Without waiting for the evening train, he would either get a lift on a passing cart or walk the six miles. Once home he had cows to milk and his turn to take in cleaning out the cow-house, pitching hay, harnessing the donkey or horse. "Until I was sixteen years of age," he was to recall, "there was nothing of any kind on a farm, from the spancelling of and the milking of a cow, I had not to deal with." When he left the school grounds and got out into the open beyond the cabins and big farmhouses, his mind could run ahead as far as the road itself. His way stretched into the Galtee foothills and the roadside banks would be covered with wild pink roses and spears of bright foxglove called in Irish fairies' thimbles. From the highway he turned into a rocky boreen winding up and down past cottages of white-washed stone and thatch till he came within sight of Maigue Castle.

At home, he paid more attention to the talk between his uncle and the other farm workers, and began to turn over in his own mind the discussions about the ancient struggle between his island and the one he had never seen. Must there always be hatred? The antagonism between people of his Church and the Protestants also puzzled him. Parnell was a Protestant and a patriot. Consternation spread through the country with the downfall of Parnell and the political split that ensued. The future seemed to hinge upon new leadership. Home rule was still the watchword as the nationalists continued to sit in Parliament.

Academic awards went to Edward during each of the two years he spent at Charleville, so the Christian Brothers recommended him for one of the public scholarships recently created by an act of the British Parliament. Going away to college would, in Bruree, be rare, but on his behalf an application was submitted to Mungret, a Jesuit institution located near the city of Limerick. Since the scholarship rules required that applicants be British subjects, the fact of his birth upon American soil raised the question of his nationality. Though his mother had been a Coll of County Limerick, his father had been a Spaniard. When the Brothers got in touch with the British-appointed Attorney-General of Ireland, he was judged eligible to compete, and he won.

With the sixty pounds he was awarded, he decided to go even farther away than at first contemplated and matriculated not at Mungret but at Blackrock College run by the Holy Ghost Society just outside the city of Dublin. When he came up from the country to the Irish capital in 1898, he was a tall, thin, awkward lad just sixteen years old. On his long neck, his head was held erect and a crest of very dark, silky hair rose from his high forehead. Neither handsome nor particularly Irish-looking, his features were prominent with a long nose, an upper lip deeply indented at the centre, a wide and mobile mouth and a chin cleft with the suggestion of a dimple. An intentness and a self-restraint not common among Irish boys made his appearance arresting.

To him the trim impersonality of the campus of Blackrock College looked strange after the natural and untended countryside around Limerick. It lay a few miles south of Dublin in the suburb of Booterstown behind well-kept lawns along the main road to the port of Kingstown, in full view of Dublin Bay. The college's battlemented stone edifice had a central tower faced with a clock, and the inner courtyard was laid out in symmetrical walks around a statue banked by formal flower-beds. Against homesickness the Limerick student fortified himself by remembering the confidence the Christian Brothers had placed in him. After all, many boys and girls were leaving home in search of work to go farther away than he.

His mother had been only a few years older than he when she had crossed the Atlantic Ocean. A few years after he had been sent back to Ireland had come the news of her marriage to Charles E. Wheelwright. His stepfather, an Englishman and not a Catholic, was employed as groom by a well-to-do family in Rochester, New York, and the Wheelwrights had living quarters over the stables in the garden of the estate. Edward had heard of the birth of a half-brother, Thomas, and a half-sister, Annie, both of whom had been baptized like him in the Church of their mother, but the summer before he had left Bruree to go to college had come the news that the little girl had died as a result, it was thought, of heart trouble. To Edward this sorrow seemed remote, though he must have sensed the comfort his mother took in her faith and in her reliance upon the will of God.

For the fact that things would not seem the same at college as at home, Edward was prepared. He applied himself to his new studies with the same industry and soon caught the notice of his teachers. He was to look back upon the regimen of their college community as "an invaluable preparation for life." In examinations he continued to excel in spite of the wider competition. Every day that the schedule permitted, he donned jersey and shorts and was on the track, 220 yards round, practising the mile and the half-mile for the meets. Agility was not his only asset; he had a stubborn determination to win.

The trips which he took home from Dublin in the mail train to Charleville across the fertile midlands and past the lonely way-stations were frequent during these years when he was finding a place for himself in Dublin's larger world. Once out of the city, he could see from the train window the sights he knew so well: figures stooping to cut turf in the bogs; deep meadows where cattle waded in the grass; a distant country house. At the cottage hearth he found more signs of comfort. The passage of a land act in the early 1900s alleviated some hardships, though it did not satisfy the people. Edward's uncle with his tall, spare figure and bearded face commanded respect in the vicinity, being elected for successive terms to the local Board of Guardians. During his holidays Edward spent less time with his childhood friends playing football and hurling, and went hunting instead by himself in the hills and marshes along the banks of the River Maigue for snipe, duck and partridge. Though nothing of a fisherman, he was a good marksman and occasionally brought home with him some special rifle on which he demonstrated his skill for his uncle by taking it apart and reassembling it.

Continuation toward the University degree which he wanted after completing the prerequisites at Blackrock depended upon the help of the Holy Ghost Fathers. They considered his record brilliant, for he had led his class and in the country-wide examination given each year by the Intermediate Education Board he had placed tenth from the top. Finances were his only hindrance. The Wheelwrights in America had their own needs and were sending his half-brother to St. Joseph's School, conducted by the Redemptorist Order in Rochester. His "Uncle Charlie," as he referred to his stepfather, was easy-going and content to ride his coach-box dressed in livery and top-hat. The boy's Uncle Edward, for whom he had been named, and his Aunt Annie both had families of their own in America. The Holy Ghost Fathers, entering into the situation, gave him a part-time appointment as a junior master at Blackrock College and in 1901 he enrolled in the institution in Dublin then known as the Royal University, which was preferred by the young man's Church to Trinity College.

At the Royal University, the classical programme was still in full sway but the reforms being demanded by nationalists included instruction in the Irish language. A Royal Commission designated to study the curriculum was holding hearings and a professor named Dr. Douglas Hyde appeared before the commissioners with a comprehensive proposal, namely "the aim to reform all education in Ireland, from the National Schools to the University, upon native and autochthonous lines." Some such steps were imperative, Dr. Hyde was warning, because University graduates were leaving the country by the first boat to seek their fortunes elsewhere.

The city of Dublin which the student from Bruree came to

know little by little was emerging at the turn of the century in all the freshness of its own local colour and was trying out its wings after long confinement in the British chrysalis. The political disillusionment after Parnell was being superseded by a cultural regeneration, and the literary revival was getting off to a flying start. The patriot Thomas Clarke, whom the British had arrested for nationalist activities the year that Edward was born, was released after his long imprisonment and this gave a spur to the independence movement. The Abbey Theatre was burgeoning, but the Abbey people, those for whom Ireland was a green and poetic field, like William B. Yeats, George Moore and George Russell, moved in a set apart from the strictly disciplined, work-a-day world of Edward de Valera. Whimsical Irish plays written by Dr. Hyde such as *The Tinker and the Fairy* were being performed by enthusiasts in the revival of native arts, and a winsome girl with light hair and upraised eyes played the part of the fairy. She was very young and her name was Janie Flanagan, though she preferred the Gaelic version of Sinead ni Fhlannagain.

All this was going on behind the high wall of Moore's garden, a stone's throw from the Royal University, but the student from Blackrock, hurrying to lectures and conferences, had little contact with actors and actresses, with poets and playwrights, or with any of the prime movers in the cultural renascence. Reading matter more to his taste than plays or poetry appeared in the articles in the *United Irishman* written by an obscure nationalist author named Arthur Griffith. In Griffith's series entitled "The Resurrection of Hungary—A Parallel for Ireland" coming out in 1904, Edward could follow the analogy drawn for Ireland from the time when "Hungary had not five journals in which a word of the Hungarian language was permitted to appear . . . no modern literature . . . no manufactures of moment. . . ." This was the year that he completed his University work with a pass degree. Though this indicates that his standing was not at the top of the class, his University record was regarded as creditable by the Holy Ghost Fathers in view of the fact that he spent several hours every day as junior master in the Intermediate College. They had promoted him to teaching their older pupils. In his cap and gown, the twenty-two-year-old holder of a Univeristy degree now looked the part of the intellectual which he had become. The tall, stiff collar which was then the style and the heavy black robe with its furred hood set off his eager, expectant outlook upon the world. What his clean-shaven and youthful countenance lacked in roundness and regularity of feature was compensated by a sharpness of gaze and a firmness in the line of his jaw.

He had his way to make in life, a way he had to make essentially alone. Teaching was something in which he already had experience and the teacher's position was a respected one. His first full-time appointment in this field came through his Blackrock superiors. They conducted another boys' boarding-school, Rockwell College, in County Tipperary. Here the University graduate was appointed to instruct in mathematics and physics, and though the salary was low he tackled his new job with the idea that the virtues of a Catholic education could be best taught by example. The grounds and buildings, lying in the lee of the Galtee Mountains, reminded him by their symmetry and seclusion of Blackrock, but overshadowing all were the gentle mountains enclosing Ireland's Golden Vale near his boyhood home. Outside the classroom as well as in he won the respect of the boys in their games and contests on the athletic field. In the advanced classes, his students were soon taking exhibitions and prizes.

Eleven miles away was the town of Cashel to which he often bicycled, and close to the centre of this town rose the Rock of Cashel like a Celtic acropolis. Its limestone sides once fortified by Brian Boru still supported the greying ruins of King Cormac's church, floored with grass and lighted from the heavens above. None of the elegance was gone from the slender cathedral windows tapering upward towards the open air, and he could spend his free hours climbing about in the ruins and exploring the round tower that still stood guard above the Rock. With the local family that ran a public-house in the row of old shop fronts near the foot of the Rock he became acquainted and was to keep alive a friendship which he formed with the daughter of this family long after their ways had parted.

Dublin, once he was away from it, remained vividly in his mind and seemed more than ever the centre of all that was promising for his country's future and his own. He could not afford to remain at Rockwell without seeking advancement. So in 1905 he left County Tipperary, after one year, to return to the city that had become home to him, his intention being to find a way to continue his own development as a teacher.

CHAPTER II

CLIMBING THE PAINFUL STAIRS (1905–1914)

AT Carysfort Training College in Blackrock where young women were prepared to teach primary classes, Edward de Valera settled into a steady position after he returned from County Tipperary. Carysfort's gaunt, brick façade with its sharp gables and high, narrow windows was located behind an open grass park on a side road near his own college. Those in his classes who took pleasure in the discovery of knowledge were, for him, the ones who had a positive "vocation" as teachers. Making lessons attractive at the sacrifice of hard, routine work he deplored, on the grounds that children must be made to like their work in spite of its drudgery.

Beside his work at Carysfort, he taught mathematics, Latin and French at other Church schools as well: at Holy Cross College in suburban Clonliffe; at the Loreto Convent and University College in St. Stephen's Green; at the Dominican Convent in another section of the city; at Belvedere, the Jesuit college; and he substituted at St. Patrick's College in nearby Maynooth where boys studied for the priesthood. He believed in no frills at the expense of the rudiments and tried, in drawing up arithmetic problems, to take topics close to his students' lives, remembering how useless some of the examples he had been given had seemed to him. As his pupils began to take exhibitions, the Holy Ghost Fathers felt proud of their protégé. He was a versatile and energetic individual. On the playing fields he supervised the boys' athletics. The Chief Secretary for Ireland, Augustine Birrell, reported upon visiting one of the schools that he saw this tall, dark, young teacher playing the piano for a particular ceremony.

In what free time his work left him, he was developing wider interests in what was going on around him in Dublin during this first decade of the twentieth century. The older people were sitting back in the belief that the Irish Parliamentary Party as led by the senior statesman, John Redmond, would eventually secure home rule for them, but the younger people saw more promise in a new organization called Sinn Fein, "Ourselves Alone," formed by

Arthur Griffith, the nationalist whose writings the young teacher had read. De Valera became a member. Sinn Fein did not advocate force to effect changes nor did all of its members believe that the country should necessarily abandon the idea of monarchy and become a Republic, but it did hold that Ireland's elected representatives should cease to sit in the English Parliament, that the Irish should have not only their own legislature but a stock exchange, bank, civil service, courts and a protective tariff. Antecedents of this doctrine of political and economic self-sufficiency go "back much longer," de Valera was to recount, "than Arthur Griffith or anybody of recent time. . . . Go back and read up Swift. . . ."

In a country such as was envisioned he was beginning to feel that he himself might have a real future as a professor when, in 1907, his mother came back to Ireland on a visit. As for the first time, he saw her a slight, bent little woman in her fifties, plainly dressed with hair tightly knotted, her features symmetrical as in the youthful photograph of her in the Bruree cottage, but sharper now and more set and bearing unmistakable evidence of hard work. With her came his half-brother, Tom, a tall boy still in his teens, and they suggested that he return with them to the United States. It was obvious that his mother pursued a strict pattern of life, staying much in her own home except for church. His stepfather was known to be easy-going, sociable, fond of beer and companionship. Now that coach-horses had been given up, he was on a pension and the Wheelwrights had their own small home in Brighton Street. His mother's determination to be independent was as rigorous as when she first left Bruree in her girlhood, and with her sense of family responsibility she had persuaded his Aunt Annie's husband to take a construction job in Rochester and move his family there from Massachusetts. Eddie, as she still called her older son, heard much about life across the ocean and the opportunities he would find as a young man of twenty-five with a fine education, but too many, he felt, of his generation were leaving for America. Ireland was the country which had given him the only home he remembered.

That he might be regarded as a foreigner by the authorities in Ireland occurred to him when, having decided not to go to America, he sought the position of mathematics teacher in the Technical Schools in Bolton Street in Dublin. Though the selection committee listed him as its first choice, he was turned down and it reached his ear that he was thought to be partly Jewish, somehow an outsider. He also applied for a post as junior inspector of the national schools, work carried out by appointees of the British educational system. Among the references he submitted was one from Sir Edmund Whittaker, Astronomer Royal of Ireland, written on the basis of "personal intercourse with him as an advanced student": "I have been much impressed by the intellectual vigour with which he has interested himself in the most difficult problems of Natural Philosophy . . . in any educational position he will exercise the best of influences."

De Valera did not get the inspectorship. Ability to use the Gaelic language had been listed as one of the qualifications and he decided that the knowledge he had of it needed expansion. He wanted to be able to put in his lapel the metal ring called the *fainne* which was the badge of honour worn by all who could converse with one another in the old tongue. With this purpose in his mind he joined the Gaelic League which he had heard about from boyhood because of the classes it sponsored all over the country. Its avowed mission was to "render the present a rational continuation of the past." Among the several branches in Dublin, de Valera chose the one called *Ard Craobh* in honour of the League's founder, the erudite Dr. Douglas Hyde, who was affectionately called *An Craobhin* or the little branch. Its meetings in Parnell Square in north Dublin opened up a circle of friends, many of whom were Gaelicizing their names, and he himself began to use Eamon instead of Edward.

Conspicuous among the members of the *Ard Craobh* branch were two other teachers: Padraic Pearse, headmaster of St. Enda's School, an Irish-speaking academy for boys located on the rambling parkland of an old mansion, the Hermitage, high up in the mountains south of Dublin; and Thomas MacDonagh, Pearse's assistant and a University lecturer. Both were known as poets and scholars who had pledged themselves to restore Ireland to her own in every sense, and they came to meetings wearing kilts of solid green or saffron tweed woven in the cottages of the Irish-speaking West. Another member of *Ard Craobh* who was obviously at home in the literary aspects of "the movement" as the members called it was eighteen-year-old Janie Flanagan, well known to Dr. Hyde for her flair in acting and dancing and for her fluency in Irish. When Dr. Hyde founded Leinster College to help teachers learn Gaelic, she joined its staff. De Valera as a new Gaelic Leaguer decided to intensify his study of Irish and in 1908 registered at Leinster College, where she became his teacher.

In the Gaelic League, he found himself more and more at ease. He came to the classes and the social evenings like the dances, *ceilidhi*, wearing a peaked and visored cap and dressed in homespun. The dark moustache which he grew brought out a florid, Latin appearance. When his own skill in other languages was discovered he was soon tutoring his particular instructor, "Shin-ee", as her name was pronounced in Irish, in French or German. She was small like his mother and quick to smile, with fair hair parted in the middle and waved over a wide forehead. There was dignity behind her gentle expression, and the impression she gave in the white guimpes and sweeping skirts of the times was one of demureness. In the summer both he and she went to study in the West of Ireland, the Gaeltacht, on the kind of holiday many of their contemporaries were taking, convinced as they were that the most beautiful Irish was spoken by those to whom it was still the natural tongue.

At Tawin, an island close to the mainland in Galway Bay where a summer programme for Gaelic studies was being held, the sound of the Atlantic Ocean's surf and the calling of the gulls over the seaweed entranced the two young people from the city. Here they acquired the Connemara dialect in the speech they were practising. Pearse had urged Eamon to do as Pearse himself had done, to seek out the people of the West as the fountainhead of Gaelic Ireland, and Eamon declared he would willingly give up all he knew of English to talk like the natives. It was Sinead's ambition to write children's books in Irish. The couple would watch the fishermen in their hookers coming and going with the tides, nets mounded on the decks. They stopped along the streets of Galway to talk in Irish with the old-timers; the women in thick, red skirts with dark shawls mantling their hair in Spanish style; the men in their homespun trousers belted with rope and their high-necked, knitted jerseys. Fishwives turned to invoke their blessings on the tall young man and the short, light-haired girl at his side.

One old man wearing the rough *bainin* or vest of the Gaeltacht to whom Eamon put a question in painstaking Irish replied as if insulted, "Do you think I do not know English?" With Sinead, Eamon decided that the people in the West must be persuaded that they had something too precious to lose in their Irish. This and many other mutual convictions they talked over as they looked at the Spanish Arch before crossing the bridge into the old village, the Claddagh, that had become part of Galway town. On a fine day they could see the Aran Islands far out in the bay, and all their experiences they enjoyed the more for sharing them. That summer the two became engaged.

The following winter, in January 1910, Eamon de Valera and Sinead ni Fhlannagain were married and planned together a lifelong pursuit of learning. He was twenty-eight and she twenty-one, both idealists, both with a capacity for hard work. They started keeping house in a suburb south of Dublin, Donnybrook, at 23 Morehampton Terrace, an unbroken row of six identical dwellings where each varnished door was approached by a short path from its own gate. The strip of house fronts was scalloped by bay windows, a plain but modern and convenient place to live.

An application he made for a scholarship in advanced mathematics at the predominantly Protestant Trinity College was rejected and he began work for a master's degree at his own University, now reorganized by Act of Parliament as the National University with three component colleges at Dublin, Cork and Galway. New obligations made it impossible for him to be free for research, and in order to supplement his income he secured, in addition to his schoolteaching, an appointment as examiner in Irish at the Royal College of Physicians and of Surgeons and as an assistant examiner in Irish for his own Alma Mater. Work of this kind, awarded upon recommendation of senior faculty members, consisted of examining boys and girls upon completion of their preparatory work for matriculation into institutions of higher education. The eye-glasses which he put on made him look more the schoolmaster than ever with their thin chain-guard hooked behind his ear. In order to qualify as soon as possible for advancement, he gave up the attempt to finish the thesis he had commenced on quaternions and withdrew his candidacy for the master's degree, taking instead the examination for a diploma in education. For this he had to cover the history of education, school management and teaching methodology, and to compile a series of sample lessons, undergoing also routine inspections of his classes, requirements which he privately resented. When the inspector came in it made him feel, he was to admit, like saying, "For heaven's sake let me alone; do not come in while I am at my work; if you want to know whether I am doing my work well or not, come in at the end and see whether I have taught the pupils properly." At the time he said nothing. The diploma was conferred upon him in the autumn following his marriage.

In December of the same year, 1910, a baby boy was born to the young couple. In accord with the Irish custom of naming the first son after the father's father and the second son after his own father, Vivion was the name chosen, expressing Eamon's feeling for the father of whom he knew so little, the baby's Spanish grandfather.

When a professorship in mathematical physics became vacant at University College in Cork in 1912, de Valera forwarded his credentials to the college's governing board. The post offered more income and his family was growing rapidly. A second child, a daughter named Mairin, was born that year. Knowing that there was another applicant for the Cork position and that his name— de Valera—was unfamiliar in any way, he made a trip one Sunday to present his recommendations in person at the home of J. J. Horgan, the Cork member of the board which included a representative from each county council in the province of Munster. Horgan took stock of his caller with the Limerick accent; he seemed a modest individual and though he spoke of belonging to the Gaelic League, the political views he expressed classified him in Horgan's mind as a supporter of Redmond's home rule policy. Horgan backed de Valera, but the Limerick member of the board, under pressure from both aspirants for the professorship, reportedly missed his train *en route* to the meeting and without his vote the board's action proved inconclusive. De Valera, hearing that the decision was to be referred to the senate of the National University, withdrew his application and instead of moving away from Dublin, took on another assignment there, that of examiner in mathematics for the Intermediate Education Board.

So far, the couple had focused their nationalist interests on the Gaelic past rather than on Ireland's uncertain political future. Their children, they resolved, should grow up speaking the Irish language, and they made a point themselves of speaking it, of buying Irish goods, of following Gaelic football and hurling, all part of Sinn Fein's programme. Griffith as president of that organization did not favour militant or aggressive measures in behalf of freedom. One Sinn Feiner had been defeated when he ran in 1908 for Parliament against the established Irish Parliamentary Party with the idea of boycotting Westminster, which discouraged subsequent sallies into the political arena against Redmond. The convictions of the de Valeras were of a steady, temperate kind not incompatible with the interests of his profession. At nationalist meetings both would be present, conversing in Irish. The nuns and the clergy who ran the schools in which he was teaching liked his demeanour, "his devotedness to duty and manly piety" which, as the sisters at Carysfort put it, set an example. In the charitable work of the Society of St. Vincent de Paul he took part, seeing for himself the conditions in which many Dubliners were living in the Coombe, the slum he traversed going and coming from his classes. Pearse at meetings of the Gaelic League inveighed against the squalor of the Dublin tenements, saying that Ireland was a nation lying in penal servitude and that the schools, the colleges and the universities were symbols of that servitude. Social unrest was mounting in the city and a general strike of workers was led by James Larkin in the summer of 1913. Though the de Valeras themselves were not part of the labour movement or its socialist leanings, the undercurrent of social agitation, of economic reform and of political impatience began to pull at all thinking people.

The de Valeras could not help being aware that a political programme was gaining over the concept of cultural regeneration, and more than a peaceful political programme too. When conflict broke out over the direction which the Gaelic League should follow, Dr. Hyde resigned as its president. The branch called *Ard Craobh* elected de Valera as its head, so he was vitally concerned at Dr. Hyde's decision. Pearse by his own admission was not curbing his tongue: "Whenever Dr. Hyde at a meeting . . . has produced his dove of peace, I have always been careful to produce my sword." This was the Fenian doctrine of revolution, not mere parliamentary opposition.

Up in Belfast only a few hours' train trip north of Dublin, the advocacy of home rule by a young Englishman connected with the British government, Winston S. Churchill, sounded daring. His own father, Lord Randolph Churchill, had preached the very opposite of home rule, declaring, "Ulster will fight, Ulster will be right," and this remained the motto of Edward Carson, chief among those resisting home rule. The possibility that the North and South of Ireland would be partitioned over the matter of loyalty to the Crown arose by 1912. The Orangemen of the North would sooner part company from the rest of Ireland than from the monarch, and Carson was organizing a force called the Ulster Volunteers to defend union. In this he had the expert advice of an Irishman high up in the British Army, Sir Henry Wilson.

Threats of force from the North did not long go unmatched in the South. At Dublin's largest meeting hall, the Rotunda located at the head of O'Connell Street near the statue of Parnell, a crowd gathered one November evening in 1913—shopkeepers, doctors, clerks, lawyers, students, teachers, among them Eamon de Valera. He knew that a professor of Irish history from the National University, Eoin MacNeill, intended to propose that the Irishmen in the South form an armed body to protect their interests just as the Irishmen in the North were organizing to fight home rule, but he did not know that MacNeill had called this meeting through the influence of a small group of men for whom Carson's activities served only as the pretext for their own recourse to force, a policy on which this small group was already bent in pursuit of the Fenian tradition. The South, de Valera mentally agreed, must prepare for whatever lay ahead; the Southerners must stand united no less than the Northerners, for the whole prospect of home rule was being jeopardized by the unionists. Ireland must defend herself in arms as well as words, but only if peace proved unavailing would force have to be used. As enrolment cards were passed out in the Rotunda, hundreds signified themselves as being wildly willing to join. Defence not revolution was de Valera's thought as he signed up, and afterward he spoke of the reluctance with which he had "elected to act with those who were prepared to rely on force to try to win what had been denied them by peaceful methods."

In a hall in Blackhall Street loaned by the Gaelic League, 600 recruits assembled for their first drill. The Royal Irish Constabulary dared not interfere so long as the Ulster Volunteers were operating unrestrained by the British in the North. MacNeill had a provisional committee working under him but no drill manual was available, no plan for choosing officers, no equipment and no uniforms. The attempts to form squads revealed an ignorance of soldiering that to de Valera was appalling. He himself knew only from his reading about such matters. It was decided to sort the enrolment cards by the addresses on them so that companies could be made up by neighbourhoods and Pearse became director of organization. De Valera's initiative began to make itself felt with the vigour which he carried over from the playing field to the drill ground, and he was made responsible for the group practising on a field in Terenure not far from Morehampton Terrace. As the corps developed, stress was placed upon democratic methods and it was decided to choose the company officers by popular vote. De Valera was first selected as lieutenant and then as captain of E Company.

The time this required could not be taken from teaching so it meant that he had fewer hours to spend with his wife, fewer moments for his children, less chance for his pastimes like reading and chess. If he got out the chess-board, it was to ponder drilling as he moved the pieces from square to square like soldiers on a field of battle. In addition to Vivion and Mairin, a new baby was born in the autumn of 1913, a boy named Eamon. The father believed that the first teachers in life were the parents, that it was in the home that character took shape, and this meant that their mother would be all important since so much of his time was spent away from them. She no less than he believed in the cause to which the Volunteers were dedicating themselves and encouraged his undertaking. Money as well as time had to be eked out, for the recruits were financing themselves by "affiliation fees." Uniforms, which had to be made by private tailors, cost thirty-five shillings at the lowest. At Volunteer headquarters in Kildare Street, the officers attended lectures on tactical problems on Saturday mornings. Through the coldest months of the winter, the men, gathering on foot or by bicycle, continued to drill, drawing from a new weekly called the *Irish Volunteer* information on practical details such as the care of the feet for road marches, the digging of entrenchments, "the trigger squeeze exercise."

The chief handicap, the officers realized, was a shortage of firearms. Even had they had the money, regulations prevented them from buying guns and ammunition. De Valera reminded his company of the doughty pikes used in the battle of Vinegar Hill by the glorious lads of 1798 who had rebelled in Ireland's cause, enlarging as he talked upon the superiority of the long-shafted Irish pikes over the short-bladed English models. But what would the Volunteers do with such things, asked one of his Donnybrook neighbours, a prosperous builder named Batt O'Connor; how would they look today? The idea, vetoed at first, was brought up by the Captain at a second meeting and adopted. A few pikes were found, rusty relics, and a few more forged by blacksmiths. The derision of onlookers at the sight of the men parading awkwardly with them only quickened de Valera's zeal.

As antagonism between the two parts of Ireland mounted, de Valera, reasoning that he had entered into public activity because of the threat of division, kept one question in his mind, "Are we making towards having ultimately one State . . . or not?" The Northerners being mustered by Carson in Belfast constituted a focus of belligerent unionism. They were determined to separate themselves if the British Government, in response to the programme of the Irish Party, should move in the direction of home rule for all of Ireland.

England was not so much occupied with this problem as with watching the crisis developing on the continent. One publication in Northern Ireland reported an offer of "aid from a powerful continental monarch," who, "if home rule is forced on the Protestants of Ireland, is prepared to send an army sufficient to release England of any further trouble in Ireland by attaching it to his own dominion." From Germany came a consignment of Mauser rifles for the Ulster Volunteers early in the spring, landed illegally but without interference from the Royal Navy. Belfast would fight before accepting home rule and Belfast was sure she would be right.

What would Dublin do? ". . . the landing of a few guns in the North," de Valera afterwards commented, "made vain the pains of a half century's struggle." He and his wife thought back to the hopes of their elders, the oppression so long endured in the hope of self-government. Guns would put an end to parliamentary methods, they felt. Captain de Valera got orders one Sunday morning in June 1914 to march E Company northward out of the city with a day's rations. As more Volunteers kept arriving under the windswept Hill of Howth, spread with pink heather and green ferns waving in the breeze, MacDonagh took command and a lean, serious-faced man named Cathal Brugha, familiar to de Valera as a senior Gaelic Leaguer, issued cryptic orders for attention. It was one o'clock and the tide was high. Rounding the island out in the bay was a white-hulled sail-boat and almost under the eyes of the British coastguard the skipper, Erskine Childers, unloaded a cargo of Mauser rifles for the men waiting on shore. Half-way to the city, Crown forces blocked the Volunteers' road and they deployed in the fields to hide their weapons, returning later to retrieve them. But in Bachelor's Walk in the centre of Dublin, spectators threw stones at British soldiers, who opened fire, killing several bystanders. With the contraband obtained at Howth and from two other landings of arms farther south on the coast, the Volunteers resumed night-time practice sessions. Though they paid little heed to it, another crucial event transpired at the end of July in faraway Sarajevo when an archduke stepped into his death car.

De Valera went to the West again to a summer college at Tourmakeady, a village buried amongst the Partry Mountains in County Mayo where Irish was spoken. Donkeys saddled with creels stood patiently amidst the pools of brown bog water waiting for their loads, and in the cottage yards he could see small boys wearing skirts made of rough, dark homespun as in centuries gone by. Here he became acquainted with the leadership of the school's guiding spirit, Sir Roger Casement, who had come back after some years spent in the Empire's consular service to champion Irish independence. Once a home ruler, like others he was done with waiting for it. "I believe," he said of the world catastrophe growing more and more imminent, "that the defeat of Great Britain by Germany might conceivably . . . result in great gain to Ireland." They were, Casement proclaimed, climbing the painful stairs of Irish history.

The idea that England's emergency would be Ireland's opportunity underlay the Irish Republican Brotherhood, the secret body in which Casement, Pearse, MacDonagh, Brugha and others were powerful. The sworn purpose of the Brotherhood, which had been reactivated upon Tom Clarke's return to Ireland, was to carry out the original Fenian objective of establishing a Republic by means of a revolution. Now, financed through the Clan-na-Gael in America, it was becoming the driving force behind the national movement. The Supreme Council of the Brotherhood in Ireland, meeting as it did in secret and laying its far-reaching

plans, considered itself as the real government of Ireland. It was
the Supreme Council which had conceived the idea of the
Rotunda rally and had, through intermediaries, persuaded
MacNeill to be the head and front of the Volunteers. Many in the
Volunteers would have been amazed had they known that there
existed an oath-bound group. Unanimous approval had to be
given by those in a local circle of the Brotherhood before anyone
was asked to join. Eamon de Valera's name when it was brought
forward elicited the necessary consent. His neighbour Batt
O'Connor, having been empowered to approach him, divulged to
him the existence of a "physical force party" inside the Volunteers.

De Valera knew that his Church did not approve of bodies
whose members were bound by oaths; that the Church had
condemned Fenian groups like the Brotherhood both in the
United States and in Ireland, subjecting members to excommuni-
cation, not because of the Brotherhood's aim to make Ireland a
Republic but because of the clandestine and violent means
advocated to achieve the aim. Arthur Griffith, whose leadership
in Sinn Fein de Valera respected, had left the Brotherhood after
deciding that its tenets were not compatible with peaceful means.
Apart from the physical force idea, the theory of a Republic was
in itself radical. De Valera like many of his generation had been
brought up to regard home rule under the Crown as the maximum
expectation and to leave things to parliamentary measures. He
declined O'Connor's invitation to join, but the Brotherhood did
not drop its intentions regarding him. To the urgings of
MacDonagh, his immediate superior in the Dublin Brigade of the
Volunteers, de Valera acceded, joining the Brotherhood on one
stipulation. He would carry out orders only, not make them, a
distinction important in his mind. When he started attending the
meetings after being sworn in, he noticed that some ponderous
literary or scientific treatise would be placed by the chairman
upon the table as a decoy for intruders. The whole atmosphere
was conspiratorial. Because he did not want the responsibility
for manipulating the Volunteers to serve unacknowledged ends
such as the I.R.B. might have in mind, he refused to serve on the
Volunteers' executive committee. MacNeill's belief that force was
justified not for aggressive purposes but for self-defence seemed
to de Valera the logical one. His own tendencies were not of the
hot-headed, hasty kind.

Among immediate needs, military discipline seemed to him uppermost, and the lack of method and inefficiency persisting in the Volunteer body were a thorn in his side. In the advertisement columns of an Irish newspaper he read about a camp for military instruction to be started in East Donegal by Captain Jack White: "I hereby invite those willing and able to pay £2 a week for a fortnight or three-week course," the notice read, "to send me their names with the least possible delay." De Valera sat down and wrote out his application. Captain White's plans, however, came to naught when the threat of war in Europe caused him to cancel the Donegal training programme.

As European turbulence that summer increased, it was the fate of home rule which the Irish agitators watched. ". . . such as are heard to advocate home rule do so not because they consider it the best," de Valera afterward explained, "not because they hanker after the English connection, but because they think that the militarist power which has kept Ireland within its grasp for centuries can never be persuaded to let her go. . . ." At thirty-two years of age, he had had time to test his first convictions. What had been for him a vision of intellectual and economic freedom as it had been for the originators of the Gaelic League was fast accumulating political significance. Freedom had to be given to the whole country, not just to part of it; of that he was positive.

"If liberty is not entire," he told a friend with whom he was cycling through Connemara, "it is not liberty." It had been the threat of division between North and South that had brought him to the first Volunteers' meeting called by MacNeill. No river, no chain of mountains, no natural boundaries separated the two parts of the island. "You know," he insisted as he and his companion cycled from Mayo and Sligo into Donegal and Tyrone, "that it was here in this Northern Land," and he indicated with an upward thrust of his chin the hilly domes rising like giants' tonsured heads in front of them, "it was here that the flag of the Republic was first raised. . . ." Through his mind went the refrain from Thomas Davis' *Song of the Volunteers of 1782*, "God bless the Northern Land!" Scenes sacred to Irish nationalism lay within Ulster's borders. County Antrim was the site of St. Patrick's novitiate. County Down was where the saint had done his missionary work. County Armagh had been his See, and at Downpatrick lay his bones with those of Columcille. From the

North had come Hugh O'Neil and Owen Roe. It was in Belfast that the Republican movement had begun with Wolfe Tone in the eighteenth century as de Valera had never forgotten from his history lessons, and practically all of the United Irishmen who first launched the idea of a Republic were Protestants.

The double threat to British security emanating from the two sections of Ireland had to be removed as quickly as possible by the British Prime Minister, Herbert Asquith, when the European war was declared in August 1914. "The North had armed. The South was arming," as the British statesman, Lloyd George, summed up the danger at England's back door. In September, Parliament passed the Home Rule Bill so long pending, but with reservations that all but nullified it. De Valera, before he returned from the West to his school work in the autumn, knew that the red die had been cast for his country. John Redmond was advising them to concur, to win England's confidence by fighting her battles on the continent, then later to look for the reward. Redmond's own brother William, a member of the House of Commons for County Clare, joined the Crown forces and urged all Volunteers to do the same thing. Pearse stood opposite Redmond in the duel developing for control of the Volunteers, Pearse the thinker and the poet, who was urging the alternative course, a course that was only a dream as shimmering as the grail.

Hibernian Hall, used by the Donnybrook Volunteers for their meetings, filled quickly with talk and commotion one evening in September after Captain de Valera's return. Donnybrook neighbours were ordinarily good friends, especially those whose convictions had brought them together in the Volunteers. For almost a year of intensive activity they had shared a common pride in their flag with its gold harp, uncrowned, on a green field. Captain de Valera put the situation to them as he saw it. Through what Redmond had that summer done in the halls of Westminster, Ireland's liberation had been sabotaged. Real home rule had been the expectation of Sinn Feiners like himself for a decade, and of older Irishmen like his uncle for decades before that, but just as home rule had seemed about to come to pass Redmond had capitulated to pressure from the English and everything was being snatched away. The legislation Parliament had put upon the statute book would exempt the Northern sector of Ireland from home rule because each of the counties in the province of

Ulster was given the option of being in or out of the scheme. The partition of North and South inherent in the act offended and outraged the nation's historic and geographic unity. Then, on top of it all, the inauguration of the whole system was postponed even in the South on the ground that world affairs made any change undesirable at that time. Captain de Valera could not put his trust in the intentions of the British Government or in Redmond's subservience to it.

Once the issue was presented in Hibernian Hall, arguments resounded from one side to the other. The evening lengthened and the split between supporters of Pearse and of Redmond cut deeper into the company of Volunteers there assembled. The Captain held out for the original objective of a free and united Ireland, adamant against joining the British forces in a foreign war. All over Ireland, other companies of Volunteers were voting on the same issue, the majority gradually aligning itself with Redmond. But in Donnybrook when at last the roll had to be called the majority stood for Pearse, a small majority but a majority. At that, the Captain allowed himself no display of satisfaction; he felt, in fact, no sense of triumph. All Irishmen belonged together on one side. Ireland's side. Rising to his upstanding height, his dark, moustached face glowering, he gathered around him those who had indicated by their vote that they, being for Pearse, were for him. Leaving the others, till now their fellows in arms, they made their way through the seething crowd to the exit. There the Captain turned, conscious that friends and neighbours were in that instant becoming enemies. Over the heads of the anxious men going out with him he called back to the others remaining in their places, "You will want us to get that Home Rule Bill yet, and when you want us we will be there."

CHAPTER III

THE LONG EVE (1915–1916)

THROUGH the dark hour before midnight on Easter Sunday, 1915, in a suburb north of Dublin, there bore in upon the ears of the sleeping residents an uneven rhythm from tramping feet. The Dublin Brigade was marshalling at the signpost in Finglas which, three centuries earlier, had been the rendezvous for a mustering against Cromwell. The Irishmen now assembling were those who, having refused Redmond's call to fight on the European battlefields, had spent the winter drilling at home instead. At the head of one detachment marched Eamon de Valera in his uniform of brownish-green tweed, thick and fuzzy. The brass buttons were harp-embossed, the darker green collar carried the insignia of a Celtic cross, and on the cuff were three bands to denote his rank. It was that of Adjutant to which he had been appointed by the Brigade's commanding officer, MacDonagh, as a result of the leadership demonstrated in Hibernian Hall the preceding autumn.

After months of rigorous practice, de Valera felt ready for the night's manœuvres. On the stroke of the hour as Easter Sunday ended, the Volunteers shouldered their Howth rifles for the starting order and over a simulated front the five battalions of the Dublin Brigade fanned out on prearranged routes, to return home only with daybreak as had the nineteenth-century "moonlighters."

All was not yet perfect from de Valera's point of view. The officers themselves were still learning to give the proper commands. He believed in preparing organized units to take the field, but full-scale skirmishes like that of Easter night could only occasionally be risked. The regular routine consisted of evening lectures and of week-end exercises for which the men would gather in fields screened by woods. If they had no uniforms, they came in unpressed Sunday suits with slouch hats or visored caps. Ranging themselves into uneven lines, they would straighten up when the reviewing officer arrived, some in their left hands bracing pikes with spear-heads towering above them, others grasping tall bows, all holding their right arms stiffly at their sides. Stray dogs skirted the lines and over all was an air of not knowing just what was contemplated. Some might come late or not appear at all and on holidays many vanished into public-houses. Captain de Valera's company knew that smoking, blaspheming or drinking were taboo on business of so high-minded a nature.

For the most part that winter, the reconstituted Volunteers had operated without interference from the British police, for England was endeavouring to keep Ireland from rebelling while recruiting for the war in Europe. Those who responded to Redmond's pleas to fight for England made no secret of their animosity toward those who did not, and families like the de Valeras were shunned as radical, left-wing, subversive slackers. Unswayed by those around him, indefatigable, de Valera appeared aloof to liking or disliking, to being liked or disliked. He was still hard at work earning a living as a teacher, but Padraic Pearse put him down in his note-book as an eminently capable military man.

For the small group with overlapping membership on the Supreme Council and on the Volunteers' executive committee, the European conflict presented the opportunity they desired. The goal was the establishment by force of an Irish Republic. Within a month after Britain's declaration of war on Germany, the Supreme Council had met and a rising had been decided upon. Though no date was set for action, it was agreed to build up military support inside Ireland and outside as well. Sean T. O'Kelly, the secretary of the Gaelic League and an outspoken, tough-minded man who had been in the Brotherhood since 1900 and was a founding member of Sinn Fein and of the Volunteers as well as of the Gaelic League, took the proposal for revolution as a serious, practical business. Casement, going to America, persuaded John Devoy, the old Fenian, and Devoy's partner in the Clan-na-Gael, Daniel F. Cohalan, a political power in Tammany Hall and a judge of the New York State supreme court, to finance an expedition to Berlin to seek German co-operation.

De Valera, where his own responsibilities were made clear, did not hesitate to accept assignments. Happening to meet Pearse one spring day in 1915 in Kildare Street outside Volunteer headquarters, he was handed personally the letter Pearse had written him by hand on the Volunteers' letterhead: "*A Cara*

(Dear Sir), At last night's meeting of the Executive you were
formally appointed Commandant of the 3rd Batt." De Valera
would continue as Brigade Adjutant, but as Commandant he
would have charge of all recruits from the Pembroke area of the
city in which his own home lay. At the age of thirty-three, he
was no foot-loose, reckless rebel but a husband, a father, a teacher,
a regular churchgoer, one who had voluntarily embraced the
cause rather than having been embraced by it. In Ireland he had
found a warm and worthy substitute for something otherwise
lacking from his earliest consciousness. In his first schooldays, he
had begun to identify himself with his Motherland. He still looked
young and as one who knew him at this time said, like "a soft
country boy" with a boy's enthusiasm lighting up his face, but he
who had first set his course in the direction of the classroom and
the library was acquiring toughness in facing conflict. He agreed
to attend the meeting for the battalion commandants of the
Dublin Brigade which Pearse was calling after the regular lecture
for all officers on the next Saturday.

On Whitsunday, he took a familiar train trip to the vicinity
of his childhood home, only on this occasion he travelled in the
company of Pearse. The entire Dublin Brigade was going to
Limerick for the day with its bands and full regalia, intent upon
making a show of strength in a city that had been badly split by
Redmond. The solid battlements of Limerick's landmark, King
John's Castle, looked no different to Eamon de Valera from when
he had seen them as a boy. The old walls rose from the flat,
grassy banks of the swirling Shannon. As the Commandant led
the Third Battalion back toward the train after the parade, wives
of British soldiers stationed in the area picked up rocks and flung
them into the line of march. With the stones flying from the side-
lines and the Royal Irish Constabulary bearing down upon the
scene, he led his men on without allowing the ranks to break.

The occasions on which the Volunteers could with impunity
attract the public's notice took various forms. Early in the
summer, news came from Devoy that the body of the famous old
Fenian, O'Donovan Rossa, would be sent back from America for
burial in Dublin's graveyard of patriots, Glasnevin Cemetery,
and de Valera's work with the committee on arrangements
brought him into contact with men and women known to him
till then only by their reputations. Madame Markievicz, for

instance, he had heard of as the angel of the labouring people. Her beauty, he found, was matched by her fervour and her unconventionality. Behind the high and barren wall of Glasnevin Cemetery, where the odour of cypress hung over the cinder walks, Pearse delivered the peroration. To the Commandant standing at attention for the last volley over the grave must have come the first inklings of thoughts he was later to express: "I hope when I die, I will get a Fenian grave."

That summer, faith in the future was heightened for him and his wife by the birth of another son, Brian. Close as he was to his children, he had less time to spend with them. Early in the autumn of that year, 1915, he assisted at a fête to raise money for new headquarters which the Volunteers were opening in Dawson Street. The stark, square, granite residence of Pearse, the Hermitage, with its Greek columns, was usually unseen at the end of the drive curving in from its iron-grilled gate and entrance arches, and when it was opened to the public few of the spectators sensed that this was the scene of a conpiratorial movement. The paths were overhung with low-branching, twisted trees and here and there a footbridge crossed the stream running beneath the oaks and beeches. From the study window, its master could point out to de Valera and fellow commandants that empurpled mountain, Kilmashogue, amidst whose bracken—as Pearse told it—Emmet, patriot and rebel, hid the night the hostile soldiers were pursuing him. On Pearse's book-shelves stood Emmet's writings with those of Tone, Mitchel, Davis, Lalor and other "hero-sires" from whom, Pearse insisted, they of the twentieth century were descended. There, too, in more than one edition, were the comedies and tragedies of Shakespeare, Pearse's favourite writer, an avowal of preference which de Valera echoed.

On a later week-end that autumn, a mock engagement was staged in this Rathfarnham region, the advance orders for which appeared in the *Irish Volunteer* over the name of the Brigade Adjutant. The soldiers were authorized by headquarters to carry in addition to the green flag another banner, the official Volunteer tricolor of green and orange, signifying both parts of Ireland, joined by a band of white down the middle. Participating units were divided into the Red Force and the Green Force, red for the Citizen Army which was a separate body of militant workers headed by the labour leader, James Connolly, and green for the

Volunteers. For the advancing units the Third Battalion formed
the rearguard to supply connections. From the rough road
beginning at Kilmashogue Mountain de Valera led the rearguard
to Harold's Grange, then "took" Ticknock Crossroads, "occupied" high ground at Sandyford, and after making contact with
the forward lines as specified in the operational plan, pushed on
to another small community lying athwart the main route south
of Dublin. At the end of the march, the Third Battalion's
side was declared the victor, to the delight of Commandant de
Valera.

The Volunteers, as the winter of 1915 to 1916 advanced,
wondered at the intensification of their activities. They were
directed to join forces with the Citizen Army and Connolly,
known to be impatient for action, appeared to his associates in
the Citizen Army more confident as he came and went at his headquarters, Liberty Hall. Once the two armed forces in the South
had been unified, an array of trained, partially equipped and
totally convinced fighters was ready for orders. They did not
know that during the first month of the new year, 1916, the
Brotherhood's Supreme Council had met to decide when the
Volunteers all over the country would rise to oust the British;
that Easter Sunday, April 23, 1916, had been the date set, and that
Pearse was to be the Commander-in-Chief. A Proclamation of the
proposed Republic was prepared by him. To this plan, Mac-
Donagh was a party as well as the others on the Supreme Council,
but not MacNeill though he still headed the Volunteers' executive
committee and was Chief of Staff, and not Griffith though he was
still president of Sinn Fein. Neither de Valera nor any general
staff officers were informed.

Attempts to take de Valera into the Brotherhood's inner
circle had not progressed since his reluctant acceptance of membership. If he had begun to have misgivings about the promise
exacted from him of unquestioning obedience to superiors in the
secret Brotherhood, he was not alone. The O'Rahilly, one of the
founders of the Volunteers, came back from a trip to America
convinced from what he had seen of the Clan-na-Gael that secret
societies were bad for people's morale. Madame Markievicz
disliked the mystery connected with the Brotherhood and
suspected that those at the top were holding the younger ones
back. Only a few of the Volunteers had entry permits to a place

called Larkfield in Kimmage Road, south of the city. Inside this
residence, really a camouflaged munitions factory, was Roderick
O'Connor, called Rory, a graduate engineer from the National
University; an old gentleman named Plunkett, a Papal Count
whose whole family was working in the movement; and a
number of young Irishmen recalled from England to live and
work there, among them a Cork lad named Michael Collins who
had given up his job as a clerk in London in answer to the
summons.

Resistant as de Valera was to sitting in on planning conferences, he was in the forefront of overt operations. He took
part in anti-recruiting meetings held to offset Redmond, and
though speech-making was not his custom he gave a brief talk at
one held in Donnybrook in company with The O'Rahilly. In his
capacity as Brigade Adjutant he wrote out detailed weekly orders
for the Volunteers:

"1. Battalion and Company officers will ensure the attendance
at Headquarters' Special Classes of Signallers, First Aid
and Ambulance Men, Engineers, and Armourers.
2. Training for sub-officers . . . at Camden Row.
3. Inspection of 2nd Batt. . . . Cyclists to parade with
machines.
4. Officers' meeting at Headquarters at 8 Saturday.
E. de Valera, Commandant, Brigade Adjutant."

At six o'clock one wet Sunday morning in January 1916,
while it was still dark, he mobilized his Battalion, marched the
men first to mass in Rathfarnham at the foot of the hills, then
began the real march up over mountainous Glendhu. Darkness
turned only to a half light and sleet fell as they climbed. At the
end of the day, the Battalion wound up on the peak of Kilbradden
and de Valera relished the accomplishment regardless of the
complaints from his drenched men. After January, every move
the Volunteers were directed to take seemed to him in the nature
of rehearsal for revolution. They were ordered, for instance, to
train in street fighting with breaks as if attacked while on the
move. Early in February the police were able to identify nine
Volunteers who led 200 men with rifles from Blackhall Place to
Phoenix Park on a skirmish lasting, according to the police

reports, from evening till two in the morning. Among the nine listed was the name of "Edward de Valera."

Easter always meant a holiday the Monday following with men free from their work, and MacNeill saw nothing unusual in the orders which appeared over the signature of "P. H. Pearse, Commandant" in the *Irish Volunteer* on April 8, 1916: ". . . every unit of the Irish Volunteers will hold manœuvres during the Easter holidays." Commandant de Valera and the other senior officers received follow-up instructions to report Easter Sunday at four o'clock in the afternoon with equipment for a routine march. The beginning of Holy Week he had taught his last classes at Carysfort after almost a decade there.

The date for the rising and a specific request for arms and ammunition and trained officers had been forwarded to the German Foreign Office in Berlin *via* the Clan-na-Gael, and it was believed in Ireland that Germany would send help for Easter Sunday. Sir Roger Casement had, in Germany, negotiated a German-Irish treaty in which Germany, in the event of winning a naval victory, promised to send to Ireland a brigade recruited by him from among those Irishmen captured by the Kaiser's troops in the British forces and sent as prisoners of war to Germany. But Sir Roger felt stranded among strangers of doubtful intentions and wanted to return to Ireland without involving his brigade to warn that the rising under the circumstances would be folly.

By Good Friday, the intention of turning Sunday's announced march into outright insurrection and of declaring a Republic was confided by Pearse as the Commander-in-Chief designate to the senior officers. MacNeill was thunderstruck and stood his ground that the Volunteers should be used only in defence, that they should not take the initiative in combat. Consulting with the members of his executive committee on Friday and Saturday, he found them divided over Pearse's plans and did not make up his own mind immediately what to do.

Commandant de Valera, like others at his level, was in the middle of the friction generated from the top. He considered himself committed to carrying out whatever orders might be issued to him whether he approved or disapproved. On Saturday he, like many others, could read in the *Irish Independent* an item printed inconspicuously at the bottom of a column:

"A collapsible boat containing a quantity of arms and ammunition was seized at Carrahane Strand, Tralee Bay, yesterday morning by the Ardfert police. A man of unknown nationality found on the shore close by was arrested."

The man was Casement, who had come from Germany in a submarine which followed a small ship, the *Aud*, carrying a few rifles and some ammunition for Ireland. The *Aud*, when sighted by British look-outs, was sent to the bottom by its German captain. At twilight on Saturday Casement, having been picked up by the Royal Irish Constabulary where he came ashore, was spirited through Dublin and placed aboard the night mail steamer for England and the execution which he foresaw for himself. His aides got word to Dublin that the rising, if it was contingent upon German help, could not succeed.

To MacNeill's redoubled protests, Pearse refused to listen. Connolly acknowledged that slaughter would be certain but remained unshaken in his determination to proceed. By midnight Saturday, MacNeill decided on his own authority to cancel orders for the manœuvres and his countermand of all parades or marches in the Sunday morning papers threw the Volunteers into confusion. Commandant de Valera was clear about one thing: his job was to carry out the orders whatever they were; the trouble was to keep the orders straight. Early Sunday afternoon he received a personal note from MacNeill directed to him as "Commt. Eamon de Vailéara": "Commt. MacDonagh left me last night with the understanding that he would return or send me a message. He has done neither. As Chief of Staff, I have ordered and hereby order that no movement whatsoever of Irish Volunteers is to be made today. You will carry out this order in your own command and make it known to other commands." De Valera found himself catapulted into top responsibility for the Dublin Brigade.

At 144 Great Brunswick Street, where the Third Battalion had originally been instructed to assemble for the manœuvres, his men, some with carbines, shot-guns, Lee-Enfield and Mauser rifles and Larkfield buck-shot, were in a turmoil around him. He knew his immediate superior MacDonagh was in seclusion with the Supreme Council, and was able to relay to him MacNeill's message, whereupon it was decided that there was no alternative but to comply for the moment and word was hastily typed: "1. As publicly announced, the inspection and manœuvres ordered for this day are cancelled." But an additional order was appended: "2. All Volunteers are to stay in Dublin until further orders. Thomas MacDonagh, Commandant. E. de Valera." Without waiting for his signature to dry, the latter folded the paper and dispatched it to the battalions of the Dublin Brigade. The Supreme Council did not waver in its ultimate intent; MacNeill was not told that the rising had been re-scheduled for Monday. Though he did not sleep at home, de Valera returned Sunday evening for a few hours to see his wife and children. Back in Great Brunswick Street he worked preparing new orders with Captain Michael Malone, a young carpenter whom he had selected from the cyclist corps of the Volunteers to be his aide-de-camp. They slept without taking off their uniforms for a little while before daybreak, then set out to deliver the new orders.

On Easter Monday, with the holiday dawning clear and sharp, the Volunteers including those of the Third Battalion were roused by messengers at their doors with a directive signed not by MacNeill but by Pearse and MacDonagh, instructing them to assemble at 10 o'clock that morning with two days' rations. Alerted by the previous day's command not to leave Dublin, most reported by mid-morning at previously agreed-upon points. Outside Dublin the officers, at sixes and sevens because of the conflicting orders, told some of the provincial units to rise, others to lie low, and only a few attempts to mobilize around the country materialized.

In Dublin action began before noon. Commander-in-Chief Pearse marched at the head of his contingent up O'Connell Street and into the General Post Office. When armed men posted the Proclamation of the Republic, the throng of holiday-makers flocked toward the Nelson Pillar at the centre of things to see what it was all about. The converging trams stopped and fathers dragged their children off to see what was happening. The old women selling oranges around the Pillar ceased their cries of "Three-for-sixpence, three-for-sixpence." Crowds jostling into the fruit barrows knocked the feathers on the old women's shapeless hats and pulled their shawls askew as all pushed towards the posted Proclamation trying to read the bold, black type:

". . . Ireland . . . having organized and trained her manhood through her secret revolutionary organization, the Irish Republican Brotherhood, and through . . . the Irish Volunteers and the Irish Citizen Army, having patiently perfected her discipline, having resolutely waited for the right moment to reveal itself . . . now seizes that moment. . . ." It was signed by seven men listed as the members of the provisional government of the Republic: Pearse as President, Thomas Clarke, Sean MacDermott, Thomas MacDonagh, Eamon Kent, James Connolly and Joseph Plunkett.

British soldiers, not yet recalled from holiday leave, stopped in amazement on the pavements to stare at Commandant de Valera with full gear, from field-glasses to gun, leading the Third Battalion from its mustering points in Great Brunswick Street and Earlsfort Terrace to Westland Row where he directed a detail under a lieutenant to occupy the railway station. A double line of tracks entered this station on an elevated line, coming from across the Liffey at one end and at the other from a tenement and mill area. The platforms on both sides of the tracks were open at the ends and covered by a low shed. Just as the Volunteers made their way up the short incline, a boat-train was pulling in with holiday visitors from England. The lieutenant, by rapping out warnings, soon cleared the train shed and had the benches, barrows and weighing-machines flung across the entrances. The railway guards thought at first these men were mad, throwing themselves prone on the platform as they did and sighting down the tracks over their muzzles.

As soon as the station was in their hands, their Commandant deployed other Volunteers to move overhead along the railway trestle toward the gaunt, black-windowed walls of Boland's Flour Mills facing the Grand Canal Basin. Altogether he had about one hundred and thirty men. He himself led the main echelon over the roadway to meet the advance squad there. Not only were the Mills so located as to permit firing on Beggars Bush Barracks, the British headquarters, and the main road from Kingstown, but they contained supplies for bread-making on which many Dubliners depended. It was the old part of the city and the streets were thick with dilapidated buildings and cylindrical gas tanks. Close to one o'clock in the afternoon he reached the Mills and met no resistance because the employees were off on holiday, and he found only the horses used in pulling the delivery drays there. Inside the flour-coated warehouse he established his command post and ran up the tricolor.

All seemed in order as he surveyed his initial situation. Though he refused to let women from the auxiliary organization, Cumann na mBan, join in the fighting, he let them act as message-bearers and provisioners. The company officers reported to him at regular intervals and Captain Malone was at his side. When the windows were barricaded and the entrances under guard, he gave directions to open fire from the upper storey toward Beggars Bush and from outside the sound of enemy fire commenced. The British were returning his attack from Beggars Bush, shaking the walls of the old warehouse with the detonations. What, asked one of the Volunteers looking up at the roof, if it caved in? "Let it," was the Commandant's short reply. Leaving the Mills in charge of his deputy, he took a small sortie into Lower Mount Street to cut that main thoroughfare. Before returning to the Mills he left men in occupation of Clanwilliam House and in several other buildings cornering the Mount Street Bridge. By stringing out his small force he aimed to cover as much ground as possible.

The following day in the House of Commons, Augustine Birrell, Chief Secretary for Ireland, reported that grave disturbances had broken out in Dublin but "the House may take it from me the situation is well in hand." When Birrell set out to return to his post, however, he found telegraphic contact broken and regular boat service suspended. The Volunteers controlled the General Post Office, Boland's Mills and other pivotal points like the City Hall and the Four Courts. St. Stephen's Green was held by the woman Commandant of the Citizen Army, Madame Markievicz. At the South Dublin Union, Cathal Brugha fell severely wounded but, propping himself up against a wall, sang *God Save Ireland*.

The men in Boland's Mills found that their salient was vulnerable from water as well as from land on Wednesday morning when an English gunboat, the *Helga*, entering the mouth of the Liffey River, opened fire. Some of the wounded de Valera was able to evacuate with the help of Cumann na mBan, and to deflect the fire he gave orders to hoist an Irish flag over the old Ringsend Distillery standing vacant nearby. The *Helga*, moving up the river by the North Wall, then took aim at Liberty Hall and got the range of the General Post Office itself. By Wednesday evening the Sherwood Foresters landed at Kingstown, and finding the rail line up the coast cut by the Third Battalion proceeded on foot toward the city. As they tried to cross the Mount Street Bridge, gunfire burst upon them from Clanwilliam House. Volunteer Paddy Doyle, setting out from the Mills to take his turn at that Bridge outpost, called out *"Beannacht leat"*—blessing on you—as he saluted Commandant de Valera. Doyle was shot to death in the fighting that followed there.

Inside the General Post Office on Friday morning, April 28, 1916, Pearse took stock of the condition of his men. "For four days they have fought and toiled almost without cessation, almost without sleep, and in the intervals of fighting we have sung songs of the freedom of Ireland." Perched near a sandbagged window on a high stool such as was used by the postal clerks, he insisted that since they had held out this long their country was entitled by international law to a representative at any general peace conference after the European war. This would be where Ireland could make her case known to the world. The fight at the General Post Office came to a finish as the garrison retreated with the building burning over their heads. Saturday afternoon Pearse, his wide-brimmed hat still strapped under his chin and turned up jauntily on one side, surrendered, and with him went all from his staff, some on stretchers. Connolly, reporting the Republican losses, mentioned the one redoubt remaining, "Commandant de Valera stretches in a position from the Gas Works to Westland Row, holding Boland's Bakery, Boland's Mills, Dublin South-Western Railway Works, and dominating Merrion Square."

Commandant de Valera was now cut off from any support. His own aide-de-camp, Captain Malone, was killed at the Mount Street Bridge, making a total of seven lost before this crossing had to be relinquished to the oncoming British reinforcements. Though there was still flour and bacon enough in the warehouse to prevent the garrison from being starved out, their ammunition was running low and they were fixing knives on the ends of their rifles or wielding pitchforks found in the Mills' stable. "If the people . . . had risen *en masse*," de Valera exclaimed to the man who came in from the outside to tend the horses, "if they had gone out with nothing but knives and forks in their hands, they could have won the country."

On Sunday a messenger reached Boland's Mills and handed him an order which Commander-in-Chief Pearse had written out before being taken himself: "In order to prevent the further slaughter of Dublin citizens and in the hope of saving lives of our followers now surrendered and hopelessly outnumbered, the members of the Provisional Government present at Headquarters have agreed to an unconditional surrender, and the Commandants of the various districts in the city and country will order their commands to lay down arms." The writer of these words was now lying exhausted on a prison cot.

Shortly after noon on Sunday, Commandant de Valera acknowledged that the battle of Boland's Mills was over. A company of the Fifth Lincolnshire Regiment under the command of Captain E. J. Hitzen, newly arrived from England, was preparing from its post in Lower Mount Street near Sir Patrick Dun's Hospital to attack. With a British prisoner as a hostage, de Valera set forth from the Mills, hatless, his long legs wrapped in untidy leggings, his hair unkempt, his moustache bedraggled. His whole uniform had turned from green to drab with dirt and flour dust. The bright weather, premature evidence of spring, seemed strangely out of keeping with the shambles all around. Smoke drifted up from the streets which were blocked with burned trams and dead horses.

"Hello," he called out as he approached Sir Patrick Dun's Hospital and saw a doctor, Myles Keogh. The wounded were still being brought into the hospital's emergency entrance and he half expected to find among them some of his comrades.

"Who are you?" the doctor called back. De Valera named himself, and the British soldier accompanying him explained that the Volunteers wanted to surrender. The doctor sent for the British sergeant-major from the post next door and the dishevelled de Valera standing on the hospital steps was identified as the man in command of the rebel company at Boland's Mills. The sergeant-major sent for his own superior, and in a few minutes Captain Hitzen arrived.

To Hitzen, a young officer in his early twenties, this tall, severe-faced prisoner looked and spoke more like a teacher than a radical Sinn Feiner.

"You may shoot me," de Valera announced as he complied with an order to put up his hands, "but my men must be un-

molested when surrendering." Without demur he handed over
his revolver and field-glasses.

"How many men have you?" the British captain asked.

"I cannot say how many are left." His original outfit had been
augmented by youths joining in the fight during the week, but
his casualties were uncounted. "I should think about a hundred."

"Will they still obey your commands?"

"Yes, certainly," Commandant de Valera's reply came sharply,
and following Captain Hitzen's directions he returned under
cover of a machine-gun to the Mills. At a whistle from him, 117
Volunteers emerged, one of them presenting a white flag made
out of flour bags fastened to a stick. After they were disarmed and
the white flag transferred to a British bearer, de Valera deliberately
and meticulously locked the entrance to the premises before he
fell in on Captain Hitzen's right. As the straggling column was
marched off toward a military camp, it was flanked by Tommies
with their bayonets affixed. The Volunteers walked with shoulders
sagging, their old felt hats and caps pulled low, their torn coats
buttoned high over their mufflers, the whites of their eyes in
staring contrast to the grime on their faces. Captain Hitzen,
respectful of the rank of the prisoner at his side, addressed him
as a colonel. "You made a gallant stand," he ventured. "It is
a pity you were not on our side fighting the Germans."

The surrendering Irishman gave no quarter. "We have our
ideals," he replied, not turning his head from the road in front
of him, "and we only fight for our ideals."

CHAPTER IV

A GOOD MAN DOWN (1916–1917)

DUBLIN'S jails were already full of the rebel Volunteers when Commandant de Valera surrendered on Sunday, April 30, 1916, and the place to which the English captain marched him without his men was the town hall at Ballsbridge. This ornate stone building he knew well; it was not far from Morehampton Terrace, and here he was locked temporarily in a small, inner office with a sentry outside the door. The only window opened not on to the street but directly into the fire station adjoining the town hall, and at dusk one of the firemen came to the other side of the ledge to whisper word of an escape scheme. The fire engine would start up as if going to a fire; the imprisoned man could climb through, jump on to the running-board, and be away. The Commandant, troubled lest he seem ungrateful, tried to convey the idea that so long as his own soldiers were lying somewhere in jail in danger of their lives, he must pay the penalty with them. Drawing back from the window, he did not move when he heard the sound of the motor.

Early the following week, after some of the Volunteers had been deported to England, he was moved across the city through smouldering ruins, past armed guards everywhere, around coils of barbed wire, and into Richmond Barracks. The weather had turned cold and the place was damp with age. Off the drill hall, in a room without beds or blankets, he found about thirty of his friends, including Batt O'Connor and Sean T. O'Kelly, all of them men who had, the week before, shouldered arms together.

Although boatloads of Volunteers were being shipped to England daily for internment without trial, the officers were being held for court martial. "As British subjects taken in the act of rebellion with arms in hand," read the Castle's announcement, "they will be tried before military courts." Birrell, back in Dublin but discredited by his miscalculation, submitted his resignation and on one of the first mornings in May was driven from the Vice-regal lodge that for years had been his residence to the harbour, where the *Helga* took him on board. General Maxwell, assuming complete command, swore that he would make it for ever impossible for the Irish to revolt again, that treason would not be even whispered in Ireland for a hundred years. As the trials commenced in one of the rooms inside Richmond Barracks, those who had signed the Republican Proclamation were called first and charged with treason. Tension mounted among the others when the sentence of death was uniformly imposed.

For de Valera, unlike Pearse, death was not something to accept readily. Men under his command had been wounded, men killed, men who had as much to live for, he told himself, as he, and the frightfulness of war ground itself into him. Public censure was gravitating around all they had tried to do in Easter Week, censure for the failure of the risk they had taken if for nothing else. For the Pearses, both Padraic and Willie, for MacDonagh, for Clarke, for Connolly and the rest he agonized as well as for himself and for the mothers, the wives, the children left behind. He had had to carry out the orders given him, but buried within him was the knowledge that he himself would not have endorsed the fateful decision had he been called upon to do so.

Debarred from visiting her husband, Sinead de Valera knelt with many wives and widows in Church Street as masses were said in the Capuchin Church for the repose of the souls of the newly dead. Still in her twenties but faced with grave responsibilities, she had in safe-keeping the riddled flag from Boland's Mills that had been brought secretly to her the night of her husband's surrender. Her baby, Brian, was less than a year old. Like the other anxiety-stricken wives of the few who had risen, she remained undaunted in carrying on at home.

In their cold, cramped room, the men awaiting trial staged a mock performance. The dour school-teacher picked to play the chief defendant was charged with being a pretender to the throne of Dalkey Island, a place familiar from holiday outings on the coast south of the city. It had been a students' prank to elect a king of Dalkey until the English had stopped the revelry in the year before the Irish rebellion of 1798, suspecting it to be infiltrated with revolutionary French ideas. Now the game came also to an abrupt end when the defendant turned sharply to one of his supposed prosecutors. The game, he confessed, was getting on his nerves. Contrary to most of them, he was not buoyed up by a sense of security in comradeship and taking up his copy of St. Augustine's *Confessions*, he drew into himself.

Unknown as he had been outside Ireland, his prolonged stand at Boland's Mills was attracting world-wide attention in the newspapers. Influential Irish-Americans held that under the Fourteenth Amendment of the American Constitution he was an American citizen. Could he legally be accused of treason if he owed no allegiance to the Crown? "Neither technically or otherwise am I a British subject," the prisoner himself commented years later, "and please God I will die without ever being one." British nationality could not descend to him through his mother, but American citizenship would rest upon certification of his birth, and she instituted steps which resulted in her filing with New York City's Commissioner of Health a corrected birth certificate for him. By affidavit she explained that at the time her first child was born he had been registered under the name of George, but that when he was baptized he was named Edward. However, he would have had to register with an American consulate at the age of eighteen and take an oath of allegiance at the age of twenty-one to have retained the diplomatic protection of the United States. By that time he had become passionately imbued with allegiance to the land of his upbringing and he regarded himself as neither American nor British, but Irish first and last though there was no such thing as Irish citizenship.

De Valera could only anticipate the worst; all the other Commandants were receiving the extreme penalty. One by one they disappeared as a messenger each evening entered their quarters with a sheet of paper containing individual charges. When his companions asked him for keepsakes, he gave away every personal belonging including his fountain-pen and the buttons from his tunic. "Good-bye, Batt," he said to his former neighbour, O'Connor, "we may not meet again. You know I am expecting—that!" and he clapped his hands like the report of a gun. Five Irishmen had already been put to death as signatories of the Republican Proclamation, seven more as being in command of the rebels, and one other for murder, Prime Minister Asquith acknowledged to an apprehensive House of Commons.

By the end of the first week in May, the world outside Ireland, cut off by news censorship and a travel embargo, became suspicious over what was going on.

The second week of May, de Valera was handed the form summoning him to trial for violating the Defence of the Realm Act. From his place in the prisoner's box he saw behind the judge's desk Colonel Blackadder, glum and forbidding, the officer presiding. There were three judges altogether. The prosecutor was a young captain in the British Army, William E. Wylie, who had been born in the North of Ireland and educated at Trinity College. In spite of his Northern origins, Captain Wylie felt that he too was an Irishman like the man he had to prosecute, and he carried out his assigned task with all the fairness he could command. Captain Hitzen was hustled in to give his evidence against the Volunteer who had surrendered to him. No time was spent on cross-questioning and the whole thing was quickly brought to its conclusion while the prisoner with unlowered head and steady stare watched the proceedings in which he was the principal. Like the rest, he was sentenced to death.

Back in his own detention quarters, the trial over, de Valera returned to St. Augustine's *Confessions*. "*Tolle lege, tolle lege,*" chanted the voice in Augustine's vision. "Take up and read, take up and read." A messenger came again into the prison room. The judge had pronounced upon him the sentence of death but the sentence was commuted: "The following results of trials by Field General Court Martial were announced at the Headquarters, Irish Command, Dublin, on Thursday, May 11," and the *communiqué* continued, "Sentenced to death, and sentence commuted to penal servitude by the General Officer Commanding-in-Chief: Edward de Valera, penal servitude for life."

It was on this same day that John Dillon of the Irish Party was calling upon the House of Commons to put an instant stop to the executions. The *Manchester Guardian* was using the term atrocities. More than anything else, emergence of popular disapproval produced the stay of execution, and the reprieve granted him came not as a single instance but coupled with that for the commandant of Dublin's Fifth Battalion, Thomas Ashe. Of the ninety prisoners actually sentenced to death, all but fifteen were to be saved by commutation. Prominent among these was William Cosgrave, a senior officer; Madame Markievicz; and the Kerry commandant, Austin Stack. The British statesmen were becoming aware of world reaction and they were at this juncture depending on American munitions for prosecution of the

European war. Asquith promised on the day that de Valera's
penalty was modified to do what he could to prevent more
executions and, except for two remaining signers of the Republican manifesto, they were stayed.

On May 12, as the Prime Minister arrived in Dublin to
investigate for himself, de Valera was placed aboard a small vessel
for transportation to England. Hundreds like him were herded
on to decks too crowded to allow them to sit down during the
crossing. Lodged in the prison at Princetown on Dartmoor in
the depths of Devonshire, de Valera as Convict 95 initiated
a campaign of protest, demanding the rights of a prisoner of war.
Part of the tradition inherited from previous generations of rebels
was resistance to prison regulations. The stark and forbidding
walls that enveloped him on the wild moorlands had once rung
with the protests of other Irishmen. Austin Stack had a Fenian
father who had served a sentence at Dartmoor. Michael Davitt,
the one-handed ticket-of-leave man, had done his time here for
Fenianism decades earlier. The cells were infested with vermin.
For exercise, the prisoners had to circle slowly round the prison
yard, compelled to keep a yard apart in single file. There was
neither warm bedding nor were there decent sanitary facilities.
De Valera began to suffer from a skin irritation. They lacked the
kind of food to which they were accustomed at home, and having
an extra loaf of bread in his cell one day and knowing that the
prisoner in the cell opposite had none, he tossed it across the
narrow corridor. Both men involved were placed on bread and
water for three days.

At the sight of a new prisoner, Eoin MacNeill, being led into
the prison yard, de Valera noticed scorn seeping into the faces of
the other Irishmen. With MacNeill he had a bond of sympathy
and understanding, and in an instant he stepped out of the line,
turned, faced the men and before the guards could silence him
called out: "Irish Volunteers! Eyes left." The peremptory order
to salute MacNeill was obeyed by the prisoners, but de Valera,
having broken the silence rule, was led off to solitary confinement.
A pile of coarse, hard rope was thrust into his isolated cell and he
was ordered to separate its strands. Picking oakum was a penance
given his predecessors in the same place and, like them, he refused
to comply. To press his demands for treatment as a prisoner of
war, de Valera tried another method of resistance, the hunger

strike, but after a few days he concluded that if his claims were not met, only he would be the loser. "I know that I am responsible for stopping hunger strikes," he explained afterward. "I feared there might be conscientious scruples at the end."

To his family and to his country he was conscious of his own obligation to live. Early in November 1916, his wife gave birth to another son who was baptized Ruairi, the first name of the idealist whom de Valera had always respected and whom he had come to revere since the man's execution during the summer: Sir Roger Casement. Regular letters from his wife kept him reassured about his family. She had moved away from the city below the border of County Wicklow to the small seashore resort of Greystones or, in its Irish version, Craig Liath, from which trains ran back and forth to Dublin frequently. The modern type of house she rented was described in real estate language as a "semi-detached villa," and it lay on a new road not far inland in open country. At the lower end of Kinlen Road, several grey stucco homes had been built in pairs with identical gateposts. The row faced toward a slope of the Dublin mountains that rose unobstructed across the pastures at the top of the lane, and the meadows were full of sheep and horses and cows with birds darting among the fuchsia hedges and the holly bushes. Within quick access for the children under an archway that carried the railway tracks was the beach, long and pebbly. The father, lodged in very different surroundings, tried to see the new home in his mind's eye.

Before Christmas when a number of Irish internees were granted amnesty at the urging of Ireland's new Chief Secretary, Henry E. Duke, Eamon de Valera was not among them. The authorities moved him first to a jail in Maidstone, the county seat of Kent, and then to Lewes Jail in Sussex with over a hundred compatriots. Lewes, where discipline proved more moderate, seemed luxurious in comparison to Dartmoor and Maidstone with its wooden floors, hot-water pipes and baths and facilities for reading and writing. When the governor of the jail consulted him as a former mathematics teacher about a particular puzzle and he was able to solve it, the governor then procured for him Poincaré's volumes on quaternions. Not since his student days had he found time to pursue this subject, once intended as his thesis. He used the wall of his cell to write up the quaternionic formula of Sir William Rowan Hamilton, Ireland's nineteenth-century mathematician: $i^2 = j^2 = k^2 = ijk = -1$. He started to prepare a textbook on advanced mathematics to use when he returned to teaching, and other interests were even closer to his heart. As one who had not been foremost in the deliberations leading to promulgation of the Republic in Easter Week, governmental theory was a new subject and one he wanted to explore. He analysed the varying forms of Republicanism.

Among his fellows he was held in esteem as a scholar and strategist, as one of the "penal servitude" men, and the senior surviving Commandant. The prisoners in considering any new idea always wanted to know what he thought of it, and though regarded as conservative, he seemed to them to be able to look farther ahead, to hold out longer, never to waver. When the men decided to vote for a prison leader he was chosen, with Commandant Ashe as assistant. Provided he could get word of support from the people at home he was willing to launch a campaign of agitation, so when a comrade was released he took the opportunity to send for instructions. The answer came in a coded telegram; he had Ireland's backing to resist. On Whitsunday he gave the signal and the morning following, at the end of the exercise period, he handed an ultimatum to the governor demanding the rights that were claimed as distinct from the common criminals. The governor termed his action mutinous and the prisoners were locked up, but with de Valera in the lead they smashed their furniture, fixtures, even the windows in their cells. For three nights they continued till he was placed in chains and moved again.

The messages of encouragement received by devious means from relatives and friends made the prisoners increasingly aware that people outside were rallying to their support under the banner of Sinn Fein. Word came that this organization was designating one of those still incarcerated, Joseph McGuinness, to run in a Parliamentary by-election in County Longford set for May 1917. The object was to take away from the old Irish Party the seat it had held for years. De Valera, at first dubious lest this might compromise Republican principles, recalled that a member of Sinn Fein had tried long ago—in 1908—for a Parliamentary seat and had been defeated. It was true that old Count Plunkett had made a run earlier in 1917 in County Roscommon and had won, refusing as the first Sinn Fein M.P. to take his seat in Westminster in a gesture of protest. Sinn Fein now showed surprising strength in County Longford and returned McGuinness, whereupon de Valera dropped his reservations.

In the month of June 1917, he and his companions were suddenly called together to hear the warden announce that they were going to be released. De Valera in a flash made up his mind about the reasons behind the order, and, as the leader, signalled the men for silence. He knew that Lloyd George, successor to Asquith, headed a coalition government and had diverse factions to appease. It was Lloyd George's plan to hold an Anglo-Irish convention in Dublin, and in order to pave the way it was natural he should grant an amnesty. At the lack of response from the Irishmen, the warden was dumbfounded, but to de Valera the display of control was gratifying. To show thanks to a jailer would be a bemeaning thing. Rounded up from their various places of detention to Pentonville Prison in London, where less than a year before Casement had been executed, the Irish prisoners were there released on Sunday, June 17, 1917.

At the rail of the s.s. *Munster* carrying the jubilant crowd homeward from Holyhead, de Valera stood beside Eoin MacNeill watching for the first glimpse of the Wicklow Hills above the gentle, insubstantial shoreline. He was emerging with a reputation enhanced by his penal servitude and had heard that Sinn Feiners in County Clare through Sinn Fein's chairman, Sean Milroy, were requesting his candidature at a by-election due to the death in France of the incumbent, William Redmond, brother of the Irish Party leader. At the ship's rail, the two men were joined by a Dublin doctor, Patrick McCartan, whose medical work had taken second place to Sinn Fein and the Brotherhood. He broached the coming by-election and the enthusiasm for Professor Edward de Valera as scholar, statesman and soldier, referring to the successes of Sinn Fein in County Roscommon and County Longford. Granting as much, de Valera expressed doubts about his ability to win East Clare. He knew nothing, he told McCartan and MacNeill, about politics. Politics connoted Westminster, the embitterment of the post-Parnell days, the disillusionment he himself had experienced over home rule. It foreshadowed a different role altogether from military activity and he saw that the time might come when political activity would not be compatible with military activity, when these two horses might pull in divergent directions. He had undisclosed doubts about his own suitability.

When the s.s. *Munster* docked early in the morning at Kingstown, he led the released men as they marched ashore singing *The Soldier's Song*. People who recognized him saw a new rigidity about his mouth and a different thrust of the chin though he still looked the teacher and scholar. He was clean-shaven, his hair was prison-cut like the "croppy boys" of 1798, his skin roughened and sallow. The quiet harbour with its promenade was peaceful and prim. The rail line bringing the coaches right out to meet the boat had been put back into working order and when the little engine, whistling all the way to Dublin, pulled under the shed, the Westland Row railway platform looked to the homecomers vastly changed from the last time they had seen it, sandbagged and bullet-holed. Swept up by the welcoming Dubliners, they were carried down the ramp. In the carriages drawn up along the cobbled street below, they leaned back as the horses were whipped up by the jarveys. There were now no shots, no bullets ricocheting on the pavements, no scuttling of frightened children into alleys and down area-ways. The kerbs were overflowing with clamorous spectators who paid no attention to the British constabulary standing by uneasily. Boys hung on the red pillar-boxes and the iron palings by the marble doorsteps. In Nassau Street, shopkeepers and clerks stood watching, work suspended, and old men with long memories held tricolor flags up in front of them. In the eyes of some lone women there were tears. Over the general tumult could be caught the words of a new song the crowds were singing:

> " *'Twas in Kilmainham prison yard our fifteen martyrs died*
> *And cold and still in Arbour Hill they are lying side by side,*
> *But we will yet pay back the debt for the spirit is still alive*
> *In men who stood through fire and blood with Convict 95."*

The cheers in the street continued after the men of the hour were escorted inside Fleming's Hotel in Gardener Place. "Up de Valera" was a new shout, "Up Dev", and "Up the Republic". Then there were calls for speeches as those in the street caught glimpses of figures within the hotel. A tall, dark man in glasses came to a window and in the moment before he turned and vanished, someone cried, "He was de Valera!" Those inside, so long bound in common fetters, determined before separating to their homes that night to select a spokesman and to organize as they had planned in prison for the sake of the Republic. They were struck by the realization that their cause was no longer that of a small and despised minority. When Thomas Ashe, an avowed Brotherhood man as well as a former Commandant, declined the post, the senior officer to escape execution and their prison organizer was nominated. Doubts that had been troubling de Valera sprang to the fore and, rising in his place, he confessed that in 1916 he had not believed in open rebellion; that he personally had been in favour of MacNeill's attempted postponement. The room grew silent. Dev went on to say that he had gone out to fight believing it was a mistake but feeling that, as far as he himself was concerned, it was his duty to obey orders. Madame Markievicz was struck with his "candour and nobility."

Not only was his leadership of the prisoners at stake but the Clare candidature as well. To bring up at this time his past doubts about the rising seemed an excess of conscience. After a break, the proceedings resumed. "He was elected," noted one who was present, "to the satisfaction of everyone." No longer did he himself have any hesitation left; he would stand for Clare in the by-election and he would stand on the platform of the Republic and nothing short of the Republic. He affixed his name as the first of twenty-six with MacNeill's as the second on a plea they drafted for the American President stating the Irish case for liberty. Dr. McCartan was commissioned to deliver it in person and adding a covering letter of his own which asked America to help "in doing for Ireland what she did for Cuba."

Politics, a new undertaking for de Valera, was as strange to his wife as to himself, but as soon as he came home she agreed to share with him the continued sacrifices that his candidature implied. Awaiting him at Greystones with her were their five small children: Vivion, now six years old; Mairin, five; Eamon, four; Brian, two; and the baby Ruairi whom he had never seen before. The mother's own efforts in the movement had to be confined chiefly to teaching them, as soon as they could talk, the Irish language. In this her husband showed his pride, putting back into his button-hole the *fainne*. "Were I to get my choice," he told old friends whom he and his wife had known from their first days in the Gaelic League, "my choice, freedom without the language or the language without freedom, I would far rather have the language without freedom." If the people believed in their own language and culture, freedom, to his complex way of thinking, would be only a matter of time.

With less than a month until election day, there was no interlude of repose in the Wicklow countryside but instead the necessity to catch up on all facets of the movement. Not till he was out of prison did he realize how thoroughly the Irish Republican Brotherhood had been reactivated by Michael Collins. It now took in most of the men who had been interned with Collins in Frongoch, but one, named Gerald Boland, declined to join and some at home were following Boland's suit. Cathal Brugha preferred to devote himself to the Volunteers, feeling that the other secret organization was outliving its usefulness, and to de Valera working with the Dublin Brigade seemed more essential. It was as a soldier that he resolved to make his entry into politics. He did not attend the Brotherhood meetings.

General election headquarters were opened in Westmoreland Street in the heart of Dublin. De Valera, wearing the greenish jacket of the Volunteers in spite of the ban by the British upon any uniforms, took the train across the Irish midlands to County Clare. As far away as London, the House of Commons was warned by one of its members to expect some "hot stuff in the shape of speeches." The journey carried him across a changing landscape from the green-gold of washed grass in the sunlight to the West's tumbled stones as grey as the rain that fell upon them. It was only six years since he and Sinead ni Fhlannagain had spent a summer together here. Though he was coming back changed inwardly and outwardly by all that had happened to him and to his country, his sense of romance about the West was undiminished.

In Ennis, the main town of County Clare, he made his first appearance standing in an open carriage under the shaft erected to the memory of Daniel O'Connell the liberator, just where the town's old, angling streets came together in a cross. Shops lined the streets, their windows full of crockery, pots and pans and sweets. Homespuns were draped from their bolts in the doorways. The shopkeepers looked out to see what was going on and the butcher left his scooped-out chopping-block to stand in his open store-front. Clare people were reserved, as proud of belonging to that county as if the neighbouring counties were foreign soil. The strange candidate's first words were in the language still spoken in Clare, "*Nil de chead agam-sa Tosnu ar an obair bheannuighthe seo i dteanga na namhad.*" Then he dropped his voice. "I have no permission to begin this holy work in the language of the enemy." Speaking without notes, he was at the start hesitant and abrupt but soon his sentences were streaming forth, laden with an insistent challenge. "I stand for that," he declared as he pointed to the Republican Proclamation of Easter Week which he had brought with him. Over and over he repeated the word Republic. He was running, he said, to test whether the struggle for Irish freedom was to be renewed by the slow and unrewarding Parliamentary debates in which the English had outwitted and outdone them, or whether it was to be fought on the basis of severance and sovereignty. Fear of partition, he let it be known, was bringing him into politics. To the North he offered fair and just rights of minority representation in any united and independent administration. Freedom for the South was not enough, for unity must be preserved.

He was interrupted when the supporters of his opponent, Patrick Lynch, a Clare man himself, marched in a column through his audience denouncing the Sinn Feiners as socialists, anarchists, revolutionaries. At that, British soldiers rushed with machine-guns to the scene, firing shots into the air. De Valera pleaded with his listeners, some of them armed with hurley sticks, not to retaliate. "You will be described to the world as a rabble, and Ireland's name will be hurt." It was agreed at his suggestion that his backers and Lynch's would appoint their own keepers of the peace to make it unnecessary for the British agents henceforth to interfere.

The constituency was a big one stretching from Ballyvaughan in the north to County Limerick in the south, and he travelled back and forth, crossing into County Limerick when he had time to visit his uncle at the cottage in Bruree. At a cross roads in a remote district of East Clare the car in which he and MacNeill and co-workers were riding was stopped by a cluster of Clare folk who, hearing that the Sinn Fein candidate would be coming through, the one they kept hearing of as "Dev," had dropped their turf-cutting and walked, some of them for miles, to see him. He spoke a few words in Irish, then shook hands all round, and as his car disappeared over the next hill the Claremen filled in the road behind him, waving and pounding their twisted sticks. "There's the man for Clare," one old-timer exclaimed, his whiskers fringing his cheeks and chin, "for Clare and for Ireland." They thought of him as humble and poor like themselves but the fact that, unlike them, he had something in him beside Irish added to his interest. He was a man of learning, too.

Everywhere he went, they began to call him Dev, at once a name and a title. He was no stranger now, nor madman nor visionary as his enemies would have had them believe. No one, no nation, declared this candidate, was more amenable to reason, to practicality, and to law so long as that law was legitimate. He was not thinking of his countrymen as mere dreamers of dreams, he said. The time when they would be satisfied with dreams had gone. Claremen and Sinn Feiners all over Ireland threw their resources into the balloting on July 11, 1917. Dev together with his campaigners, and Lynch with his, assembled on the steps of Clare's courthouse to hear the high sheriff announce the results. For Lynch, 2,035 votes were reported; for de Valera, 5,010. "England has her answer," came a thick, country voice from below the steps and a shout went up.

Wherever Dev went in the summer of 1917, travelling by train for lack of a car, speaking at other by-elections, attending Sinn Fein meetings, inspecting units of the Volunteers, throngs came to see and hear him as the "Irish Eagle." Lieutenant Ernie O'Malley of the Volunteers, awaiting his arrival one day that summer at the hotel in the midlands town of Tullamore for an inspection of the local contingent, saw him stride into the lounge garbed in the outlawed uniform. Dev took off his cap with its silver badges, revealing a mat of dark hair growing in close to the skull. Deep lines spread from either side of his nose around the corners of the wide mouth, giving him something of the eagle's ferocity. As questions and answers began to flow between them, soldier to soldier, O'Malley saw the visitor's features acquire unexpected mobility, heard his voice take on the modulation that came from personal understanding of all the obstacles in bringing a group of untrained recruits up to parade efficiency, and O'Malley grasped his sense of discipline. If a man was not sober, the older officer advised, if he was seen to be going into the public-houses too often, they did not want him in the force.

The Tullamore Volunteers as they paraded and as they listened to what de Valera had to tell them caught his feeling of their mission. Why should they fight for England, he exhorted, they who were being called traitors? "Traitors to what?" and he turned toward the tricolor on the platform. They would be no traitors to that flag, the only flag they were willing to fight and die for, not for the blood-stained Union Jack. The Volunteers, knowing that they were mocked by some as rainbow chasers, were reassured to hear Dev proclaim that it was no new pot of gold they were pursuing. "Get every rifle you can," he told them, "and those of you who cannot get rifles, get shot-guns; if you cannot get these, get the . . . pike, a very good weapon at close fighting."

"We have got them," shouted the Volunteers massing before him.

"Then get more of them. A row of ten-foot pikes will beat a row of bayonets any day."

At the reports of his speeches in the newspapers, the British Prime Minister rose in the House of Commons. "They are," pronounced Lloyd George, "plain, deliberate, and I might almost say cold-blooded, incitements to rebellion." When the Chief Secretary for Ireland, Mr. Duke, recalled that the "honourable member for East Clare" had stated at the time of his imprisonment that his birthplace was New York, and recalled also that there was no record of his having been subsequently naturalized as a British subject, the eligibility of that individual to belong to Parliament was itself questioned. Lloyd George was pressed as to why no restrictions were imposed upon his movements.

De Valera was repeating wherever he went that his followers would have to fight in every way which prudence and common sense dictated, for they could not drop the threat of force. "Why should we?" he demanded.

"Never," came the instant retort and when pikes and hurley sticks were subsequently banned, the Volunteers drilled with broomsticks slanted over their shoulders. Down in Fermoy, a shop apprentice named Liam Lynch led the local company out to greet him and Lynch's zeal impressed de Valera with what his younger compatriots everywhere had in them. Though Dev sometimes made his inspections wearing a long, black overcoat and big black hat, it was usually the uniform. Military needs consumed him.

"Start at once and purchase shot-guns and buckshot," was his advice. "This is much more effective at close quarters than ball cartridge." By the following autumn, Volunteer units from all over the country sent representatives to Dublin to choose a chief for the coming year. Some, including Austin Stack and Thomas Ashe, had been re-arrested by the British and the latter had died on hunger strike in Mountjoy Jail in Dublin. Of those present for the Volunteers' meeting Brugha, who had kept the force alive while the others were in jail, had at his side Rory O'Connor as director of engineering and Michael Collins as director of organization. The question arose as to whether the use of violence was justifiable and latent differences of opinion were revealed, though no one was entirely explicit for or against it. De Valera, speaking as the senior officer, put across the point that military victory would not be an end in itself, that military victory had to have a political objective. Brugha, sensing that he could not exact similar agreement, withdrew his name from re-nomination for the Volunteers' headship and de Valera, as if by automatic consent, took his place.

Disagreements also asserted themselves when the annual meeting or *Ard Fheis* of Sinn Fein convened in Dublin in the same month of October 1917. MacNeill's arrival evoked protests from the newer members of the movement and from Madame Markievicz. Not only did Griffith take up the cudgels in his behalf, but de Valera said he would not participate unless the Professor was allowed to do so, and MacNeill was seated. In the preliminary sessions among key individuals Griffith, still president of Sinn Fein, re-enunciated the ideas that dated from his founding of the organization. From his study of Austro-Hungary, he derived his early theory of a dual monarchy wherein one ruler might serve as king of England and as king of Ireland. Brugha, on the other hand, wanted a Republic declared by force if necessary, and this —Rory O'Connor insisted—was the only possible goal. Collins put in a reminder that the Brotherhood's Supreme Council was watching whatever Sinn Fein might do. As for de Valera, he had not committed himself to any form of government. There was, he noted, unanimity on only one score, that Sinn Fein ought to plan a *de facto* government of some kind for Ireland regardless of what form it might take, and this basic idea he undertook to reduce to writing for the consideration of the whole *Ard Fheis*.

What came from de Valera's pen for the consideration of the delegates was a new constitution for Sinn Fein calling for a provisional government to be set up as soon as the war in Europe was over. The preamble incorporated a compromise concerning the form to be given the provisional government. "Sinn Fein aims at securing the international recognition of Ireland as an independent Irish Republic. Having achieved that status the Irish people may by referendum freely choose their own form of Government." This served to postpone the crucial decision. As soon as a peace conference could be held in Europe, the new programme could be implemented. Until then, Sinn Fein could serve as the civil arm of the nation and the Volunteers as the military arm.

For all his present willingness to postpone decision on a permanent form of government, de Valera did not conceal from the *Ard Fheis* that he was prepared to use physical force if it should be necessary to put the new constitution into effect when the time came. Each Sinn Fein club, he recommended, should get one rifle and all members of the club should learn its mechanism and operation. His head and shoulders, as he spoke, were thrust forward with his stiff, dark hair as it grew in again falling over his forehead, his face unlighted by any smile, his right hand upraised with fingers clenched, his left hand plunged into the pocket of his baggy jacket. England, he told them with a hollow resonance, was pretending that it was not by the naked sword that she was keeping Ireland in duress. "We will draw the naked sword to make her bare her naked sword."

Arthur Griffith, who had been written off long ago by one university student, James Joyce, as a man who had no go in him for the mob, was conscious that his old, passive programme must be re-shaped for action. Feeling that he himself could not do it, he exclaimed to those seated near him, "Thank God for de Valera, heaven must have sent him." The constitution as drafted was adopted by the delegates. When the *Ard Fheis* proceeded to the business of electing a president for the new term, Griffith declined to be considered again. This was the signal for the other candidate, Count Plunkett, to eliminate himself and the way was cleared for what was obviously in the delegates' minds. Eamon de Valera was by acclamation chosen. So that he would not have to resume teaching, Sinn Fein arranged a salary of £500 a year. His only fear was whether he had it within him to move fast enough. "No one need ever tell me," he replied to one well-intentioned adviser, "to go slow. What I want is someone to tell me to go forward."

In his speech accepting the office, Sinn Fein's new president repeated his reservations: "It is as an Irish Republic that we have a chance of getting international recognition. Some of us would wish, having got that recognition, to have a Republican form of government. Some might have fault to find with that and prefer other forms of government." Doubt on one score at least was settled when he added that "there is no contemplation of having a Monarchy in which the Monarch would be of the House of Windsor." If it did not prove possible to "find a form of words to meet the wishes of all parties," he himself would have to side with the Republicans, he made it clear. Brugha and Griffith, neither of whom relinquished his own convictions, both came forward to congratulate him and he sensed that he had become, as he was to put it, "a sort of connecting link between the two." With the assumption of leadership in both Sinn Fein and the Volunteers, he gathered the reins into his own hand. "I combined therefore in myself," as he was to look back upon this moment, "the political headship and the military headship."

CHAPTER V

RAINBOW CHASERS (1918–1919)

TO prove that he recognized no dividing line between North and South, Eamon de Valera, M.P., set out with a bodyguard on St. Patrick's Eve in March 1918, over roads leading up to the mountains of Mourne in the Orange North. He had, according to reports, told one audience in Bessborough that "The Unionists are a rock on the road . . . we must, if necessary, blast it out of our path." Before midnight he and his cohorts arrived with hurley sticks and flaming torches outside the hall in Belfast where local Republicans had called a rally. Finding the building barred and bolted, they moved on to a field outside the city where the "professor" from Dublin—Professor Moonlight this time— began to address the several thousand Northern nationalists who had followed the cavalcade out from the city. Out of the darkness Belfast police officers appeared but the crowd, emboldened by the bravado of Professor Moonlight, refused to disperse. Clubs flailed out in the red light of the torches. Rioting ran wild but by morning Dev was back on home territory, free and unharmed.

Now that he was the indubitable chief of the military and civil movements alike, the Press became one of his growing concerns, and to an American journalist from the *Christian Science Monitor* he gave what he said was his first interview with a foreign newspaper. The conversation took place in an old house off St. Stephen's Green, the entrance being just another dark, scuffed doorway along Harcourt Street's flat brick frontages. The hall was grimy and in the room itself there was a paucity of furniture, no files, no documents, with signs like "Beware" and "Walls have Ears" hanging on the drab plaster. This, the reporter knew, was the inner sanctum of the organization being mentioned in fearful whispers all over the world, Number 6 Harcourt Street, the headquarters of Sinn Fein. "Newspapers, you know, are the devil's chief agency in the modern world," the Sinn Feiner began.

It was understandable that he should resent the news that was going out of his country, censored as it was by the British, and the reporter, ignoring the rebuff, turned to the subject of the war in Europe. "If you were free tomorrow, you would not hand over your ports to Germany?"

"If England took away her troops and our independence was acknowledged," he parried, "we would fight to the last man to maintain that independence." It was not the Irish ports which the British needed in the spring of 1918 so much as it was Irish manpower. Sir Henry Wilson, Chief of the Imperial General Staff, was urging that Irishmen be drafted without further delay. The British civil officials, however, who were stationed in Ireland thought there were too few troops there to enforce anything so unpopular. Prime Minister Lloyd George tried to secure the backing of the Anglo-Irish convention for conscription but when, by April 1918, that attentuated assembly refused, it was allowed to die and without further delay a bill was presented in Parliament to require the enlistment of Irishmen at any time by a mere order in council. The threat of conscription roused the animosity of Sinn Fein and the Irish Party alike, making the two as one on this issue. When Lloyd George's measure passed, Dillon, who had become head of the Irish Party following Redmond's death, led the Party out of the House of Commons.

In Dublin the Lord Mayor invited both de Valera and Dillon to the Mansion House in Dawson Street for a conference of all Irish factions to deal with the subject of conscription. Griffith and MacNeill were summoned and from the Irish Party, O'Brien and Healy. Labour leaders were included so that the British for the first time were confronted by a solid front. De Valera arrived with Griffith, deep in conversation, looking all the more striking by the side of the short, moustached founder of Sinn Fein. As the pair walked up Dawson Street de Valera, clutching a small professor's satchel, scarcely seemed to note from his downcast eyes the people following at their heels. The exterior of the eighteenth-century Mansion House was familiar to him with its gravelled approach and old-fashioned lantern-posts; the iron lace trimming over the great front windows; the glass *porte cochère* beneath which carriages used to discharge their dignitaries; the whole having the look of a birdcage. Inside he saw that it was part of another world, the rooms being hung with portraits of British rulers, including Queen Victoria, and pictures of Dublin's be-robed and be-wigged Lord Mayors. De Valera was unawed by the older nationalists in whose company he found himself.

The Irish Party leaders were at the same time taking his measure. Healy, curious about the "Castilian" features of the younger man, described him as "tall, spare, spectacled, schoolmasterly, of Jewish cast, and as chatterful as Griffith was reserved." The ebullient Sinn Feiner could not, Healy noted, pronounce either the thick or thin "th" and his "dats" and "tinks" grated on the ear. "Still, a resourceful fellow." William O'Brien was impressed by "his transparent sincerity . . . his gentleness and equability."

De Valera drafted in his fine, controlled script a communication elaborating the united point of view on compulsory military service to send to the United States, but it did not at first suit Dillon. The author, as he resisted changing it, said, "You will bear with us, won't you?" His smile made him look to his older colleagues almost boyish. "You know I am an old schoolmaster." He surprised them by the good humour of which he was capable. "Even the obstinacy," and it was sometimes trying, O'Brien admitted, "with which he would defend a thesis as though it were a point in pure mathematics with more than the French bigotry for logic, became tolerable. . . ." Healy sensed that he and his contemporaries were in no position to pit their prestige against this new idol. When he proposed to his *confrères* with his energetic resourcefulness that they present their case to the Irish bishops who were sitting with Cardinal Logue at St. Patrick's College outside Dublin in Maynooth, they did not deny the value of this idea but none was eager to accompany him. "I am not accustomed," Healy demurred, "to meeting bishops or archbishops."

"Oh," retorted de Valera easily, again glad to have a ready source of self-confidence, "there's nothing in that." He was at once deprecating and debonair. "I have lived all my life among priests." The pledge taken in Irish parishes on an April Sunday following against compulsory military service was again the work of his pen.

The claws of Sinn Fein would be cut, Lloyd George persisted, by removing the likeliest young Irishmen to France as conscripts. England was fearful of another rising and he was determined to eliminate the threat at his back door. With Germany on the march in France and nearing the Marne as spring of 1918 advanced, he could afford no weakness in his armour. "I would suggest,"

General Bryan T. Mahon, who was at the head of the Irish command, wrote the Prime Minister confidentially, "that the first thing is to get all known leaders out of the way at once; extra troops should be on the spot immediately, and everyone, irrespective of who he is, arrested on the first sign of trouble." Lloyd George thereupon took the precaution of securing a change in the Defence of the Realm Act so that it would be possible to deport Irish violators without public trial, a change which was not publicly announced. German-Irish collaboration was suspected again.

In contacts between Dublin and Berlin, a direct part had been played by the Irish in New York who, before de Valera had been released from prison, had again requested Germany to land an armed force in Ireland. Berlin had offered to send rifles, machine-guns and cartridges to Galway and Tralee, but to this the reply had come from America, "Project declined, as without landing (i.e. of troops) it would be useless." Off the coast of Galway on April 12, 1918, nevertheless, a German submarine put ashore an Irish prisoner of war named Joseph Dowling, the commanding officer of those Irishmen who had enrolled in the late Sir Roger Casement's brigade. Dowling like Casement before him was apprehended on the shore. English allegations about a plan to land German arms and ammunition gained credence and the West of Ireland was promptly declared a military zone. The *Clare Champion* was suppressed; Tommies moved in; the mails were censored.

De Valera, when approached for a statement, asserted that, "If the Germans came to Ireland to hold it, those who are now resisting English power would be the first to resist the Germans." He neither owned nor disowned any knowledge about Dowling's landing, though some among the Volunteers knew that the man had been sent by the Germans. De Valera suggested later with a hint of irony that the Irish in America might know more about the movement than some at home. MacNeill gave out the opinion that the Chief was strongly anti-German; that he would not be a party to any German intrigues, and others working closely with the Chief were sure it was a complete surprise to him, to Collins, and to the Brotherhood as well. When Lord Wimborne and his associates in Dublin Castle expressed their conviction that de Valera was not in any plot with the enemy, he and the Chief

Secretary, Mr. Duke, both of whom had differed with their Government in London as to the wisdom of conscription as well as over the likelihood of German-Irish collaboration, were on May 11, 1918, summarily replaced with Sir John French and Mr. Edward Shortt. Within a week the new Lord Lieutenant prepared a proclamation in which it was asserted that a German plot had been uncovered in Ireland.

On the evening of May 17, 1918, de Valera, arriving at Volunteer headquarters in Dublin to preside over a regular meeting of the executive committee, was surprised to find some of the clerks removing material from the files. The reason for such activity at that hour was explained when Michael Collins appeared with news secured by his scouts from inside Dublin Castle. Certain prominent Sinn Feiners were about to be taken into custody. De Valera had with him in his satchel a "Memorandum on Irish Army Organization" covering "General Problems of Irish Defence" and various papers for the agenda. Other reports were discussed and turned in to him, but when the regular business was finished, the men returned to the report which Collins had brought. If it were true, they asked each other, would it be better to try to avoid arrest or to submit? The latter course would attract world-wide attention. The Chief had no car of his own, and though Collins advised him to spend the night in the city, he decided to go home to Greystones. His own arrest, if it happened, might do the cause more good than harm. What else was there for him to do by way of action till the war in Europe ended? "Quietly reasoning the situation out on these lines we decided unanimously," reported a lawyer who was present, Darrell Figgis, "to stand to our arrests and take the consequences." Dev caught the 10.15 train out of the Harcourt Street station. At Bray he had to change and two other passengers from Dublin did the same thing. In an hour or less the engine reached the quiet Greystones platform by the side of the sea. De Valera put his hand out of the carriage window to open the door. The two who had travelled on the same train, Head Constable Mulligan of the Royal Irish Constabulary and his assistant, revealed their identity and Dev in the dark stepped down into the hands of District Inspector Molony, waiting for the train there.

In the waiting-room his bag was seized, its contents hastily examined. The paper on army organization seemed to be in his own handwriting. Though he was not given a chance to explain at the moment, he denied later that it was either composed by him or at his suggestion. "The document . . . attributed to me and said to be in my handwriting, is not in my handwriting." Among other papers he was said to be carrying were "extracts from a statement of Ireland's case before the powers to be assembled in a peace conference," and a letter with suggestions about how to avert conscription. This he insisted was not in his handwriting either but had been handed to him that evening while he was presiding at the Volunteers' meeting and, to protect the author, he had "pinched off" the signature.

He was put in an automobile and driven up the coast to Kingstown where the official waiting in the lighted shed on the dock handed him a paper signed by the new Chief Secretary, Mr. Shortt. It was an order of internment without trial. Other persons were being driven out on to the wharf in big lorries. Before being taken aboard the gunboat lying in the harbour, he turned to reassure a sympathizer who was watching the commotion. "Be calm and confident," he urged. After all, the leaders were submitting to what they called the "Pretence of the Realm Act" by their own decision and for their own purposes. Climbing down a ladder into the small hold of the vessel, he saw in the dim light of a lantern the upturned faces of Count Plunkett and Griffith; there too in her place with the men was the dishevelled but still beautiful and very elated "Madame." Dev stretched himself out to try to sleep but new arrivals kept climbing down to join them and he jumped up to greet each one. Michael Collins, bicycling round Dublin to spread the warning, was not found by the police. When daylight sifted into the stuffy hold, mugs of tea were brought down with biscuits, but not until eighty or more were aboard did the crossing begin.

Two years to the month had passed since Eamon de Valera had come to England before, but the circumstances of his arrival were hardly different. The country to which he was being brought was still at war externally with Germany and internally with Ireland. While the Irish prisoners debarked in Holyhead on Saturday night, searchlights played over the darkening scene and all were marched off to a military camp to sleep on straw. On Monday morning de Valera, Griffith and a few others prominent among the prisoners were started off by an early train for

Gloucester. At the stations along the way they could glimpse pictures of themselves in the papers and lists of their names headed by "Edward de Valera, M.P.". They searched the newspapers sent in to them in Gloucester Jail for word about their arrests but found little or nothing in the nature of an official explanation until the Saturday following. Then the British Government released what Chief Secretary Shortt called the evidence of a German plot: "According to documents found on his person de Valera had worked out in detail the constitution of his rebel army and hoped to be able to muster a half a million trained men." Further, the official statement said, an agent from Germany had been landed by submarine and a new rising, contingent upon the landing of munitions from submarines, had been planned to follow a German offensive in the West when Great Britain would be stripped of troops. Uncertainty and incredulity spread in England as well as in Ireland. "You could not hang a dog upon the evidence," commented one Englishman in the House of Commons, "in this plot." De Valera voluntarily gave his own answer later: "There was no such thing as this German plot of 1918. . . . From July 1917 I was intimately in touch with all the major activities both of the Sinn Fein political organization and of the Irish Volunteers, and so I speak with knowledge and authority."

Transferred within a week to Lincoln Jail, de Valera was soon encouraging his fellows to plan their prison regimen of reading, religious devotions and physical exercise. Among a group of English prisoners at Lincoln who, like the Irish, had resisted conscription—the conscientious objectors—he discovered a kindred spirit. In the prison yard he ran races and took a delight in being able to beat men younger than he. He heard that the British had tried once more after the mass deportation to conscript the Irish but that Dillon had held out against it, whereupon Lloyd George had abandoned the idea. When he thought about conditions in Ireland, he knew that the direction of the Volunteers would be taken over by Collins. Harry Boland, himself a Brotherhood man whom Dev knew from their days in Dartmoor together, the brother of Gerald, both being the sons of a Fenian, could step into the breach left in Sinn Fein by the imprisonment of both himself as president and of Griffith as vice-president.

So far as his family in Greystones was concerned, his mind

was at rest because supporters in County Clare were helping his wife. Being unable to perform the duties of the presidency for Sinn Fein, he would not permit payments to be made from his salary, but the small sum earned by the publication of his statement of the case against conscription was being deposited to Mrs. de Valera's account. This, when he heard of it, worried him; he wondered what Healy and the others with whom he had worked at the Mansion House on the anti-conscription pledge would think. His wife was not allowed to visit him in England, which would have been difficult for her to do anyway, but letters were permitted. Members of her own family were near at hand in Dublin to help when, in the summer of 1918, another baby arrived, this time a girl called Emer from Irish folk-lore. Away in prison, the baby's father wished that he might see his second daughter—his sixth child.

"I know you will be glad," he wrote to his mother in America, "that I have served all our masses here. I feel like a little boy again and I pray that my childish faith may ever remain with me. I tell you this because I know it will give you more pleasure than anything else I could write." In his own solitude he could sympathize with his mother, knowing that his half-brother had gone away to join the priesthood. "I hope you will see Tom soon. You must feel lonely without him, although I am certain you do not regret you reared him for such a calling." Father Thomas Wheelwright, after being ordained at Mount Saint Alphonsus in Esopus, New York, had gone to teach mathematics at St. Mary's College in North East, Pennsylvania. Letters from him and from his mother arrived to greet Dev in October when he celebrated his thirty-sixth birthday in his prison cell. "Tom mentions references to me in the Press," wrote Eamon. "I once remember balking at an essay, 'The Press', in an examination. I often regret I had not then my present experience of it! What a power for evil it is, setting classes and nations at each other's throats. . . ."

The course that world events were taking he followed more closely than he had had time to do before. "I read the English papers here a great deal," he wrote in one family letter. "Were I an Englishman I'd feel rather proud of the *Manchester Guardian*. It is sane in general. As far as its views on Ireland goes, that is another matter. . . ." His old wrath gorged up at the comments printed on Ireland. " 'Cowards!' 'Shirkers!' 'Skulkers!' screams the British Press," he quoted, infuriated at the lack of attention to the Irishmen's reasons for refusing to fight on the side of England.

The news in November 1918 of Germany's surrender made little immediate change in the monotony inside Lincoln Jail, but to Sinn Fein's plans, laid over a year before, the return of peace meant the time for action. The Sinn Feiners had agreed to wait only till the war ended before re-proclaiming the Irish Republic. Shortly after the armistice was signed, de Valera sent through his wife a letter to be forwarded to Rochester, New York:

Lincoln Prison,
Nov. 28, 1918.

My dear Mother,

    . . . I hate writing to you from a place like this—and yet when I am at liberty I have so little time to write. . . .

I am sure you are all relieved that the war is over. If America holds to the principles enunciated by her President during the war she will have a noble place in the history of nations—but will the President be able to get them accepted by others whose entry into the war was on motives less unselfish?

I hope uncle's children and aunt's have come through the fighting. It is particularly hard on those who are now receiving the news of the deaths of relatives. After the armistice it seems so awful. Whoever caused the war, humanity has paid a heavy price for it. . . .

This life is so short in comparison with the future it counts for little what sorrows and inconveniences it brings. Were it not so short who would be ready to die. With love to yourself and Uncle Charlie, I am dearest mother,

Eddie.

He got word from Dublin that Sinn Fein intended to put up a slate of candidates when Lloyd George after the armistice called a general election—an election which, of course, included the Irish seats in the House of Commons. By voting for or against the candidates nominated by Sinn Fein, the Irish people would indicate whether they approved of establishing a *de facto* government. De Valera's name was put up not only in his original constituency in East Clare but in County Mayo, in County Down in the North and in Belfast itself. The electoral register had, he knew, been revised so that a portion of the Irish women would have the franchise and many women were Republicans. Feeling almost in harness again, he drew up a manifesto to send back to his constituencies calling attention to President Woodrow Wilson's advocacy of self-determination. "As you are aware," he wrote, "my views I may not give," and his manifesto, intercepted by the censors, never reached the voters. It was not needed.

At the polls early in December 1918, Sinn Fein overwhelmed the Irish Party. Sinn Fein, having held only 6 out of 105 Irish seats in the House of Commons, won 73 of them. The British statesman, Winston S. Churchill, lamented that the old nationalists, the Parliamentarians, had not come forward in defence of their pre-war agreement on home rule, and Churchill called Ireland the "sick and ailing child of the British Empire." The popular vote, instead of endorsing the act that was upon the British statute books waiting only for the declaration of peace to go into operation, ratified the Sinn Fein programme for a native Irish government. The old Irish Party was blotted out of existence and de Valera personally triumphed in East Clare, defeated Dillon in East Mayo, and carried all the other constituencies where he had been up besides. Inside Lincoln, he received cabled congratulations from New York sent by the Clan-na-Gael leader, Judge Cohalan.

The message came at a significant moment because the English were saying that suspicions of German-Irish collusion had put a damper on American sympathies. De Valera knew that if Ireland was going to set up her own government, help would have to be obtained from America. An idea crossed his mind, one that he could not then carry out but an idea he remembered, the possibility of making a trip to America to enlist aid for his cause.

Duly elected Sinn Feiners who were not in prison assembled without any secrecy in Dublin's Mansion House on January 21, 1919, to convoke the first session of the Irish Republic's legislature, Dail Eireann, and on the roll were formally inscribed the names of those unable to attend because of "the foreign enemy." De Valera, reading of the occasion in the papers, longed to be back across the Irish Sea. Sinn Fein interpreted the vote as a mandate to implement its constitution. Sean T. O'Kelly was in the chair as speaker. Though old Count Plunkett was present as a link with the oldest fighters, the majority in the Round Room were younger recruits to the political ranks. Richard Barton, an Oxford-educated landowner and a Protestant, was reported present. He was, Dev recalled, a convert to Sinn Fein from the days of 1916 when, as a young lieutenant in the British Army, he had been assigned to guard the Irish prisoners and, being so impressed by their faith, had since made common cause with them. Now he had risen to the rank of Commandant in the Volunteers. In the Mansion House also sat Richard—Dick— Mulcahy, known as a precise, correct disciplinarian who had fought at the side of Thomas Ashe in Easter Week and had helped resuscitate the Irish Republican Brotherhood inside Frongoch with Collins. Another of the Sinn Feiners present was a nephew of Timothy Healy, Kevin O'Higgins, sharp of mind and tongue who, though still a law student, had served a prison term.

First order of business reported from the Mansion House was the adoption of a declaration of independence ratifying the fact that the Republic was constitutionally established. The *teachtai*, as the deputies called themselves, appointed three of their members to represent them at the peace conference scheduled for Versailles: de Valera, Count Plunkett and Griffith. Cathal Brugha was designated as the President of the Dail *pro tem*. "The President," noted one of the *teachtai*, "in this case means the President of the Ministry," it being assumed that a President of the Republic as distinct from the leader of the Government could be elected only by the people as a whole, not by the Dail.

Though Brugha was to serve for the moment as President of the Dail, it was inferred that the real Chief would be available as soon as he got out of Lincoln. In the longest and darkest days of the year, restlessness grew upon de Valera from the cumulative effect of confinement for some twenty-two months within less than three years. Lincoln after all was but one of the many English jails he had come to know too intimately. At Dartmoor, remote and forbidding, he had begun in May of 1916 his penal servitude. Next had been Maidstone Jail in Kent. When Christmas of that year had brought release for some of his fellows, he had been moved instead to Lewes in Sussex. From Lewes he had been transferred again before being sent to Pentonville and thence released in June 1917. Then, after less than a year, he had found himself back in England in Gloucester Prison. At the end of one week there, he had been lodged in Lincoln Jail and there he had remained throughout the spring, the summer, the autumn and on into the winter of 1918 to 1919.

About a week after the Dail's inaugural session Collins, known in Brotherhood circles as the director of escapes, with Harry Boland's assistance brought to culmination certain carefully laid plans. Dev, by saving candle stubs from the prison altar when he served at mass, had got a wax impression of the chaplain's key from which the making of duplicates was undertaken inside and outside the prison walls. On the night of February 3, 1919, he saw the signal he was expecting flashed by a light from the black fields outside. With two companions and a rope-ladder, he made his way to the gate which Collins and Boland were trying to open from the outside. Their key broke in the lock. De Valera had another duplicate and he and his companion walked past the sentry unobserved into the winter night. "I got out of Lincoln Jail," he was to relate, "through neglect of routine." By private automobile he was taken to the town of Newark some miles to the north where, outside the local hotel, a taxi picked him up and the driver, though chary of his petrol ration, was persuaded to take him as far as Manchester. There Dev went into hiding as stories about him grew in the Press. When he had to go out on the street, as it was recounted, he wore a red beard. Police notices were posted describing the fugitive as aged "35, a professor, standing 6 ft. 3 in.". Coastal towns were watched, outbound ships searched, and as far away as Holland warrants were sworn out at the request of the British for his apprehension.

When Collins came to confer with him in Manchester, Dev broached his idea of going to the United States. Liverpool, close by, had frequent sailings and along its waterfront were many Irish seamen friendly to the Republic. A twofold purpose would, as Dev explained it, be served: first, obtaining American recognition for the *de facto* Irish Republic; and second, raising funds to support the Republican government. Dev pointed out that he would not be an outsider in the country where he had been born and where his mother still made her home.

To be sure, not all the prosperous and powerful Irishmen in the United States were of one mind among themselves about Ireland's future and had not been for years, but that was another

reason for his going; perhaps he could unite the factions. Dr.
McCartan was at loggerheads with the Clan and so was Liam
Mellowes, who had taken refuge in the United States after the
Easter rising. Mellowes' letters were full of the feuding among
the Irish-Americans. The latter reported his own admiration for
Joseph McGarrity, who had risen from immigrant boy to wealthy
distiller in Philadelphia. McGarrity was aiming for nothing short
of American recognition for the Republic, and though he was
a member of the Clan-na-Gael he was not in control of it as was
old John Devoy. Devoy was backed by those who were carrying
on the Fenian tradition, the "irreconcilables." Closest to Devoy
was Judge Cohalan, who was talking about self-determination.

The hazards to which Dev exposed himself by one abortive
attempt to leave for America left Collins aghast. "You know
what it is," Collins remarked to his Brotherhood confidants back
in Dublin, "to try to argue with Dev." The others nodded. "He
says he . . . thought it all out while in prison and that he feels the
one place where he can be useful to Ireland is in America."
Already the secret publication of the Volunteers, *An tOglach*, had
announced that Commandant de Valera was at large, was well-
informed, was taking a leading part in the councils of the Republican Government. Cathal Brugha, apprehensive over further
absence of the Chief at a time when his influence was needed
at home to prevent factions from forming, crossed over to
Manchester and told him outright that the people were expecting
him back to take his rightful place in the new government. He,
Brugha, had accepted the headship of the Dail, fully conscious
of his own inability to supply the necessary integration, on the
assumption that it would be for a brief interval only.

The Chief yielded, agreeing for the time at least to return and
when, a few weeks after his escape, most of the other internees
were voluntarily released by the British, the coast seemed clear
for him. His transformation into herodom had been completed
by the magic of his jail-break and Sinn Fein planned to welcome
him home publicly. "Why, to use the famous word, it would be
'unthinkable,' " he wrote in consternation and sarcasm cancelling
the plan; Britain would never permit a public reception for him.
"We who have waited know how to wait. Many a heavy fish is
caught even with a fine line if the angler is patient." Character-
istically, he not only sent a copy of his dictum in this matter to

the Sinn Fein executive committee and another to the Lord Mayor, but on top of that requested the former to check with the latter.

When he arrived back, the reunion was as quiet as he wished it to be. Brugha got a car to drive the Chief home to Greystones though the latter demurred at the extravagance when he could, he said, as easily take the train from Dublin. He found Vivion, Mairin, Eamon, Brian and Ruairi grown almost beyond recognition and saw his baby daughter Emer. His wife surmised that he would never be content to go back to teaching. At first he stayed in seclusion, but the British had ceased to hunt for him. Griffith was worried by the man's impetuosity to get ahead with destiny and by the risks he took. Dev refused to speak to members of the constabulary who crossed his path; they were in his eyes tools of the British. The extent of his calculating determination surprised one of the newly elected Republican deputies, Dick Mulcahy, who understood the Chief to say to him when they met one day in Fitzwilliam Square: "You are a young man going in for politics. I will give you two pieces of advice—study economics and read the *Prince*." Griffith, fearing the effect of long imprisonment, urged de Valera to take a real holiday with his family in the West of Ireland where a friend would place his house at the de Valeras' disposal, a place that would ensure real privacy, something Griffith knew would suit the Chief. "That's enough," the Chief rapped out. "I'm not going to have my personal life interfered with in this way." Griffith desisted, convinced of the younger man's selflessness and unreserved in his praise of him. Such "rectitude," such "wonderful judgment," said Griffith. "Since Parnell there has been no man equal to de Valera."

At the door of the small stucco villa in Greystones, a reporter from an English newspaper presented himself armed with a note of introduction from Collins. Mr. de Valera, he was informed, was taking a walk, so he waited. Along the stretches of stony shingle scooped out of Ireland's coast below Dublin, de Valera could walk in solitude, head down into the wintry weather, a figure as bleak as the fog-bound shore. His mind worked fast where there was no one to accost him. When he finally came home, exhilarated by the sea air, his good humour and punctilious courtesy set his caller at ease. His face seemed thinner, his sallow cheeks trenched with lines, his features fallen, but his eyes behind the lenses of his glasses burned with the same zeal.

To answer a question about the charges of the German plot and his own internment, he cast about for an example to make clear the absurdity of the affair. What would the world think, he propounded, if he were to kidnap Mr. Shortt on some vague and unprovable charge just as Mr. Shortt had kidnapped him? Hypothetically he put forward the crime of adultery, only to retract this as offensive. "Supposing I were to accuse Mr. Shortt of dealing with the Devil." Shades of St. Augustine and the Manichean heresy crossed his mind and he took up his pencil like a school-teacher. "That example," and he smiled, "should perhaps appeal to the English more. Though they do know adultery exists, they are not quite so sure about the Devil!"

Ireland was capable of friendship not only with the world as a whole but with England itself, as he put his case, offering to prepare a written statement for the newsman. "Give us freedom," he picked his next words slowly, "freedom to enter voluntarily into whatever associations with England we may desire," he paused to imply full purport to the word association, "and all natural and inherent affinities will for the first time be free to find full expression." His country should not become an isolated Utopia apart from the rest of the world. Provided the equality of nations great and small should be recognized his Government, he told his caller in conclusion, was ready to make Ireland a constituent unit of a league of nations such as the American President had in mind.

Now that there was an official Irish government in operation, he saw no need for an underground administration such as the Irish Republican Brotherhood was perpetuating. From the day he had first been elected a public representative, he had had little to do with that organization. Rory O'Connor had dropped out of the I.R.B. and Brugha had tried to stop it altogether when the Dail came into being. Griffith, originally a Brotherhood man, had left it, but Stack did not resign. Collins was unwilling to abandon all the machinery he had constructed. He and Harry Boland of the Supreme Council begged the Chief to renew his own affiliation but Dev refused, set against taking further orders from any source but the electorate and the electorate's chosen representatives.

To mark the Chief's return to public life, an extraordinary session of Dail Eireann was convoked on the first of April, 1919, and upon Brugha's resignation as President *pro tem.*, the *teachtai* by acclamation made de Valera *Priomh-Aire*, a title translated literally as "first minister" but more commonly as President. Before retiring from the rostrum, Brugha also pushed through arrangements enabling the new President of the Dail to designate a "President-Substitute." De Valera opened his remarks accepting the office in Irish, injecting the note of inspiration which the deputies had missed while he was gone: ". . . the people of Ireland are marching on the road to freedom," he encouraged them. ". . . we have taken the highway let others think it good or bad." To enable him to give the Government all his time the Dail provided him with a salary which, at his own decision, was fixed not at £1,000 as Brugha proposed but at Sinn Fein's old figure of £500. Spartan living was his preference and always had been. Anything that smacked of luxury like the silk hat so long affected by the Parliamentarians of the Irish Party roused his disdain.

In appointing his Ministers, he took care to include the two distinct points of view about the Republic that had become apparent to him in 1917 after the drafting of the Sinn Fein constitution, and which were now represented respectively by those in the Brotherhood and by those out of it. Griffith became Minister for Home Affairs, Brugha for Defence, Collins for Finance, Cosgrave for Local Government, Barton for Agriculture, MacNeill for Industry, Count Plunkett for Foreign Affairs, Madame Markievicz for Labour, and Mulcahy the Chief of Staff for the Volunteers. At President de Valera's behest certain amenities were introduced into the legislature's proceedings. Deputies were to be referred to in the Dail by the names of their constituencies and he forbade them to make personal remarks against each other.

The adamancy of President Wilson and of Prime Minister Lloyd George against hearing the Irish case at the peace conference gave new impetus to de Valera's idea of seeking a hearing in America and he reopened the matter in the confidence of his Cabinet. "Ireland is bound to the United States by the closest ties," he stressed. Griffith questioned whether anyone else but Dev could hold the reins at home with the driving forces of nationalism reaching breakneck pace. Dev's principal purpose, as he stated it, was to secure recognition for that nationalism, "recognition of the Parliament and the State." His Ministers were fearful of the risks such a trip entailed but this he refused to

consider; had he not come into public life when the only reward
for those who did not succeed was a noble death? Money needs
were pressing, all admitted, and Collins was interested in floating
bonds in the United States. Without more than was to be found
in the pockets of Irish Republicans at home, English opposition
could never be overcome. America held the promise of aid and
nothing that Collins could say any longer deterred Dev from
planning the journey that, to him, offered the only promise left of
political and financial fortification in the impending battle for
nationhood.

CHAPTER VI

MISSION TO AMERICA (1919–1921)

WHEN President de Valera said good-bye to his family in Greystones on the last Sunday evening in May 1919, his wife knew that if once he reached his destination he was not likely to return for many months. To get as far as England, no passport was required. Unrecognized and unaccosted, he crossed to Holyhead and in Liverpool spent the night in the house of an Irish family. Early Monday, with a black muffler pulled up from his jacket collar, a visored cap over his eyes, and only a small bundle under his arm, he took a tram, mixing with the crowd of men *en route* to the day's work. Arrangements had been made at the docks by Collins, who had been in touch with Irish seamen there. The s.s. *Lapland*, a twin-screw steamer of the International Navigation Company, was due to sail for New York, and by following the men signing on as crew de Valera had no trouble in boarding the ship and by departure time he was deep down in the hold.

Once the voyage got under way, Irish members of the crew managed to move him to a small utility room in the forward quarters, but rats gnawed the only extra clothing he had brought and the close air and motion of the vessel made him seasick. When the ship docked on June 11, 1919, he was slipped ashore by night, back in the city where he had been born, empty-handed. Near the dock at the dark corner of 11th Avenue and 14th Street, he spied the familiar form of Harry Boland waiting for him with another man. This was Joseph McGarrity, who had been, Dev knew, friend and protector to other Irish crusaders. They took him directly to Liam Mellowes' room on East 39th Street.

It was decided that his coming should not be publicly disclosed till the Clan-na-Gael's directorate was apprised of it and until announcement could be made by the Clan. Cohalan and Devoy, once they were informed, threw themselves into elaborate arrangements. At a private visit in Judge Cohalan's house in New York, he was introduced to the Clan's leaders. They saw that the small brown booklet he had with him contained the

record of the Dail's first meeting, and on the fly-leaves they
noticed that he had pasted the Proclamation of the Republic from
Easter Week, the constitution of Sinn Fein, and the manifesto
prepared from the 1918 election. This "little testament of the
Republic", he told any who asked, constituted chapter and verse
of his political creed. He had also brought with him, some
reported, Machiavelli's *Prince*.

McGarrity, impressed by the man's vigour after the hardship
of his voyage, said to himself, "A man who can do that must be
a great guy," and took him home to Philadelphia. In the big house
on Chestnut Street, where Pearse and Casement had in their day
found a haven too, McGarrity looked after his needs even to
providing a new suit of clothes. For two weeks from the time he
landed, while details were mapped by the individuals backing him
in the United States, no confirmation of his whereabouts was
given out. There was time for a private trip to Rochester, New
York, on which Boland accompanied him to guard against
premature newspaper publicity.

The Wheelwrights were living in the small home which they
owned at 18 Brighton Street, a quiet, shady side-street a block
or two off the main thoroughfare. Round the front of the dark
frame-house ran a verandah to the side where the entrance was
located, but it offered little privacy. From "Charlie" Wheelwright,
known as a "character," the neighbours got the impression that
he was in touch with the notorious Sinn Fein leader who was his
stepson, but Mrs. Wheelwright turned aside all inquiries with
a smile at once knowing and forbidding. When mother and son
were reunited this white-haired woman, now more than sixty
years old and dressed in black with only an old-fashioned brooch
for ornament, looked to her son slighter than ever and stooped
from hard work, but her face would light up with understanding
of his aims and aspirations. There was no frivolity about her and
even her sister and her sister's grown children stood in some awe
of "Aunt Kate." They could not catch her up on the name of
a single plant or flower or bush in the fenced-in garden behind
her house. To see his half-brother, the traveller went to Boston
and spent a Sunday at the Redemptorist Mission Church to which
Father Thomas Wheelwright was at the time attached.

Finally, news correspondents were informed by Boland that
President Eamon de Valera would appear in New York on

June 23, 1919, at "five-thirty on the dot." As the man himself picked up the new suitcase from the Chestnut Street hall in Philadelphia, McGarrity ordered him to put it down. "Remember, from the moment you leave this house, you go as the President of the Irish Republic." The tweed suit and loose, blue tie which de Valera was wearing for his American *début* were quite unlike his ordinary black. Throughout the reception in New York's old Waldorf-Astoria, Judge Cohalan headed the receiving line, big, bluff and jubilant, presenting those prominent in the Clan and in the larger organization, the Friends of Irish Freedom, which was really the open front for the Clan. "From today," began the long statement de Valera handed to reporters, "I am in America as the official head of the Republic established by the will of the Irish people in accordance with the principle of Self-Determination." The correspondents were more interested to find out some of the things their readers were clamouring to know. "I believe you feel somewhat hurt," he tried to mollify them, "for not being able to find out how I got into this country, but the seriousness of my business makes me keep it from you."

"Are you an American citizen?" they asked, disregarding Boland's prior pronouncement that he was.

His manner was punctilious. "I am an Irish citizen."

The point was not allowed to drop. "Did you forswear allegiance to the United States?"

"I ceased to be an American when I became a soldier of the Irish Republic." In his mind, allegiance to the Volunteer force had automatically terminated his status as an American. Late in the evening, after bidding good night to the Press, to Cohalan and Devoy, and to other dignitaries, he was free. "I wonder," he said as he drove around Central Park with McGarrity and with McCartan who had come from Washington, "what Griffith will say when he reads that I came out in the Press as 'President of the Republic'." Nowhere in the written minutes of the Dail was his title specifically spelled out this way, but the Irish-Americans surrounding him had insisted.

The matter of political titles and forms de Valera had staved off since 1917, knowing from the Sinn Fein *Ard Fheis* that it threatened to cause controversy in Ireland. Now he saw a similar rift imminent in America. Some seemed to him to favour self-determination and others wanted Ireland recognized as a Republic and nothing short of that, but it was not politics alone but personalities that contained the disruptive potential. There were apparently two groups. Devoy, still in control of the newspaper, the *Gaelic-American*, but past his prime and very deaf, relied upon Judge Cohalan, who obviously expected to dictate to the Clan-na-Gael. McGarrity in his way was equally fixed, and through his wealth as a distiller and his generosity possessed of his own influence. Premonition of conflict was so disturbing that Dev wrote Griffith, who was acting in his place at home, that he was tempted to turn around and come back. Instead, he made up his mind to be equally friendly with the "Cohalan-Devoy group" and "the others"—Joe McGarrity and his friends.

Before an audience of 40,000 in Boston's ball park, he commenced his American tour on the day after the Peace Treaty was signed in distant Versailles. "Peace was nominally signed between two great combating sides yesterday," he said, "peace—peace that gives us twenty new wars instead of the one that it nominally ends." His accent, neither British-influenced nor brogue, had something like a lisp and he looked foreign even to the Irish-minded crowd in Boston with a face pale and erudite, neck long and thin, shoulders narrow and sloping. He wore eye-glasses attached to a fine chain, and in the button-hole of his suit was the *fainne*. "The idea of a community of nations," he declared, "is today a possibility if America does what the people of the world pray America will do." Controversy over approving the Peace Treaty and League of Nations intensified in the United States Senate. De Valera argued that it would become an "unholy alliance" unless an explicit reservation was added to the Covenant compelling the British to apply its provisions to Ireland. America, he urged, should act quickly. When the Senate decided to adopt a reservation approving the principle of self-determination for Ireland, de Valera in his enthusiasm cabled Deputy-President Griffith, "A Te Deum should be sung throughout all Ireland." No sooner had this message been dispatched than the American Senators, putting the whole peace plan to a vote, rejected it, the Irish reservation included.

In spite of the overturn of the League of Nations in the United States, Americans' loyalty to their war-time allies still ran high, causing doubts over de Valera's record in relation to Germany. "As far as England is concerned," he remarked in one speech, "the Irish people wished and hoped that Germany might win the war." Newspapers accused him of hitching his wagon to a fallen star and demands arose from American Legionnaires that he be deported. To those Americans who had only recently laid down arms against the Kaiser, his views verged on the traitorous. Because, he explained, no master could have been worse than the English, the Irish people had not been afraid of being conquered by any other nation, meaning Germany, but now there had been a great war and he himself had changed his ideas. The whole problem came down to a simple fact in his interpretation of it: Ireland could not make good alone in her struggle against England. She had been and was willing to take help wherever it might be offered.

No practical resource could be overlooked, for de Valera prided himself that his was the hardest-headed generation in Ireland. "The dreamers," he said, "are those who think they can raise the solid edifice upon the shifting sands." The Union of Socialist Soviet Republics was at the time seeking American recognition just as Ireland was doing, and McCartan was in touch in Washington with an engineer named Ludwig Christian Alexander Karlovich Martens and his assistant, Nuorteva, who were representing Russia unofficially at the American capital. De Valera, believing that the Moscow government was a coming power, met the two Russians in company with Boland, and although he was not ready to ask the new Russian regime to recognize the Irish Republic, he was willing to further their friendship by practical means. From the treasury of the Irish Republican mission, $20,000 was loaned secretly, for which Martens transferred to Boland as security certain pieces of Russian jewellery which had been smuggled into the United States after the Bolshevist revolution. De Valera, who was keeping in close touch with his Ministers in Dublin, was able to forward a memorandum of Dr. McCartan's, suggesting the formation of another kind of league of nations, one embracing the two Republics, the Irish and the Russian. The idea of grouping a league of nations around "R" was capable of development, he wrote, and suggested that the Ministers send to Moscow "the doctor". Though de Valera refused to give McCartan complete power to act as plenipotentiary, certain credentials were provided; the envoy was given funds out of American contributions; and he sailed from

New York to negotiate with the Soviet Government. What interested de Valera were the principles of disarmament, of international arbitration, and of a world league.

If Ireland was to be officially recognized, American diplomatic representatives would have to be sent to Dublin, and hearings on the appropriations that would be necessary actually began in the House of Representatives' Committee on Foreign Affairs. Pending action on the overall matter of recognition, Dev did not attend the hearings in Washington personally, but a member of the committee asked if "The executive department of the government there, the president of the Irish Republic, is now in the United States?"

"He is up at the Raleigh Hotel," it was acknowledged by one of the Irish-American delegation which was present in full force for the hearings. One prominent Irish-American proposed a parallel out of American history: ". . . conditions in Ireland today are analogous to those under which we intervened in Cuba twenty-one years ago. And I venture to say the people of Ireland have more in common with us, are bound to us by ties far deeper than the people of Cuba."

The United States' recognition of Cuba was noted by de Valera as a possible precedent for the recognition of the Irish Republic by Great Britain. America's grant of freedom to Cuba had been mentioned once before by McCartan when the latter wrote to the United States Congress in June 1917, and John O'Dea of Philadelphia, the national secretary of the Ancient Order of Hibernians in America, picked up the recurrent parallel: "The recognition of the Republic of Cuba was but a more complete emulation of the proposal of Henry Clay to accord diplomatic recognition to the Republic of Rio de la Plata. These are but a few of the political precedents that legally justify recognition of the Irish Republic by our Government."

The intricacies of Congressional hearings could not keep the Chief hotel-bound long. Unless he got money soon, his Government would not be able to carry on at home. Cohalan was reluctant about a new campaign, fearing it would compete with his own Victory Fund, but the Dail had authorized the issuance of bonds to individual subscribers and McGarrity made the initial purchase with $10,000. To subscribers who wanted to know whether the bonds would be redeemed, de Valera did not give a guarantee because, he admitted, he could not foresee the result of Ireland's struggle, but he promised that any Government in Ireland which was representative of the people would assume the obligation to pay back the money.

News of the drive heartened Collins, serving in Dublin as Minister of Finance. The home Government was in need of the proceeds for current operations, and Collins as a Brotherhood man was determined further that the old Fenian bonds be repaid. Uncertain heretofore whether de Valera agreed on the latter point, Collins now wrote his Chief, "It was worth (your) going to America to be converted to that idea." De Valera in surprise replied: "What did you mean by saying it was worth going to America to be 'converted' to the idea of paying up the Fenian bonds? Surely I never opposed acknowledging that as a national debt." Accustomed as they were to settling any differences face to face, it proved more difficult at a distance. Minor misunderstandings were aggravated and in a later letter Collins said he was "sorry to be always fighting with you on these matters."

Removed from the simple life of home where comforts were measured, away from the steadying influence of academic tradition, de Valera was undergoing the heady sensation of an American welcome with all its accoutrements of milling crowds, marching bands, parades and headlines. He travelled up and down the seaboard, then across the continent, addressing tumultuous audiences. Presented with keys to cities, invited to address state legislatures and invested with honorary degrees by a half-dozen universities, he stood before his enthusiasts as the living symbol of the revolution, overwhelmingly serious with no time or thought for jest. Just as with those who were for him, so it was with those opposed. The Governor of Alabama demanded that he be deported. In Los Angeles, newspapers declared that he should be mobbed and arrangements for his use of the Shrine Auditorium were cancelled by officials.

Things seemed, on the surface, to be going well in spite of the anti-Irish manifestations. In the mornings he would be up early to play handball whenever a court could be found with his genial and untiring companion, Boland. During a period when Boland was unable to be with him, Mellowes substituted and the letters Mellowes sent back to friends in Ireland reflected apprehension: "Gang not pulling with Dev. Want to run him down."

Mellowes himself had suffered both illness and disillusion because of his own adversities in America. "All conceit gone from him ... since he discovered condition," he wrote home. "Never saw a sicker man as a result. Disillusionment isn't the word. ..."

When de Valera's travels brought him again to Rochester, secrecy was no longer needed for he came as the Irish President. The Wheelwrights' neighbours saw him go to Mass with his mother in her Church of the Blessed Sacrament, his prayer-book open as he followed the ritual. Father Thomas Connors, the parish priest, who already knew something about the visitor from the letters he had sent his mother while in prison, was invited to Brighton Street. Mrs. Wheelwright refused to sit down at the meal-table with them, preferring to wait upon them, unobtrusive and content. Proudly she permitted visits from other members of the family, not only her sister Annie's family living in Rochester but from those farther away. From Canada came one of the daughters of his Uncle Edward Coll. Ever since childhood this cousin, Elizabeth Coll Millson, had heard stories of the little boy named Eddie and of his trip across the ocean in the care of her father. She saw him grown into a solemn-faced man with penetrating eyes, tall, dignified and thin to a degree she thought painful. Even within the circle of relatives his conversation was consumed with one subject, the maltreatment of Ireland. She found it hard to understand his attitude in the light of her own experiences living under British rule in Ottawa and could not resist saying to him, "You certainly must hate the English."

From her Irish cousin she got a lofty rejoinder, " 'Tis not that I love Caesar less but Rome more." It was easier to talk of other matters. His mother was the focal point of the whole family, and she wanted to hear more about her grandchildren and about her daughter-in-law. Boland, who had been back in Ireland to report to the Cabinet for the President, told of motoring down from Dublin to Greystones and of taking Mrs. de Valera for a ride, even of broaching the possibility of her coming to America. Collins, who was a frequent and favourite visitor at the Greystones household, did not rule the idea out so far as transportation went. "I was at Greystones on Thursday evening last," he wrote Dev. "All well there too, and cheerful in spite of everything." And then a little later another bulletin: "I was at Greystones on Sunday evening. . . . It would have been edifying for you to have seen me fooling with the children."

To his relatives, de Valera's preoccupation with official business was apparent. He was seeking some formula that would solve the differences over Ireland's status, some formula that would enlist the approval of all the Irish partisans as well as of the British. Rumours were afoot that Britain wanted to make peace but any solution would, so far as he was concerned, have to keep the North and the South of Ireland together. There was still time, because the Home Rule Act with its partition clause had not yet gone into effect. A new approach had crossed his mind at the time of the hearings in Washington, and he seized the opportunity of giving expression to this idea, so far undiscussed, when, in February 1920, an interview was arranged for him with a representative of a British journal, the *Westminster Gazette*.

"Why doesn't Britain do thus with Ireland as the United States did with Cuba?" he proposed as one of a series of possible solutions that he intended to outline. This parallel between Ireland and Cuba had been drawn in the Congressional testimony he had followed in Washington. The people of Ireland would, he intimated, co-operate with their whole soul if the Cuban precedent were followed because it would not, as he saw it, infringe upon the idea of a Republic. Among the parallel factors in the situation, he pointed to defence: "The United States safeguarded itself from the possible use of the island of Cuba as a base for an attack by a foreign power by stipulating: 'That the Government of Cuba shall never enter into any treaty . . . with any foreign power . . . for . . . control over any portion of said island.' " It was permanent neutrality he sought. This proposal would hinge upon settlement of the specific questions of defence, sovereignty, taxation and titular headship. In speaking for a British reading public as he was doing, he exerted himself to be as conciliatory as possible. Britain could, as a second alternative, create a Monroe Doctrine for Ireland: "The United States, by the Monroe Doctrine, made provision for its security without depriving the Latin Republics of the South of their independence and life." Casement in one of his pamphlets had commented that the Monroe Doctrine ought to apply in the old world as well as in the new, and de Valera had looked up President Monroe's original statement about the western hemisphere. "Why could not England," he went on, "acknowledging Ireland's independence, still assert herself against interposition of any other power there?" As a third alternative, de Valera suggested to the correspondent that "An international instrument could easily be framed—as in the case of Belgium—an instrument that meant more for the safety of France, as the last war proved, than the actual possession of Belgian territory. . . ."

Finally, the peace conference and the creation of a League of Nations had given England another opportunity, he pointed out, though that now seemed to have been lost. By any of these four methods, Britain—a timorous tyrant in his parlance—could make provision for her national safety if fears for her security constituted her reason for denying Ireland her independence.

As soon as Cohalan heard about these recommendations, his antagonism leapt into the open. The Cuban proposal would, the Judge sent word to de Valera, make Ireland an ally of England and buttress the British Empire. To Cohalan, de Valera, the interloper, was getting all the attention while he and Devoy, who had so long directed Irish-America's course, were no longer in command. Devoy joined the attack in the *Gaelic-American*, deriding the proposal as a white feather, a surrender, a bolt from the blue, a betrayal of the cause. "I cannot and will not support him," announced Devoy, "in the radical change of policy."

In contrast to their opposition, Joe McGarrity remained unshaken in the friendship he had shown from the moment he had welcomed de Valera. The McGarrity's newborn son was baptized Eamon while de Valera stood as godfather in Philadelphia, an occasion which carried him back to Ireland and the baptism of his own children. The chance to be part of a family group made him feel closer to his own and helped him to disregard stories spreading in America because of his prolonged absence from Ireland. He was separated from his wife permanently, it was being whispered, and to this he was unable to divulge the answer that would have spoken for itself. Mrs. de Valera had succeeded in getting across the Atlantic to be with him, but the trip had to be executed by Collins with the utmost secrecy to avoid British interference. Travelling on a passport made out in another name, she reached Rochester unrecognized where her husband's mother welcomed her into their warm circle with much talk about their

children. "Shin-nee," as they called her, charmed them both by
manner and appearance with her crown of braided hair, and a
natural sweetness of expression. She could not stay away from
her own small children long and soon returned in company with
a woman friend.

In the personal and political enmity which her husband was
encountering, his determination to see it through toughened.
The time was coming, he wrote early in the year 1920 to Griffith,
"for plain speaking." The rigid schedule of work that he adopted
left him scant time for relaxation, and a grimness of manner belied
his human qualities. Once only he went to the theatre in New
York, though he confessed that this gave him great pleasure. To
a dramatist and compatriot who happened to visit the United
States, William B. Yeats, Dev seemed to be "a living argument
rather than a living man. All propaganda, no human life, but not
bitter or hysterical or unjust." Yeats predicted that he would be
persistent but that he would "fail through not having enough
human life to judge the human life in others. He will ask too much
of everyone and will ask it without charm. He will be pushed
aside by others." Cohalan and Devoy were the ones who, in
America, were trying to push him aside.

A deadly attempt by Cohalan and Devoy to ruin him began,
he wrote Griffith, ascribing the motives of the two Clan chieftains
to "jealousy, resentment of a rival, some devilish cause"—he was
not sure just what. When he managed in spite of them to keep the
sale of bonds going, the same pair tried to make a rubber stamp
out of him, as he put it in his letters. What they really wanted, he
was convinced, was to drive him out of the country altogether.
For the hostility that had developed he did not hold himself
responsible, explaining that his presence only gave a new twist to
the Irish-Americans' old quarrels. He endeavoured to answer his
detractors by concentrating on the cause itself as the proper source
of unification for them all, and with the instinct of the student he
undertook with Boland to compile all the coercion acts passed by
Britain against Ireland throughout the long course of history.
One evening in the spring, while they were working in their
rooms at the Waldorf-Astoria, came a telephone call from Joe
McGarrity at the Park Avenue Hotel where, McGarrity said,
Judge Cohalan was at that moment denouncing the Irish President
before a large meeting. McGarrity wanted permission to use in

rebuttal a letter of Devoy's to which he had gained access, revealing a scheme to send the President home. This, de Valera decided, was the opportunity for the plain speaking he had had in mind.

At the Park Avenue Hotel, he pushed open the closed doors of the room where Cohalan stood at the forefront, flushed and gesticulating. The man named de Valera, living in royal suites at hotels, spreading discord everywhere, knew nothing of American history or politics and would consult none, the tirade continued. But silence fell upon the Judge when de Valera, stalking straight toward the platform, seized the floor, plunging into the abuse which had been heaped upon him, attributing it to a struggle for power and nothing more. He turned to McGarrity. "Produce the letter, Joe." This was the breaking point. Cohalan, less flushed now than pale, stepped forward before the letter could be read to withdraw his accusations. The audience watched, astounded, as the hand Cohalan proffered was calmly taken. Dev, having prevailed, did not look surprised. By will-power he had subdued, if not persuaded, those who had arrayed themselves against him.

To de Valera and to Cohalan both had occurred the idea that the 1920 American political conventions set for that summer would offer a chance to raise the Irish question to the national level in the United States, for it was the opportunity to get an advance commitment from whatever party might wield the power in Washington for the next four years. The President proceeded on the assumption that Cohalan, having been cowed, would support whatever he decided to do, but to avoid appearing beholden to the Clan he secured from the Dail authorization to spend up to $500,000 in connection with the impending American election.

If the Republicans, whose convention came first, could be persuaded to include recognition of Ireland in their platform the Democrats, de Valera reasoned, would have to do the same. On a hot summer night, he rode slowly into downtown Chicago, his limousine flying the Irish tricolor, and with the eloquence of his most visionary mood he addressed his mass meeting: "We are the spear points of the hosts in political slavery—we can be the shafts of dawn for the despairing and the wretched everywhere." He was going to call upon the convention for all-out recognition of an independent Republic. At his quarters in the Edgewater Beach Hotel, de Valera found a deputation waiting for him, sent by Cohalan who had arrived independently in Chicago for the convention with a different Irish plank for inclusion in the Republican Party's platform. Cohalan's spokesmen demanded outright that de Valera leave the city and the country. At the sight of Cohalan's draft asking for an expression of sympathy, no more, he did not hide his disgust. "This declaration," he exclaimed, "leaves the Irish question exactly where it was." The time for half-way measures was gone, and what he wanted was a pledge of action. The rival Irish planks were put in the hands of the proper convention committee but the platform, upon being reported out, contained neither plank. The party delegates were by then so excited over the new Presidential candidate named Harding that there was no way of recapturing their attention.

De Valera, making it clear that he would not be driven out of the United States, turned next toward the Democratic convention in San Francisco. There, the Irish question was brought to the floor by the Democratic delegates and won some votes but not enough to get a plank into that Party's platform. In the end, only the Farmer-Labour Party adopted any provision for recognition, and de Valera was urged as the electoral campaign got under way to recommend this third party to Irish-American voters. "It is not for me to suggest how they should vote," he said in irritation. "That's their business. Besides, this question of America's policy toward Ireland is one that concerns every citizen and not merely those of Irish blood."

Scourged anew by Devoy's newspaper, he had to work in the teeth of overt opposition. It was alleged that his Chicago expenses were paid out of money raised in the bond drive, and he had to deny misrepresentations not only of the Chicago trip but of his Cuban statement and of the bond drive. The difficulty, as he saw it, was that the Tammany Judge was seeking all authority. "I cannot feel," he wrote home after the recurrence of discord, "confidence enough in a certain man to let him have implicit control of tactics here, without consultation and agreement with me." When the Friends of Irish Freedom, Cohalan's organization, cut off and insulted him, he formed the American Association for the Recognition of the Irish Republic with headquarters in Washington. Liam Mellowes in reports to Ireland insisted that, in spite of all attempts to undo him, the Chief was achieving miracles. There were tangible as well as intangible assets now on

hand from his mission that needed safeguarding. The bond drive
had put some six million dollars in American banks which
Cohalan was already manœuvring to control. As secretary for the
new Association, de Valera engaged a bright-eyed, pretty, quick
young Irishwoman whom Boland introduced to him. Kathleen
O'Connell had come over from Ireland to an uncle in America in
order to continue her schooling and had been working for
McCartan in Washington.

As soon as the Association for the Recognition of the Irish
Republic was established and staffed, Dev's thoughts turned more
and more to the state of affairs at home. The Lord Mayor of Cork,
Terence MacSwiney, was persisting on the hunger strike he had
started in an English prison. "MacSwiney doesn't want to die,"
de Valera rebuked those who argued that MacSwiney's death
would be suicide, "no sane man looking on the sweetness of life
does." His perturbation over conditions across the Atlantic was
such that, late in the summer of 1920, he announced that he would
soon go home to lead his people by his own example.

MacSwiney's ordeal was only one of the sorrows afflicting
the Republican Ministers whom Dev had charged with carrying
on the Government. The Dail, which had been meeting without
interference at the time of his departure and which had set up
a system of Republican courts, had sent diplomatic representatives
abroad, and had taken other actions symbolic of civil administration in an attempt to carry out his parting instructions, was
now suppressed by the British. Griffith, dubious from the start
about his own ability to keep unity and peace at home, had backed
up the absent President when the *Westminster Gazette* interview
precipitated consternation among some of their colleagues in
Dublin. Dev sent word that his purpose had been to start the
British talking terms, and Collins then recommended that the
Ministers accept this explanation.

One morning in November 1920, the Chief read in the
American newspapers that his President-Substitute had been
seized and put in jail. Collins immediately took charge and it was
clear to Dev that the government for which he sought recognition in the United States was a government on the verge of
war. Whether the English could be defeated in a contest of arms
he wondered. Troop reinforcements, reported to have arrived at
the behest of the new British commander-in-chief for Ireland,

General Nevil Macready, numbered around 40,000. The special auxiliaries that Britain recruited were dubbed in Ireland the Black and Tans from their makeshift uniforms. Neither the English nor the Irish permitted the other side to outstrip them by so much as one shooting. While the British fired from their armoured vehicles, the Irish fought from hedges and ditches. "Sinnfainery," as Dev saw it called in the papers, was answering with street ambuscades, night forays upon barracks, hit-and-run attacks upon Crown forces. Members of the Irish Republican Brotherhood were smuggling ammunition from Liverpool and Glasgow and, by the use of an explosive called Irish cheddar, were manufacturing grenades and mines. The Volunteer Army was organized into divisions, battalions and companies under young officers like O'Malley, now a Commandant in the Southern area. When stores and farms of Sinn Feiners were burned and when Kevin Barry was hanged in Mountjoy Jail, the Irish revolutionaries reciprocated by wrecking communication lines and throwing bombs into the British barracks. Late in November, a number of British officers suspected by Collins' agents of espionage were massacred as they slept and on the same afternoon, at the football match in Dublin's Croke Park, vengeance was taken when the Black and Tans fired fatal shots into the crowd of Irish spectators. Bloody Sunday, this day was named.

"Can we," demanded the Irish President from his distant post, ". . . afford to fling away any weapon by which nations in the past have achieved their freedom? . . . If ever the sword"— it was Pearse's sword of which he thought—"If ever the sword was legitimate, it is in such a case as ours." But hope remained on both sides of the conflict that it might be brought to an end by negotiation. A British spokesman let it be known that if Eamon de Valera was in the vicinity of London and desired to confer, no obstacles would be put in his path. A message to Dev from his Cabinet informed him that the Irish ecclesiastic, Archbishop Clune of Australia, had intervened to propose a truce. For the legal head of the nation to remain longer away seemed impossible.

As his sojourn in America entered its eighteenth month, fatigue as well as anxiety caught up with him. Another winter was advancing. He was so hoarse he could hardly make himself heard at the meeting held in New York to mourn MacSwiney's death. He stood before the weeping Irish men and women with his own shoulders bowed, his head low. Interminable travelling from taxi to train, from hotel to public hall, was beginning to tell upon him. His hope that Wilsonian internationalism would be exerted had been dashed for ever by Harding's victory of the preceding month, and the election, he said, put a natural end to his mission. Any idea of joining with the Russians in a joint campaign for recognition was cancelled by the fact that Martens was about to be deported from America. As far as the inveterate Cohalan and Devoy were concerned, the flush of the welcome originally accorded him had taken on the deeper hue of anger. Woodrow Wilson had failed to effectuate his own war-time ideals, ending any expectation of help in that quarter.

From the Waldorf-Astoria on December 9, 1920, the Irish President dictated a defiant statement: "If Britain wants to continue to overrun Ireland with the Black and Tans, and to massacre the Irish people until even British generals and British statesmen themselves are compelled to cry out that their barbarities are worse than those of the Bashi-Bazouks, surely Britain does not expect that the people of any self-respecting nation can covet her friendship." This was the last the Press or the public heard from him in America. Two days later, undetected, he boarded the s.s. *Celtic* at its New York pier. Waiting for sailing time deep down in the ship where sailors had concealed him, he scribbled on the only scrap of paper he could find a farewell message which Boland, whom he was leaving behind him in America, took ashore with instructions to hold.

During the wintry voyage eastward, Dev spent his time thinking about the political situation which would confront him in Dublin; about the need to reassert his leadership among his own cohorts, Collins and the others; about Griffith awaiting release from jail; about the feelers from Downing Street. The American people had done everything they could, he assured himself, except to force their Government to recognize the Irish Republic, and although recognition had been denied, he felt he had gained much for which his people should be grateful. He clung to the reasons that had led him to present the Cuban analogy as one solution for Anglo-Irish relations. The Clan-na-Gael's opposition he had countered as best he could. In Kathleen O'Connell, who was to stay with the new Association till it was on its feet, he had great confidence. Success was undeniable in one respect: Dail Eireann's first external loan had been amply subscribed and money lay in American banks for the needs of the Republic, whatever those needs might be; that they would be great he could not doubt. According to the news over the ship's wireless, the Black and Tans were burning the whole city of Cork.

As soon as his absence was noted in the United States, new headlines emblazoned his name. British authorities searched the s.s. *Aquitania* for him in Southampton. When the s.s. *Pontia* out of New York tied up at a Dublin quay, machine-guns were trained on its decks and gangplank. In New York City, Boland remained on hand to talk to the reporters, shrugging off rumours that President de Valera was *en route* to England to negotiate. He was, the secretary repeated, tired out, ailing, in need of peace and quiet and was resting at a private home outside the city. Mrs. de Valera was interrogated at her home in Greystones by reporters who told her they were surprised to find her there instead of at her "Chicago home," as Press stories had it. This she laughed off. Yes, she had received letters and cards from Dev, as she referred to her husband, but no word would she say as to where they had been mailed.

Three days before Christmas while the *Celtic* docked in Liverpool, Dev hid in a storage room behind a bin of potatoes till midnight and, in spite of the waiting police, got ashore dressed in the jersey and dungarees of a seaman, as when he had last left this port. He made his way to Manchester, which had offered refuge once before. Collins had arrangements prepared for the last lap home. On the day before Christmas, the Chief lay in a berth aboard a small channel freighter as if in a drunken stupor while the sailor whose cabin it was explained that this was an intemperate friend he was shepherding home for the holidays. Dev from the porthole saw the grey and low-lying shore rising like a wraith from the foothills of fog. Sea and sky and the air that lay between made a grey panorama such as he had seen nowhere else in all his journeying. After the small ship, edging into the Liffey, tied up near the Custom House, he found himself on a quay in the centre of Dublin and Collins waiting with news for him. For all the gunfire and the smoke in Ireland, there was hope of peace. The English, he learned, wanted to talk terms.

It was Christmas Eve and the Chief refused to be rushed into any decision. His mind and heart were too full. The old city to which he was returning, beneath its weight of fear and pall of winter, looked to be putting forth an attempt at Yuletide, but after the colossal grandeur and night-time brilliance of the American metropolis that he had left, it appeared small and still. Even the Nelson Pillar seemed like a needle rather than the tall shaft he remembered. In the turn and twist of every familiar street and in the shadows of every ancient landmark, he recognized his real home. Spanning the River Liffey and leading to the road for Greystones was O'Connell Bridge, which he picked out from the murk by the candelabra that were its street lights, four branching out from the centre globe, coroneted with fluted metal that glistened in the rain. The early curfew rung down by the Castle had left the city's thoroughfares early to their puddles and phantom reflections.

Sinead de Valera realized that it would not be safe for her husband to remain with his family, though he took the precaution of disguising himself so far as his height and singular features permitted. His uncertainty as to what the police would do upon his return she shared. Hopes of the family's settling down together were put off again. All the children were being brought up in awareness of their father's cause even though what they knew of him came chiefly through their mother. The older ones could understand the Gaelic language in which they knew he placed such stress. To their upbringing she had and would devote her skill as a teacher and all her intuitive perception.

By cable on the first day of the new year, 1921, de Valera sent Boland permission to announce that he was back in Dublin and to release to the American people the farewell written before sailing: "I came to you on a holy mission, a mission of freedom. I return to my people who sent me, not indeed, as I had dreamt it with the mission accomplished, but, withal, with a message that will cheer in the dark days that have come upon them. . . ."

CHAPTER VII

PEACE BY PEN OR BY SWORD (1921)

IN the fighting which had convulsed Ireland during the President's absence the people had turned to guidance close at hand, to Michael Collins, young and hale and full of fight. De Valera, eager to assume his old responsibilities but not at first sure of his initial moves, listened as Collins informed him of the contacts which had been made surreptitiously by London; a truce could actually have been had except that he, Collins, and Griffith had not been willing to surrender arms. Martial law remained in force in certain counties. Some of their best guerrilla fighters had been killed, captured and wounded, Liam Lynch among the latter. Collins was hitting back with all the fury of which he and the Brotherhood were capable. The country was in a weak position and the position of weakness was not, in Dev's game of chess, the cue to move decisively. It was the unarmed, political approach to the English that would be at once more difficult and more dangerous. So, to warn Harry Boland against making any precipitate statements in America, he wrote, "Don't let this talk of peace influence you. . . ." It might be months till he as President could be sure of where he stood. After all, the British had let almost a year pass since his Cuban proposal and he did not trust the present, undercover approach. "Deal with it," de Valera concluded his letter to Boland, "as a trick of Lloyd George."

As for himself, Dev said, he never felt so free or so safe as when he had a gun in his hand. The search instituted for him when he had disappeared from the United States made it foolhardy to go to Greystones, so he slept at hiding-places which he changed frequently like the Georgian house of Dr. Farnan in Merrion Square, or the Strand Road residence named "Loughnavale", or the big house—"Glenvar"—at the end of its own driveway in Blackrock. The early dark of the winter afternoons shielded him as he bicycled back and forth to an old house in Mount Street off Merrion Square where, in a camouflaged room with a secret door in the panelling, he set to work.

Stories that he had made more enemies than friends during

his American sojourn had preceded his return, and the members of the Dail were impatient to hear what he himself had to say. When Collins undertook to arrange a session in spite of the British ban upon any gatherings of six or more persons, Brugha at first induced the President to oppose it lest all the deputies be exposed to arrest. Collins' resentment at Brugha's action flared up and Brugha, for his part, resented Collins' assumption of power after Griffith's arrest. The Brotherhood, Brugha suspected, was only too ready to serve as a Government within the Government. But within a few days, a score or more of the deputies succeeded in assembling at the house of one of their number, Walter Cole, and President de Valera decided to join them there. He had little to say of the high hopes for American recognition with which he had set out except that he could not, he said, if he were President of the United States, recognize Ireland as a Republic; that President Wilson's primary obligation was to his own citizens, which meant he had to preserve amicable relations between Britain and the United States. So far as policy at home was concerned, Dev suggested that since the British had superior force, they in Ireland should perhaps "lighten off" their attacks on the enemy though he thought they should at the same time "stick on." How long the people as a whole would keep up their resistance he questioned after their months of suffering, but so far as negotiations went he recommended delay. Collins' attention, as the Chief talked, waned; the same ground had been covered in many letters. "The President went into matters connected with his wanderings at some length," Collins wrote in a note he managed to slip in to Griffith in prison, ". . . all the points are well enough known to you."

The Cabinet Ministers, whose offices were scattered all over the city, up back staircases and off dark hallways, could meet only precariously, so de Valera undertook to see them separately and to send them notes by couriers like Mellowes, who was back from America. The mails could not be used since the postal authorities were under British control and opened letters at will. When Kathleen O'Connell returned to serve as his secretary, he relied more and more upon her help in the innumerable letters he had to write. When the Cabinet did meet together, it was in private homes. Dev, noticing that the Minister for Local Government, William Cosgrave, did not appear with the others, was given to understand that he had gone to England. Some, insinuating desertion, demanded Cosgrave be removed from office, but the President sent for him to return and named the young lawyer, Kevin O'Higgins, to act in the meantime.

At one of the rare meetings of the Ministry, the Chief indicated that if Michael Collins would go to America, he might be able to win over the "irreconcilables" like Cohalan and Devoy. De Valera pursued this possibility by writing Collins a long letter to prepare him for the proposed assignment, seeking to counteract in advance any idea that he himself had caused the split among the Irish-Americans. "You will not, of course," the letter read, "make the mistake of thinking that the division began with my advent in America." Collins was not interested in what might be said about the Chief in the United States, being more concerned about what would happen if he left Ireland to the military operations against the British. The conclusion of the letter, predicated upon his going, failed to move him: ". . . whatever coup the English may attempt, the line of succession is safe, and the future provided for." Brugha, unconvinced of Collins' indispensability to the guerrillas, was stressing the fact that he, not Collins, was Minister of Defence. Certain of the Ministers suspected that the Chief wanted to get a rival out of the way, while others regarded Collins' unwillingness to go as an act of insubordination. De Valera himself, unable to persuade "Mick" to cross the Atlantic, decided to drop the idea; the Irish would have to stand alone against the British Empire.

No official support was to be anticipated from the American Government and even the faint hope of Russian help dwindled. Unknown to the deputies, the Russian jewels remained in private hands in Ireland against the repayment of the loan that had been extended in Washington to the Soviet representative. Though word came back from Moscow that Lenin had spoken encouragingly of the part labour might play in the fight for Irish freedom, and though Martens had become a person of influence in the Bolshevik regime as a member of the supreme economic council, Russia seemed, de Valera told his colleagues, more interested in "getting in" with a big manufacturing nation like the United States than in helping Ireland. Suspicion of the Soviet was growing in many parts of the world and England capitalized on this by publishing a White Paper entitled *Intercourse between*

Bolshevism and Sinn Fein. The transaction in money and jewels remained, however, a secret shared by Dev and a very few others. As time passed, the Dail postponed its hope of Russo-Irish collaboration. De Valera realized that his first task lay on his own doorstep, that of uniting his Ministers around his own authority.

There was reason to be concerned for his own prestige as leader. The *Weekly Summary*, published by Sir Hamar Greenwood, Chief Secretary for Ireland, and the Dublin Castle authorities, launched a personal attack upon him. "Valera," the publication stated, "belongs to a race of treacherous murderers and has inducted Ireland into the murderous treachery of his race." Reluctant as he was to take cognizance of personal matters, he forwarded a copy of the article to the Spanish Ambassador in London with the message, "Circulation of the infamous libel in a British Government publication is an official insult to the Spanish nation." The result was to stir public sentiment for rather than against him. The less that was known about his private life the greater grew general interest in it. A Republican who lived near Bruree, David Dwane, started to gather material for the President's biography and took his notebook and pencil to Patrick Coll's cottage where he filled page after page of notes from the uncle and from the neighbours who had known "Eddie" as a child. The earlier hero-worship was reviving in the country, and verses could be seen pasted up in the shop windows:

> *When we were little children Johnny Redmond was a fool,*
> *He bade us to be satisfied with something called Home Rule,*
> *But we have learned a thing or two since we went to school,*
> *And we'll crown De Valera King of IRELAND.*

Castle police, though still referring to him as "somebody's child from Spain," and as "the half-breed Spaniard," ceased to harry and hunt him. De Valera suspected that Lloyd George was singling him out for special treatment to induce him as President to come to terms. With partition due to go into operation in that spring of 1921, the British Government had scheduled an election for May to choose the members for two separate legislative bodies, the Northern Irish Parliament in Belfast and the Southern Irish Parliament in Dublin, as prescribed in the Government of

Ireland Act. Sinn Fein undertook at Dev's bidding to contest every constituency, the voting process being his key to Irish destiny: "It was by the elections that we placed ourselves upon a foundation of certitude and made the Republic unassailable." He himself was a candidate from County Down in Northern Ireland though he did not intend to take a seat in Belfast, and he also ran from his original constituency in East Clare for election to the new Parliament of Southern Ireland.

He needed someone to help him with publicity though he insisted on checking and revising every paper and statement himself, and Michael Collins introduced to him Robert Barton's cousin, the man who had piloted the yacht into Howth Harbour in the summer of 1914. Erskine Childers had, since that time, served in the British Army but had left it out of sympathy with the Easter rising. When the Chief suggested that he take over the editing of the Republicans' publication, the *Irish Bulletin*, Childers, agile of mentality and tense of manner, threw himself into the job with zest.

The Irish people as a whole would never, the President forewarned in the manifesto prepared for the electoral campaign, accept a border drawn between the counties in the South and the counties in the North as the Act contemplated. To show that the South would not knuckle to the forces of partition, the Dail had already instituted a boycott of goods from Northern counties. That the disagreement was due to religious differences Dev denied; the fact that the lines of potential political division coincided with religious lines did not mean that religious differences were the cause of political differences. Never had he gone so far in the direction of conciliation as he did in this campaign in order to win votes for the Northern nationalists versus the partitionists. In a message to Northern voters he announced that, if England could show any rights with which Ireland's rights would clash, he would be willing to adjust them by negotiation and treaty. Mindful of Lloyd George's fears for the security of the Empire in case of future wars, he gave assurance that Ireland would not serve as a jumping-off ground for an attack upon England by any other power.

Shortly before the polling day, he received from the Northern leader, Sir James Craig, a note offering to talk matters over. Sir James, unionist and exponent of Empire who had adopted

Carson's credo, had long been connected in minor capacities with the British Government and had been requested by Lloyd George to see the Southern leader. He came in secret to the headquarters of the Chief Secretary of Ireland, Sir Hamar Greenwood, was picked up by Republican escorts and driven to the home of a lawyer in Clontarf where de Valera awaited him. The Southern leader was nervously alert, more spirit than substance in his sparse and tenuous appearance. The Northerner was heavy-featured, ponderous, immovable in mind as well as manner. To them both the prospect of partition was abhorrent and Sir James opened the conversation by asking what could be done to avert it. "Sinn Fein," commenced de Valera like a teacher ready to expound his views, "stands for Ireland undivided with regard to other nations and states, but in home affairs for such devolution of administration and authority as would make for satisfaction and contentment of all sections of the people." Devolution was an idea not so far generally considered in either North or South.

Craig, politician instead of teacher, lit his pipe while the Southerner delved backward into Irish history, elaborating upon the country's historic unity and his plan of governmental devolution. "We believe that the men of Ulster reft from us by statute but retained to us by higher laws, look upon Ireland as their country and in their hearts cherish the Irish name." It was Belfast Protestants, de Valera pointed out, who first conceived the idea of an Irish Republic after the French Revolution. At the end of four hours Sir James rose, tore a bit of paper from a sheet of music standing on the piano rack, and jotted down a few innocuous words to release to the Press. No basis of fellow-feeling had arisen between them, no joint course of action set. They had, on the contrary, become more conscious of the differences between them due to birth, upbringing and bias. To the people living north of the projected demarcation line de Valera sent a final appeal to vote so that there might be an end to boycott and retaliation, to partition, disunion and ruin: "Orange and Green together can command the future. Ireland one is Ireland peaceful, prosperous and happy."

On election day, Ireland was anything but peaceful. In the North, stones were hurled on the streets as persons of suspected sympathies went to vote; polls were rushed; fraud was charged; all in spite of the patrolling of the Black and Tans. Sinn Feiners

swept everything but the six counties of the North where the
unionists retained control, though de Valera with Collins,
Griffith and one or two others captured seats in both unwanted
houses—the Parliaments of Northern and Southern Ireland. The
President's legislative entanglements after this election were
multifold. He held seats simultaneously in the House of Commons, in the Parliament of Northern Ireland, in the Parliament
of Southern Ireland, and in Dail Eireann. He, and with him all
but a few of the members elected to the new Southern Parliament, ignored the summons to its first session issued by the Lord
Lieutenant in accordance with the new law. Belfast unionists for
their part engaged a firm of lawyers to seek ways of declaring de
Valera's election to the Northern legislature void on the old
ground that he was not a British citizen.

Partition went into effect with a separate government in
Belfast. The North would now have to be persuaded, not co-
erced, de Valera saw, and to some of his co-workers he intimated
that they would have to agree to a connection with England.
One day early in the summer while talking with Collins, Childers
and several others at one of their retreats, he took a compass and
drew one big circle to represent the British Commonwealth.
Inside this, he drew five smaller circles to represent Canada,
Australia, South Africa, New Zealand and Newfoundland—the
dominions. Then, to show Ireland's position, he described another small circle separately, connecting it by a line to the big
circle. Collins, watching, said nothing. The partitioning of the
country after the election did not end force and violence. Coastguard stations, lonely lighthouses, telephone exchanges were
being raided, deeds for which Republicans were executed by
firing squads. One of the most daring fighters, Commandant
Ernie O'Malley, was captured and jailed after months of
bivouacking in the fields and hills. To get first-hand information
concerning military activities, the President interviewed individuals whenever he could get them up from their outposts.

Commandant General Tom Barry was summoned from the
south-west and spent two hours answering questions about
specific engagements. The British propagandists were representing such men as bandits and outlaws. Since Ireland had now
a Government of its own in operation, the President came to the
conclusion that it would be only fitting to give the armed body

of Volunteers the status of an official militia and he reorganized them with Mulcahy as Chief of Staff. "The Government," announced the President, "is responsible for the actions of the Irish Republican Army. It is not, as the enemy would have you believe, a Praetorian guard. It is a national army. . . ." He wanted no imputation that the belligerent acts were not duly authorized by himself and his Cabinet. "If the British use tanks, why shouldn't we use stone walls and ditches?"

After O'Malley escaped from jail, the President sent for him. In the three years since they had talked in Tullamore, this fighter had lived on the run, in peril of his life, several times wounded and once tortured by his captors. In the small parlour of a house near the sea, the President received him. Seated also round the table in the centre of the room were Collins and Mulcahy. "They tell me," began the Chief, "that you know most of the actual situation in the South."

"Things have changed since I have been in jail, sir," replied the cautious, thin-lipped man with the beaten face. He looked at the others nervously.

Mulcahy spread a map on the table and the President's finger fell on Tipperary. "Tell us about the county," he commenced. "What are the military and police strengths?" O'Malley himself, grown ruthless under long fighting, was full of information on raids and ambushes and for three hours Collins and Mulcahy sat and listened till the President suddenly straightened up from the table. "What time is it?" he ejaculated. "There's a Cabinet meeting this evening." The three visitors left and O'Malley felt uncomfortable as Collins and Mulcahy did not conceal amusement at some of the questions Dev had put.

President de Valera exerted all his energies to take control of the Army's policies, and when a meeting of the General Headquarters Staff was called at the home of Madame O'Rahilly in Herbert Park, he made it a point to be present. The plan under discussion was to destroy the Custom House standing on Eden Quay on the north bank of the Liffey, the architectural pride of all Dubliners. The President was quick to agree that it was "a Custom House where customs were not collected." The British were sending into Ireland such goods as they wished without duty. Free trade, the nationalists argued, had been forced upon Ireland to her disadvantage and to Britain's gain. "I knew the history of that building," the President later recalled, "one of the most precious gems of architecture." Its classic portico centring the spacious symmetry of the structure's wings he had first seen through the aura of his student days. The President, careful to participate in the decision as the one wielding the ultimate authority over the civil and military branches of the Government, agreed that if as a result the enemy were to lose a chance of dominating the Irish economy it would be a good bargain. "I was a party to that decision," he wrote afterward, "and not without a certain sorrow and a certain sadness of heart." On May 25, 1921, in a swift gambit the granite pile was gouged and gutted by fire and its records consumed. Where de Valera used to look upon a landmark of history, he saw a blackened stone carcass standing stripped and charred against a smoked sky and débris-strewn river. ". . . Why did I give my sanction?" This was the question he had to answer in his own conscience for a long time. "Because I said it was better to destroy that work of art . . . that this nation might have a Custom House where customs would be collected for this nation."

Indication of differences of opinion over such tactics would naturally be magnified by the British, who sought to cut off the extremists and force a call for negotiation. The British Prime Minister, weighing human foibles, had waited throughout the spring to see the effect in Ireland of the President's return, to see whether de Valera had come home because he was discouraged over Ireland's failure to win by use of force, or perhaps because he wanted to be the one to get a favourable settlement, to be able to say to the Dail—and Lloyd George was ready to put the words into the Irishman's mouth—"Look what we compelled them to give you." But the Irish President, being fully aware of this possibility, had since January striven continuously to bring about unity in his Government. To refute rumours of rebellion against his authority, he drew up a formal statement: "We, the entire membership of the Ministry of Dail Eireann, individually declare . . . that we have not, nor have we had . . . either individually or collectively, any difference with the President who speaks authoritatively for all of us. . . ." To this statement he secured the signatures of each member of the Ministry and put it in his coat pocket where it would be quickly available upon any occasion.

At hurried and hazardous conferences with his co-workers, in multitudinous memoranda, and in all the carefully reached decisions, he had endeavoured to hold his Cabinet together by the cohesive strength of the old aim and objective. By early summer in 1921 he felt that if London should offer officially to open negotiations, he could afford to listen. With secret overtures he had no patience. After Lord Derby, disguised behind horn-rimmed glasses, came to Ireland to see him and registered under another name at the Shelbourne Hotel, Dev sent London a sharp message of how business would have to be done. Prime Minister Lloyd George must understand that if he had anything to say it would have to be according to proper international usage and not through subterranean means or go-betweens; if a written communication were to be addressed directly to him as President of the Irish Republic, a straight reply would be forthcoming.

Lloyd George for his part concluded that this man, if approached as the *de facto* leader and chieftain of his people, might come half-way and bring in his train all the rest of the Republicans. De Valera and Collins might, he suspected, react differently to British plans. The question of who should speak for Ireland was important if he, Lloyd George, were to make an offer of dominion status. Lloyd George's indecision was resolved for him when the King decided to go to Belfast at the end of June to speak at the opening of the Northern Parliament: "I appeal to all Irishmen to pause, to stretch out the hand of forbearance and conciliation, to forgive and forget." Among the officials drawn to Belfast for the panoply of this occasion was the Commander-in-Chief of the British forces in Ireland, Sir Nevil Macready, who risked leaving his post in the South to witness the North's ceremony.

The Worcestershire Regiment was left on guard in Dublin, a squad of which undertook a routine search of premises. They entered a walled garden at the end of a long driveway in the suburb of Blackrock—"Glenvar," as it happened—and saw several Irishmen deep in conversation, actually the Republican Ministers, drawn to meet by the feeling that Downing Street might be planning some proposal to coincide with the opening of the Belfast legislature. One member of the group who seemed to the search-party to be in disguise was placed under arrest by the soldiers and removed to Portobello Barracks. In his pocket was found an official-looking document, seen upon examination to be a testimonial of some kind to the unity of the Irish Government, a disclaimer of rifts and a vindication of the powers of "the President who speaks authoritatively for all." The signatures appended to the paper were those of the Republican Ministers. Hastily, the prisoner's disguise was removed and the soldiers realized they had in their hands the President of the Irish Republic, the man whom they had for weeks been enjoined from touching.

"The very night the British arrested me in Blackrock," Dev regaled his comrades, "they found something which . . . taught them that there are no differences of opinion amongst us." Certainly the raiding party was not stretching out the hand of forbearance as the King in his speech was reported to have asked. His arrest "put in their way at the last moment," Dev inferred, "a certain temptation to change their plans and try the terror for a further period." Assistant Under-Secretary, Alfred W. Cope, hearing of the identity of the prisoner at Portobello, set wheels in motion as fast as he could, and the day after he was seized the President was set free with the advice that he go back to the house in Blackrock to await a communication.

There, two days later, a letter was delivered from Lloyd George: "Sir: The British Government are deeply anxious that so far as they can assure it, the King's appeal for reconciliation in Ireland shall not have been made in vain; . . . I write therefore to convey the following invitation to you as the chosen leader of a great majority in Southern Ireland. . . . That you should attend a conference here in London in company with Sir James Craig to explore to the utmost the possibility of a settlement. . . ." De Valera wired in reply that he would consult his colleagues— such, he indicated pointedly, as were available. When Lloyd George set Griffith free from Mountjoy on the last day of June de Valera at once went to talk with him at his home in Clontarf. Another of the Ministers on whom de Valera had relied, Eoin MacNeill, was also released from jail, and Robert Barton, who had been held in penal servitude in England, arrived in Dublin. Arrangements were made to transfer Dev's secret headquarters from the house in Blackrock to an official address in the Rathgar district at 53 Kenilworth Square. No longer need he worry about being seen in public and he doffed his disguise.

The Republican advisers agreed upon being reunited that too much was at stake in Lloyd George's invitation for precipitate acceptance or refusal. Their Chief disliked the idea of going over to London side by side with his Northern counterpart. It would look to the outside world as if the two of them were going over, he said, to be spanked and told by their master to be good boys. So, remembering his talk of a few weeks before with Sir James, he wrote to the Ulsterman suggesting they meet together again, that Ireland's differences be settled inside Ireland. Craig telegraphed that it would be impossible for him to arrange any meeting.

If advance agreement with representatives of the other Irish factions could be reached, the Republicans were convinced that they could secure more concessions from the British. Lord Midleton, well known as a Southern unionist, and other prominent unionists like Andrew Jameson, the whiskey distiller, also received an invitation from the President to a conference in Dublin beginning on July 4. On the Sunday evening before, Lord Midleton, uncertain about the wisdom of accepting, called at the Mansion House to get more information. The courteous attention paid him by the only person there, a tall, dark man who introduced himself as the Lord Mayor's secretary, impressed him and he resolved to attend. Though Dev did not introduce himself, it was he who had answered the door, having come in to prepare for the next day's session.

Next morning, the Stars and Stripes were flying at the Mansion House in honour of the American independence day, and pink and red geraniums were blooming in the baskets that hung from the glass-paned *porte cochère*. Dev, the first to arrive, got out of his taxi smiling and looking, to the people on the pavement, who saw him for the first time in months, to be in good health and spirits. Griffith, pale and aged after his recent imprisonment, followed the President amid more applause, and even Lord Midleton's arrival was cheered. The latter, upon being presented to the Irish President, discovered to his surprise that they had already met. General Smuts, Prime Minister of South Africa, came over from London at the request of Lloyd George and de Valera, taken by this towering, fine-featured statesman with the trim, pointed beard, could not deny that Ireland had something in common with South Africa. Lord Midleton read aloud a letter from Lloyd George indicating that the British would agree to a cease-fire without the surrender of arms. When General Macready, hurrying up the steps of the Mansion House on July 8, exchanged salutes with the Irish Republican sentries, the hopes of the anxious watchers rose, and at eight o'clock that evening came a bulletin that President de Valera had agreed to discuss with Prime Minister Lloyd George the basis on which a formal peace conference would be held.

Commandant O'Malley, searched out in the hills of the south-west by a dispatch-rider with instructions to hold fire, was incredulous and suspected that there were two sides to what had happened in Dublin, that not everyone favoured the move. Still, the President was in command and O'Malley saw refuted the rumours of disagreement within the Cabinet in the President's published statement: "Those who hope for disunion will be disappointed now as so often before."

In the group chosen to accompany him to London—Griffith, Barton, Stack, Count Plunkett and Childers—he included the varying points of view that had been expressed within the circle of leadership. Collins was to stay at home and take charge of affairs there with the difficult duty of preserving the truce. Dev confided to his Ministers that he had in mind a specific plan which, so far as he explained it, appeared to them to be a compromise between pure Republicanism and association with Britain. "External association" for Ireland with England was what he called it. He took upon himself the odium, as he said in retro-spect, of suggesting this idea because he was convinced that an independent Republic for the whole of the country, a Republic that was in association with Britain, could be a prosperous one.

At the Grosvenor Hotel in London the President registered with a flourish, putting after his name the words "Irish nation-ality." Lloyd George had returned from Chequers to be ready for the coming conversations and had notified the Chief of his Im-perial General Staff, Sir Henry Wilson, of de Valera's visit: "You will have a chance of talking to him." Sir Henry, whose own Irish roots were Northern roots, considered even home rule too soft a policy.

"I do not speak to murderers," the latter replied.

"You have often done so," Lloyd George upbraided him.

"Never, and if I meet Valera I will hand him over to the police."

In contrast to Sir Henry, Lloyd George's frame of mind was cordial, and he addressed his guest as "de Valer-era, Chieftain of a great majority of the Irish race." For several hours at the first meeting, the two leaders were left alone at 10 Downing Street. Lloyd George owned to being baffled. ". . . When I tried to bring him down to the present day, back he went to Cromwell again. It reminded me of a circus roundabout when I was a boy," he told his secretary in exasperation. "I used to sit on a rocking-horse that raced round and round after the horse in front, and when the roundabout came to rest I was still the same distance from the horse in front as when I started."

De Valera, sitting down at the desk in his hotel room, wrote on July 15 to Collins: "The position is simply this—that Lloyd George is developing a proposal which he wishes me to bring in my pocket as a proposal to the Irish Nation. . . . The idea on which we, the Ministry started out, remains unchanged. . . ." He signed himself intimately, using the name by which he was best known—Dev. Hearing that Lloyd George had compared dealing with him to picking up mercury with a fork, his sense of mischief was roused. So the Prime Minister wanted to lay the blame on the mercury! ". . . if he thought a little of the instrument he was using," de Valera commented, "a fork. . . ." Several days later, he advised Collins: "Things may burst up here suddenly. . . . I intend adhering to our original plan as closely as possible, but the changes in the situation have to be met as they arise." In reply to this, Collins reminded him that any terms should be submitted to the full Cabinet.

Dev had not formally presented his own plan when, on July 20, Lloyd George handed him proposals for an Anglo-Irish accord approved by the King and the British Government which offered dominion status, subject to specific limitations. Britain was to receive access to Irish harbours, financial contributions for imperial defence, the right to recruit for the Crown. There were to be no protective tariffs and Ireland was to be responsible for a share of the United Kingdom's debt. There was no reference to the North and partition, de Valera saw at a glance, was to remain in effect. To him personally, he told the Prime Minister, the terms were not acceptable; they were, in fact, impossible. At that, Lloyd George's control gave way and he threatened immediate war upon Ireland. De Valera was unmoved. "Because they [the English] adopted the attitude of the bully," he recounted, "we answered back that we would resist the bully if they spoke so." Lloyd George, at once menacing and conciliatory, called upon the Irish leader to reconsider, at least to take the terms back with him and send a written reply. The latter, though having to agree to this procedure, felt his worst fears being substantiated. "I have been all along in favour of peace with England, and . . . could have carried it all right," he lamented, "if Lloyd George had placed me in a position to offer the young men"—young men like Commandant O'Malley, for instance—"a measure of national independence for the whole country on reasonable terms of external association."

The President upon his return did not conceal from Collins and the other Ministers the fact that he had broken personally with Lloyd George. The lesson Ireland had learned in the last couple of years, he said, was "that acts, not talk, achieve nations' freedom." One of the first things which he did upon sitting down in a new office opened at the Mansion House was to write to the South African Premier, recognizing in him a man who, though believing in the British ties, also believed in the freedom of his own people. "My dear Smuts," he began, ". . . the proposals of the British Government will not be accepted here. . . . Unless the North-East comes in on some reasonable basis no further progress can be made." This was a frank, rock-bottom statement. "An Ireland in fragments nobody cares about. To the principle of self-determination our people are devotedly attached. . . . The Republic is the expression of that principle in their regard. . . . The British do not seem to realize this at all."

"Full dominion status," Smuts wrote back at once, "with all it is and implies, is yours . . . if you will but take it." If anything could have converted him Smut's letter would have done it, de Valera admitted, but every member of his Cabinet voted against its recommendation. Canada's situation which had been held up as analogous he discounted, because Ireland's proximity to Britain was made a basis for restrictions unheard of in the case of the other dominions. Some in the Cabinet like Austin Stack urged that the final rejection to be dispatched to Lloyd George should be unqualified, and Brugha was emphatic that no threats of John Bull should deter them. It was the practice of the Cabinet to discard all suggestions that did not win unanimous support. Collins, Griffith and—for the Army—Mulcahy—argued for a refusal more mild in tone.

The Government as a whole had no wish to terminate negotiations. The general concept of external association was something upon which the President believed he could get all to agree, and a counter-proposal embodying this idea was authorized by the Cabinet. The secrecy which surrounded it prevented others in Ireland including the deputies from knowing about it. "External association of Ireland with the group of free nations in . . . the British Commonwealth as it is called," de Valera wrote Lloyd George, "would leave us with the Republic unless the people wished to change it. . . ." Ireland would be rid of the English King and all allegiance to him. It would make Irish citizens out of those who were otherwise British subjects and would free Ireland in a short while of all occupation forces without committing the country to anything more than consultation with the representatives of Great Britain and the dominions on matters of common concern.

In the middle of August, the deputies gathered at the Mansion House for the convening of the Second Dail, and at a private session held first the President mentioned dividing the headship of the Government into a nominal executive or President plus a working executive or Prime Minister. Difficulties loomed ahead if further negotiations devolved upon the Government in keeping the office of the Presidency above partisanship, but Dev was persuaded that some less formal way than his proposed reorganization might be found. When he expressed reservations about swearing the oath to the Republic which Brugha had previously put into effect, deputies like Mary MacSwiney took alarm, jumping to the conclusion that the President believed it was out of the question to secure recognition for an Irish Republic as such. Uninformed as a body about his idea of external association, they could not foresee the embarrassment he might face at some future date of being charged with inconsistency for having taken an oath to the Republic. Resolving in his own mind that he would interpret the oath as a pledge to act faithfully and honestly in the best interests of the Irish people, no more, he raised his hand when the public session opened to say with the other deputies, "I do solemnly swear . . . that I . . . will support and defend the Irish Republic." What had been suggested to him in London, he explained, did not even amount to dominion status because Ireland as a whole would not be recognized. "Where is Ireland?" he propounded. "There is no Ireland. There are two broken pieces of Ireland. . . ." By unanimous vote, the Dail formally confirmed the Cabinet's rejection of the British offer.

In words ringing with acclaim, de Valera was nominated for another term of office by Commandant Sean McKeon of the Irish Republican Army. It was more than re-election to the Presidency of the Dail that McKeon proposed, for the motion was by pre-arrangement stated so that the title henceforth should be President of the Irish Republic, as he had been known in America. General Mulcahy seconded the motion and de Valera was unanimously returned to office. Exuberant, he rose from his place of vantage in the Round Room. He felt, he said, like a boy among boys with a "heaven-bound" mission. "I have enough of common sense to know that it is not when one's heart is full that one should talk." Schooled in repressing his emotions, he steadied his voice to protest that credit was being given him for work which was not his alone but the work of those whose lives had been expended in heroism, and of living heroes like Cathal Brugha, like Michael Collins—he mentioned both by name. It was as a team that they had worked, he proclaimed, and it was as a team that they would continue to work. "Remember," he cautioned, lest any might later come to feel their present confidence in him misplaced because of what he might propose, "Remember, I do not take, as far as I am concerned, oaths as regards forms of Government." Mary MacSwiney looked about her in trepidation. He was thinking of his strictures concerning this moot subject in the private session the day before when he had tried to make it clear that he was binding himself only to act faithfully in the interests of the Irish people.

Pursuant to the convening of the Second Dail, the President of the Irish Republic designated the members of a small, six-man Cabinet within a larger Ministry: Griffith as vice-president and Minister of Foreign Affairs; Collins, Finance; Stack, Home Affairs; Brugha, Defence; Cosgrave, Local Government; and Barton, Economic Affairs. At the first meeting of this new Cabinet, the plan of association with the British Commonwealth was reintroduced, the President specifying as he had done to the preceding Cabinet that what he had in mind did not mean the same thing as an isolated Republic. "I was honest," he reflected as he thought back upon what he said at this Cabinet session. "I have not a face of brass."

All hopes depended upon prolongation of the truce till permanent settlement could be ensured, but August of 1921 ended without England's reply to his own proposal. The soldiers on both sides showed signs of restiveness. One of the conditions of the truce had been the retention of arms and the men of the I.R.A. were utilizing the time to refurbish their equipment and recoup their depleted strength. At mountain retreats in the southwest, Dev personally reviewed the Cork and Kerry Brigades, and with Commandant Liam Lynch toured the scenes of I.R.A. engagements.

For the English as well, the last days of summer were uneasy ones. General Macready, who still had 30,000 British soldiers in Ireland under his command, decided the delay presaged renewed warfare, especially after Austen Chamberlain, the leader of the House of Commons, declared that the British were ready to raise 100,000 additional men besides putting every available soldier into Ireland to wage the kind of war which he called the cruellest of all forms of civil war, guerrilla war. Lloyd George had told de Valera outright that if settlement was not forthcoming, warfare would be renewed, and Churchill, Secretary of State for the Colonies, threatened that, if dominion home rule, as he called it, was rejected by the Irish, it would be real war, no mere "bushranging."

Rather than allow the opportunity for peaceful settlement to pass by default the Irish President, taking into account the known obduracy of Sir James Craig, composed another letter reassuring Lloyd George that "Ireland, so far from disregarding the special position of the minority in North-East Ulster, would be willing to sanction any measure of autonomy which they might desire. . . ." Boland and Barton were commissioned to carry this letter direct to Gairloch in the north-west of Scotland where Lloyd George had retired after Parliament rose. Boland, though not taken into full confidence by his Chief as to the nature of the missive, was given to understand that the isolated Republic would have to enter into some sort of an association, something Boland gathered "that would be consistent with the position they were maintaining". In Scotland, the Irish emissaries were handed a sealed envelope to take back to Dublin which, when de Valera opened it next day, extended an invitation to confer without further interchange of notes at Inverness on September 20. This de Valera was quick to accept but, in spite of its express caveat against additional preliminaries, added, "Our nation has formally declared its independence and recognizes itself as a sovereign state." Then the Irish President signed his name and sent Boland back to Gairloch with the acceptance.

With negotiations in the offing, de Valera consulted with his Ministers as to who should go as delegates. If he stayed at home himself those whom he sent would be protected, he reasoned, from being rushed into decisions by the necessity of reporting back to him in Dublin. "When," he said, "such a time comes I will be in a position, having discussed the matter with the Cabinet, to come forward with such proposals as we think wise and right." He was not as free as he had been when he went to London in July because, since his designation in August as President of the Irish Republic, he considered himself the symbol of that Republic, a symbol which he had to keep pure "even from insinuation lest any word across the table from me would," as he explained later, "in any sense, give away the Republic." The final decision would, it was agreed, be up to the Dail, but his own preference frankly was to remain in Ireland. He had been once and had not got what he wanted from Lloyd George.

The natural person to head a negotiating team as the President saw it would be the Minister of Foreign Affairs, Griffith. When these two talked about it, Dev brought up again the matter of external association and, more mathematician than politician at the moment, picked up his pencil to draw a diagram:

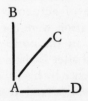

The A–B line stood for the strait jacket of the Republic, he explained to Griffith, but the A–C line represented external association. As for the A–D line, the President went on, that was where their action would eventually lead them. Griffith, persuaded in his own mind that someone should take from the President's shoulders the onus of criticism which might arise from further negotiations, consented to go to London. He would, he cautioned, be unable to bring back a Republic but if Dev did not expect that, he was willing.

Having found his chairman, the President next turned to Michael Collins. As key man in the Brotherhood, he had much to lose by sitting down with the enemy. The sagacious old Tim Healy, still active though his party of Parliamentarians was long dead, warned Collins privately not to go unless de Valera also went. Collins, having pleaded with his Chief for several hours to be left out of it, gave in, telling himself that he did not care if his popularity had to be sacrificed for the sake of peace. Austin Stack was not considered as he was unsympathetic toward the parley, and Brugha declined any thought of participating unless the talks were held on neutral soil. The President's remaining nominations were based on special qualifications: Barton, the Minister for Economic Affairs, would be able to speak not only on economics but for the Protestant minority; Eamon J. Duggan, a legal expert, was a member of the truce committee; Gavan Duffy, bearing the name of his Fenian forbear, had been Casement's counsel. In addition to the five delegates, de Valera picked Erskine Childers to be head secretary.

When the Dail in private session received the names for confirmation, one deputy moved that the President should take a place on the delegation himself, but there was no second and most of the deputies agreed it was logical for the head of the state to remain with his people. To send a properly accredited delegation headed by the Minister of Foreign Affairs seemed more correct to Dev, who was becoming a particularist in the niceties of statecraft, than to go himself. He was now the head of a nation like the King of England in addition to being a political leader like Lloyd George, combining in his person both the nominal and the actual executive functions. If he went to London in his dual capacity he would run the risk of having to pronounce decisions on the spot. So long as he stayed in Ireland, there would be someone to whom Griffith would have to refer decisions and so would not be stampeded. All the names proposed were ratified and the President wished them designated as plenipotentiaries, a term already used in his letters to Lloyd George. When the extent of the delegates' powers raised some doubts, Dev threatened to resign with his whole Ministry, and at the end of the discussion the deputies gave to the delegation the full latitude on which he was insistent.

Boland, meanwhile, at Gairloch presented the acceptance of the invitation to negotiate, but he felt unable to delete at Lloyd George's demand the last sentence containing Ireland's presupposition of sovereignty. The plans for the conference were then summarily cancelled by the English, the bid withdrawn, this less than a week before it was to open. The British Cabinet Ministers, irritated at repeated summons to Scotland from their holidays, had the satisfaction nevertheless of being on hand when another letter arrived from Dublin. "We have had no thought," wrote the Irish President, "at any time of asking you to accept any conditions precedent to a conference." Days ensued after de Valera's letter setting aside conditions, ten days of tension, until on September 29 the Prime Minister, ruling out previous correspondence, reopened contact: "We send you herewith a fresh invitation to a conference in London on the 11th October." Each letter and wire of the many exchanged during September, 1921, was but another move in a month of diplomatic hedge-hopping. The Press called this not an ultimatum but an "ultimatissimum." The following day de Valera notified Lloyd George that the Irish envoys would be in London on the given date in October. The sending of this word, Collins concluded to himself, was the forerunner of compromise. With this final upshot of the summer's dealings across the Irish Sea, hope unbounded returned to the mass of people in both nations.

CHAPTER VIII

THE PRICE TO PAY (1921)

WHEN the Cabinet assembled for a farewell session with the London-bound delegates, President de Valera passed around the table confidential copies of something he and Childers had prepared. It was the incomplete draft of a treaty with England—Draft Treaty A, he called it. Of the two main issues it outlined, the first was independence. His solution on this was definite—external association—and he wanted the delegates to take as much of the draft as was ready with them because it set forth external association as the price he was willing to pay for a united Ireland. "I proposed it," he explained afterwards, "I take full responsibility for it." The second issue was the unity of Ireland and though he had not had time to write that portion, it was his plan to replace partition with devolution.

While the men around the Cabinet table scanned the draft, de Valera was making rapid notes with his pencil and in a moment he handed to Griffith what he had written: "It is understood, before decisions are finally reached . . . that a dispatch notifying the intention to make these decisions will be sent to members of the Cabinet in Dublin, and that a reply will be awaited by the Plenipotentiaries before final decision is made."

In addition to the pencilled memorandum and Draft Treaty A, the President turned over to Griffith, Collins, Barton, Duggan and Gavan Duffy their formal credentials entitling them as "Envoys Plenipotentiaries from the elected Government of the Republic of Ireland to negotiate and conclude on behalf of Ireland, with the representatives of his [sic] Britannic Majesty George V, a treaty or treaties of settlement, association and accommodation between Ireland and the community of nations, known as the British Commonwealth."

After his envoys departed, he resumed work on the Treaty's draft in consultation with the three Cabinet members who were remaining at his side—Brugha, Stack and Cosgrave. He still had to find a way round Brugha's antipathy for any link with the

British throne. Though the idea of external association had been in de Valera's mind during his own talks in London, and though the processing of it with his own colleagues had been a continuous preoccupation since then, he had not found a formulation of it in regard to the North to which all the Ministers would be willing to subscribe. Sending Boland back to the United States to keep Irish-Americans in touch, he impressed upon him that there was to be no mention of external association by anyone anywhere—in Ireland, England or America—until it actually materialized.

Eagerly de Valera awaited the reports of his envoys from London which were to be sent to him nightly by special couriers. The plenipotentiaries with their secretaries, advisers, and an Irish cook settled themselves into the tall, ornate, red brick corner house at 22 Hans Place set in a ring of substantial dwellings and fronting on a large, oval green in London's Belgravia. It had been leased by the Dail for three months with option over a longer period. Collins, with his own bodyguard, was established nearby at 15 Cadogan Gardens. Griffith's first Press statement sounded exuberant: "Now is the night before the tomorrow of Ireland dawns. The business of the day is to prepare the country for the glorious future which awaits her."

De Valera, in a different tone, undertook to stiffen public opinion on the day negotiations opened, October 11, 1921: "The peace that will end this conflict will be secured, not by the skill or statesmanship of leaders, but by the stern determination of a closeknit nation steeled to the acceptance of death rather than the abandonment of its rightful liberty." Since the calling of the truce some months before, he had been able to live at home in Greystones, going and coming freely in a small Ford car from his office in the Mansion House and the other one in Kenilworth Square, no longer worried about being recognized and arrested. The National University installed him with ceremony in the honorary, lifetime post of Chancellorship and in his black and gold robe he became the nominal head of its three colleges at Galway, Cork and Dublin, entitled to preside over the Senate of the institution where he had been a struggling student and which had once passed him over for a professorship.

The first full letter he received from London was encouraging. "The meeting of today," Griffith wrote him, "has left on my mind the impression that the English Government is anxious for

peace. . . ." The British team, de Valera reflected as he read the
letters, was headed by the Coalition's Prime Minister, Lloyd
George, and composed of "practised parliamentarians": Austen
Chamberlain, unionist leader of the Conservative Party in the
House of Commons, son of the quondam home-ruler, Joseph
Chamberlain; Winston S. Churchill, Tory-born ex-Conservative,
originally a home-ruler, now a Liberal and Secretary of State for
the Colonies; Lord Birkenhead, prosecutor of Casement, unionist, ardent member of the Conservative Party and now Lord
Chancellor; Sir Hamar Greenwood, Chief Secretary for Ireland;
Sir Laming Worthington-Evans, Conservative politician, solicitor
and Secretary of State for War; and Sir Gordon Hewart, Lord
Chief Justice and Attorney-General. Many in Britain, de Valera
knew, still thought of the Irish as Hottentots, but he did not
know that Birkenhead had prepared himself by studying a
memorandum compiled for his personal use from "private
sources." "All the delegates," ran this memorandum, "with the
exception of Gavan Duffy, will be nervous and ill at ease. They
are absolutely without world experience. . . . In overcoming their
nervousness they may be a bit rude, and extravagant in speech."
Griffith, according to these private sources, would be "more
clever than de Valera but not so attractive."

"I note that Lloyd George is covering again the ground he
covered with me," de Valera replied to Griffith after the latter's
letter summarizing initial developments. The opening discussions
harked back to the July offer of dominion status. "You will have
to pick him up soon on this 'further than this we can't go' stunt,"
he wrote Griffith. The existence of Draft Treaty A had not yet
been mentioned by the Irishmen, whose strategy was to hold off
the primary problems and get agreement on the secondary ones
first. The lack of the unfinished part of the Draft Treaty dealing
with the North, de Valera realized, forced Griffith to play for
time, stressing the unfairness of retaining within the Empire
Republican majorities in certain parts of Ulster. To this the
British, he was informed, retorted by pointing to the unionist
majority in other parts, and Michael Collins then spoke of the
possibility of setting up a group to study the boundary line
between North and South, "a Boundary Commission or local
option whatever you may call it." Griffith's report to his Chief
at the end of the first week contained a note of urgency: "If we

cannot have the Ulster and other omitted clauses by ten o'clock Monday at the latest, we must fight them on grounds of their own choosing."

De Valera, sensing that the "battle royal" was going to take place in the week ahead, rushed work on the details of his plan of devolution. His Cabinet had agreed to recommend an All-Ireland Parliament with jurisdiction over a Northern legislature such as was already in existence in Belfast. Power over local affairs would devolve from the All-Ireland Parliament upon the regional legislators. For "the skeleton draft treaty," as he called it, he submitted this wording: "The following constituencies of North East Ireland [and he enumerated the disputed border areas] . . . may by vote . . . elect to be directly represented in the Irish Parliament, provided that if all of them or a smaller number contiguous . . . do not so elect, they shall be entitled to maintain a legislature possessed of the local governing powers set out in the . . . 'Government of Ireland Act, 1920', and provided they shall be entitled to the same representation . . . in the Irish Parliament as they would have been entitled to in the British Parliament under the provisions of the above-mentioned Act." This would give local autonomy to Northern areas if the majorities therein insisted.

Griffith, fortified by arrival of the additional clauses from Dublin and by several letters as well from his Chief, and armed with maps and charts delineating the border areas, came to Downing Street to present the alternative to partition. As soon as mention was made of local option, Lloyd George pounced upon it. The value of the 1920 Government of Ireland Act would, he exclaimed, be vitiated as he pointed to maps of his own showing unionist preponderance in the doubtful counties. Local option was not only unacceptable; it was unnecessary.

Endeavouring to avoid a break, Griffith told the Prime Minister that he would submit in writing on the following Monday, October 24, the composite draft which the Irish themselves had in mind for settlement. Sub-committees dealing with trade, finance and defence were forging ahead in London. Over the week-end in Dublin, President de Valera put into the hands of Collins personally the drafted treaty with the stipulation that it was to be put forward as their irreducible minimum. It gave consent "to adhere for all purposes of agreed common concern, to the League of Sovereign States associated and known as the British Commonwealth of Nations." No mention of the King appeared, for though de Valera was clear in his own mind that the Crown was the symbol of association that would have to be acknowledged, he had not yet put this in writing. Brugha, still resistant, could not agree with his Chief's point of view that it was possible to have a Republic in association. When the full draft which Collins carried to London was presented to the British delegation as promised, Griffith stated verbally that the Crown would be accepted as the head of the association. With the submission of the Irish terms, the plenary sessions of the London conference ended.

That London was bringing pressure to bear for acceptance of the Crown in Ireland's internal affairs seemed apparent to de Valera, not only from the minutes of the sessions which Childers sent but in Griffith's dispatch following presentation of the Draft Treaty. "Told them," the latter wrote of the British negotiators, "the only possibility of Ireland considering association of any kind with the Crown was in exchange for essential unity—a concession to Ulster." The Ministers whom Dev called together in Dublin were apprehensive. For purposes of external association, the Crown would be one thing; for internal affairs, it was quite another. "The President," noted Madame Markievicz who was Minister of Labour though not in the Cabinet proper, "was seeking for some formula by which he could express our loyalty to our agreement with His Britannic Majesty." He still had to get agreement on details including the words defining the degree of association, and asked Brugha to put in writing his opinion as to how some expression of allegiance to the Crown could be reconciled with the Irish claims. "We are all here at one," the President wrote his representatives in London, "that there can be no question of asking the Irish people to enter into an arrangement which would make them subjects of the Crown or demand from them allegiance to the British King. If war is the only alternative we can only face it. . . ." Prospects had taken a turn that might necessitate his going over to help, and in his next letter he offered to join the envoys at 22 Hans Place.

By now Griffith and Collins were deep in private meetings arranged by Lloyd George at which the question of Ulster was rampant. What Griffith and Collins wanted was a freer hand in their task, not more supervision. Lloyd George had heard that the moderates wanted a settlement whereas "the gunmen" did not and this gave him new impetus. The British hinted that the North might come into an All-Ireland Parliament if the Northern boundary was not altered. "This was a new proposal," Griffith wrote him, "and while we did not hold any hope that it might be a basis, we, between ourselves thought it might be a possible basis." De Valera sensed that his going over would be resented and dropped the idea, assuring Griffith that his offer had been nothing more than an attempt to keep the delegation in touch with the views of the Cabinet: "The main thing now, it seems to us, is to clinch with them on the Ulster question without delay, and get the basis for representation in the All-Ireland Parliament agreed upon definitely—and after that the make or break question. E. de V." The question that would make or break the conference was unity versus partition, and unity entailed external association with the Crown.

De Valera's hands were full enough in Dublin for he had yet to get Brugha to modify his adamancy against the Crown's entering into the settlement at all. Griffith sent word that if the Crown were accepted, Ulster would be required by the British to enter an All-Ireland Parliament. "Surely, Cathal," the President then urged Brugha, "you can't object to taking an oath if you agree to association?"

President de Valera had another reason for being relieved at not having to be away from Dublin. The annual *Ard Fheis* of Sinn Fein of which he was still the head took place at the end of October. The envoys, he warned its delegates, might come back from London having found what seemed to them a way out of the impasse. "It might happen that we would differ, not only in the Dail, but even in the Cabinet itself, on certain conceivable lines of policy." What would happen then, he declined to predict. "I am anxious that you should realize the difficulties that are in the way, and the fact that the best people might legitimately differ." His listeners felt a knife-point at their hearts. "I am not an extremist," he reiterated, "I believe I take an average view of things." The difference, if it came, he warned, would be over "the decision as to whether the price at which peace can be purchased is too high." Though the Sinn Feiners had been aware that the Army was showing signs of renewed activity, they were scarcely prepared for his final tocsin: "Whether it be peace or truce, I think this question will be decided one way or the other within the next five days. . . . Although there is an arrangement for a seventy-two hours' notice of a termination of the truce, we cannot be sure the enemy will act up to the condition. The minute you hear of a break take measures for your own safety at once. . . . There will be no unknown graves for Irishmen here as in Suvla Bay. If we have to die we will die gloriously."

Brugha was moved by the critical nature of the situation and before the end of October, out of loyalty to his Chief and love of Ireland, he gave his word in writing, a word which was harder for him to give than life itself—his word for limited recognition of the Crown. This word, for which de Valera had been waiting and hoping and praying, reached him in the form of a note in Brugha's handwriting—a priceless note, the President called it: "All other matters being satisfactorily settled, we are prepared to recommend to our people that the accepted head of Great Britain be recognized as the head of the new Association. . . . In matters that do not affect the group, we continue to act independently, our form of government remains the same as at present. . . ."

Now, even the extreme Republicans like Brugha and Stack seemed to the President ready to accept what he had known all along would be a compromise, what he was to call in so many words, "the compromise of External Association." On October 29, 1921, the Irish envoys in London were able to inform the British that Ireland would, "for purposes of the association, recognize the Crown as the symbol and accepted head of the combination of signatory states." The Sinn Feiners had dispersed from the *Ard Fheis* to their homes throughout the country, and as the deadline Dev had foretold for the decision in London came and went without the news he had led them to expect, they worried afresh. The President, also waiting with anxiety, threw himself into the reorganization he had instituted of the armed force. Brugha, in the task of preparing for possible resumption of action against the British, had to work in the shadow of Collins who was coming back to Ireland every week-end. To revive morale among those idled by the truce, the President appealed for total obedience. "There are unfortunately no methods for war but dictatorial methods," he explained. "Even the democratic Celts chose a king dictator for war, Caesar tells us. If war is to be waged successfully, you must concentrate power in a single authority."

Inertia induced by the protracted truce had dampened the soldiers' spirits, but the inspection trips which he undertook put new zest into their drilling. The Dublin Brigade, to which he had retained his own special allegiance ever since 1916, staged a tactical demonstration for him. An old lorry was started down a country road at a fast clip, and as it passed over a given point mines were exploded, demolishing it. His boyish satisfaction pleased the Volunteers. Whether the brigades were on marches over the muddy, slick, bog roads or at rain-sodden camps hidden up in the hills of the south-west, his appearance walking briskly down the rows of saluting men, always a few steps ahead of those accompanying him, his shoulders seeming to push ahead as he bent forward from the waist, eager to quicken the pace, evoked wild enthusiasm. He would speak a few words on the spur of the moment, his sentences long and cumbersome, his words obscure, but his emotion clear and positive. As he talked, each soldier felt Dev's dark eyes looking directly at him through heavily rimmed glasses. Young men, hearing his authentic note of courage, knew and said to each other as they stood in ditch-water and under the rifted skies that it was an experience to lift the heart and sweeten life. "Each man on parade," one soldier related, "felt the direct, personal appeal of his message."

Keeping half his mind on the Volunteers and the other half on the plenipotentiaries, the President was in and out of Dublin all autumn. On the first week-end in November, Gavan Duffy returned from London in order to discuss something he would not put in writing. The delegates, he reported, had been persuaded to sign their names to a letter requested by Lloyd George summarizing certain concessions Griffith had made personally. Since the plenary sessions had been concluded, Griffith and Collins had been holding private meetings with the British intermediaries and Gavan Duffy asked the Chief to put a stop to these *tête-à-têtes* and actions taken without inclusion of the whole delegation.

De Valera as he listened did not forget that the preceding July he himself had conferred in private with Lloyd George, leaving his own advisers behind him at the hotel. Confidence in the man he had appointed as chairman in London must be preserved. He had, as a matter of fact, already received a copy of the missive mentioned by Gavan Duffy directly from Griffith in which he, Griffith, assured Lloyd George that he would "recommend that Ireland should consent to a recognition of the Crown as head of the proposed association of States" and would "agree to any necessary safeguards and to the maintenance of existing parliamentary powers. . . ." Dev knew enough about British politics to guess that the precarious nature of Lloyd George's own position was driving him to exact such commitments from the Irish envoys. The Coalition Government was hanging in the balance and a vote from the diehards to censure Lloyd George in the British Parliament would follow upon any failure to satisfy Ulster.

Craig, Griffith notified de Valera on November 8, 1921, was opposing the plan for an All-Ireland Parliament. The Irish delegation was given to understand by the British that if, under the circumstances, they would relinquish that idea for the North, a boundary commission would be set up to delimit the area remaining under the jurisdiction of the Northern Government. "This would give us," Griffith wrote hopefully in his letter, "most of Tyrone, Fermanagh, and part of Armagh, Down, etc." The President replied immediately without any of the sanguinity apparent in his chairman's mind. "I think," de Valera wrote, ". . . we should not budge a single inch from the point to which the negotiations have now led us." As for the boundary commission which Griffith mentioned, Dev did not refer to it at all in his answer. At no time had he contemplated any settlement in which the North would remain apart from the rest of Ireland and attached to the United Kingdom. If the negotiations had to be broken off, he directed, the break should come on the question of Ulster and not on the Crown. The whole world would sympathize with Dublin if Belfast thwarted the natural unity of the country after the South had gone so far to meet the North's claims.

By means of their regular exchange of letters, de Valera in Dublin and Griffith in London had held themselves together for the month since the Anglo-Irish negotiations had opened. De Valera felt that he had sent Griffith the final word in the form of the completed draft of the Treaty. Each sought fortification for his respective position in the opinions of those closer at hand.

The processes of fellow-feeling set in between men working across the table from one another in Downing Street, absorbed in the same daily task, trying to accomplish a hard and hazardous undertaking in the face of a doubting world.

De Valera got word from Griffith that Lloyd George was sending a further offer to Ulster to create an All-Ireland Parliament under the terms of which Ulster would have the right to vote itself out within twelve months but should the North do so, a boundary commission was to be set up to delimit the area. If, Griffith wrote, Ulster refused this offer Lloyd George said he would fight, summon Parliament, appeal to it against Ulster, dissolve it, or pass an act establishing an All-Ireland Parliament. "I told him it was his proposal, not ours," de Valera read from his chairman. "If the Ulsterman accepted it, we would have to discuss it with him. . . . I could not guarantee its acceptance as, of course, my colleagues knew nothing of it yet." In another off-the-record talk with Lloyd George, this time in a private house in Park Lane, Griffith had agreed not to repudiate the idea of a boundary commission, a commitment the Prime Minister had pledged him to keep secret from the other envoys. Lloyd George's secretary had made a written summary of the conversation which Griffith had by request checked for accuracy. De Valera felt at a loss as he put down the latest communication. Only afterwards did he comment: "How he [Griffith] allowed himself to be deluded by the Boundary Commission idea I have never been able to understand. This part of his letters dealing with this make pathetic reading."

De Valera had assumed that the negotiations would end early in November, but it was the middle of the month before Britain's codified proposals for settlement were put in the hands of his envoys. Ireland was therein offered dominion status again. Ulster was given the right to vote itself out of an All-Ireland Government with the provision for a commission to determine the boundary between North and South in accordance with the wishes of the residents. Griffith informed his President that "our reply . . . should be, I think, that it won't do but that we'll have in an alternative Treaty proposal on Saturday or Monday." With this, de Valera at once sent off word of his impatience: ". . . there has been so much beating about the bush already that I think we should now get down to definite business and send them as far as possible our final word." The moment had come when Draft Treaty A must be brought up to date and in that form presented. "You have no doubt been working on your draft," he continued to Griffith, referring to the revisions in the original Draft Treaty that were in process at Hans Place, "so that possibly the best course is to let us have yours and then we can give you our views on it. This document will, of course, be of tremendous importance. . . . We expect, therefore, that we will have an opportunity of seeing it before you send it."

Griffith as chairman took over from Childers, who had been the amanuensis, the finishing of the revisions, and the form in which they were actually submitted to Downing Street on November 22 was his. Although they did not tender allegiance to the Crown, the Irish terms for the first time carried an offer of recognition of the Crown for limited purposes as "the symbol and accepted head of the Association." Unspecified safeguards were promised "the North-East." Griffith apprised his Chief that the crucial question, Crown or Empire, was upon them. "If Ulster gets to break on them she will have re-won the game." What the British received was Draft Treaty A with modifications. Within an hour after the document was delivered, the Prime Minister ruled it out as unsatisfactory.

Informed at once of the deadlock, de Valera called a full Cabinet meeting, to take place in Dublin on November 25, and Griffith returned home for the first time. He and the other delegates, upon sitting down with their fellows, reaffirmed approval of limited recognition for the Crown. Dev, all of them comprehended, was standing on the theory of external association and when the week-end was over, Griffith prepared another memorandum for Lloyd George clarifying the Irish position. The Prime Minister, while sticking to his point that the Crown must be recognized internally as well as externally, thereupon asked if Ireland would accept the same status as Canada? To Griffith, this seemed to offer new prospect of accord. In short order, Lloyd George then put in writing the formal British point of view and on December 1 the Irish received from him certain "Articles of Agreement." Simultaneously, Sir James Craig received a promise from the Prime Minister that a copy of the terms would be sent to Belfast with the final decision thereon no later than Tuesday, December 6.

A note informing de Valera that the British proposals had been delivered to his envoys reached him by special courier in the remote town of Scarrif, County Clare, on his Army inspection tour. Immediately he started back for Dublin, taking Brugha with him, and another Cabinet meeting was called for Saturday, December 3, when the delegates could be present. Griffith, returning again to Dublin, waited alone late that Friday evening in the President's Kenilworth Square office with the British set of terms. De Valera, scanning it, read that Ireland was to receive "the same national status in the . . . British Empire as the Dominion of Canada . . . and shall be styled and known as the Irish Free State." Northern Ireland was to continue under the Government of Ireland Act, if she chose, without becoming part of the new Free State, in which case a commission would be set up to determine the boundary. De Valera was amazed. He could not recall giving any indication that he would sanction Northern Ireland's voting itself out of the whole. The very purpose of external association was to restore the basic unity of the country. The only reason for offering any recognition of the Crown was to overcome partition.

He continued to skim through what Griffith had put before him. Pending future arrangements, the defence of Ireland was to be undertaken by His Majesty's Imperial Forces, and the harbours of Berehaven, Queenstown, and Lough Swilly were specifically set aside for them. Long ago de Valera had made clear his opinion that England wanted to keep the ports for "a pirate's rendezvous" from which to sally forth and strangle any rival. Only if England did not make use of such Irish facilities could Ireland remain neutral in the event of general war. Lloyd George seemed to have gone back to the partition policy of the Government of Ireland Act, and the previous July de Valera had returned from London because Lloyd George had made this kind of a proposition. No doubt was left on the matter of the Crown by the Articles which stipulated that there be an oath of allegiance to "the King as Head of the State and of the Empire." No oath whatsoever had been written into any of the proposals submitted from the Irish side.

"I would never consent to sign such an agreement," de Valera exclaimed in constricted voice, putting down the papers. Griffith's only comment was that, as for himself, he had not felt he could break off the negotiations because of the provisions regarding the Crown. Collins and the other delegates, having lingered in London to iron out minor details in the Articles of Agreement, landed back in Ireland the following morning and the Cabinet was immediately called to order in the Mansion House by the President. Though no minutes were to be taken, Colm O'Murchadha, acting as secretary to the Cabinet, kept a running record as arguments began freely and frankly. Dev launched at once into a critique of the British proposals, his voice rasping as he insisted that the Articles meant "British dominion status nominally with an oath of allegiance to the British King as an organic part of the Irish constitution, and a recognition of him as head of the Irish State."

The oath, de Valera pointed out, capitalized his main objections: "inclusion in the Empire, the British King as King in Ireland, Chief Executive of the Irish State, and the source from which all authority in Ireland was to be derived." As he made his points O'Murchadha noted, "He [President de Valera] personally could not subscribe to the oath of allegiance, nor could he sign any document which would give North-East Ulster power to vote itself out of the Irish State." Brugha and Stack, like their Chief, spurned the Articles placed before them. The plenipotentiaries interposed that the British would insist upon some sort of oath, to which the President replied that he would not be unreasonable; once the relationship between Ireland and England was rightly set forth, he would swear to uphold that relationship. If the British wanted an oath, "we could easily frame one that would be in accordance with our proposals." Hastily, he assayed the wording of such an oath, unaware that O'Murchadha was trying to catch his words, "I do solemnly swear true faith and allegiance to the Irish constitution of the Irish Free State, to the Treaty of Association, and to recognize the King of Great Britain as Head of the Association."

It was his opinion that the original recommendation of external association ought to be put forward again in London, but Griffith and Collins insisted that the British had ruled out external association absolutely. Neither felt it right, in view of the Irish Cabinet's willingness to enter into an association of some form, to withdraw from the negotiations over details of allegiance to the Crown and they with Duggan favoured signing the British terms.

The oath was for them no more than "sugar coating" to make the settlement palatable to the people on the other side.

The President declared himself ready, if they could not get better terms, to renew the armed battle. Lloyd George had threatened him with war in July. After an hour's recess for lunch, Collins called to his colleagues' attention the fact that "in England it is the intention . . . if hostilities between these two nations are resumed, to send 200,000 troops . . . in the enterprise of completely subjugating our country." Fear and fatigue caused irascibility as Saturday's daylight hours waned. For a group accustomed to acting on the basis of unanimity, a crevasse seemed to the Ministers to be widening under their feet.

At teatime, the Ministers who were not members of the Cabinet were summoned. The disagreement could no longer be kept from them. Brugha turned upon Griffith. "If you sign for the King, you split Ireland from top to bottom." Stack and Barton nodded in vehement concurrence. Brugha, bent upon expressing what he had long suppressed, denounced Griffith and Collins both for falling in with Lloyd George's schemes. The London sessions, he charged, had been broken up into small, private parleying for the Prime Minister's own purposes. "Yes, the British Government selected their men," Brugha lashed out, ". . . they knew they were the two weakest men we had in the team, and Lloyd George and his friends pretty soon discovered that."

The chairman of the delegation, white of face, made no direct reply. Perhaps, he suggested, the President would wish to go to London himself to take the responsibility on his own shoulders since he, Griffith, was not willing to risk reversion to force? They were scheduled to present themselves in Downing Street the following afternoon with a definitive answer on the Articles. Barton seconded the suggestion that de Valera go to London so that he would be there to break with Lloyd George in person. "I actually . . . made up my mind," Dev explained afterward, "to go over to London."

As the hour arrived to start the journey, Griffith spoke again and offered his word not to sign the Articles as they stood, and confidence in the man serving as chairman swept back over the President. Though little time was left, last-minute efforts were made to outline specific changes to place before the British next

day, the changes without which Griffith had promised not to
sign. Unless the oath, for one thing, was revised the Articles were
not going to be accepted by the envoys. The understanding was
that the envoys would, if the changes were not adopted, insist
that the terms be submitted to the Dail. They agreed to break,
if they had to break, on the Ulster issue, not on the matter of the
Crown. No longer did it seem necessary to de Valera to go
personally and putting that idea to a vote, a majority decided
against it. The Cabinet session which had lasted seven hours
adjourned finally in haste and confusion.

In view of the critical state of affairs, it seemed essential to
de Valera to return to the troops concentrated in the west and
south-west. By driving most of the night he reached Galway, got
a few hours' sleep at the Bishop's residence, and on Sunday spoke
at a muster of Army cadres from Clare and Galway. ". . . the
country must be prepared now to face sacrifices as it has been in
the past." No word came from Stack who had remained in
Dublin to relay any messages, and the official party continued
southward on its prearranged tour. Chief of Staff Mulcahy,
travelling with the President, sent telegrams in code in the course
of that Sunday to all brigade posts throughout the country in
which he gave the I.R.A. units the signal to revert to a war
footing. He knew that General Macready was reinforcing the
British auxiliaries.

Monday, December 5, the President was scheduled to review
the Mid-Limerick Brigade. When a certificate conferring upon
him the freedom of the city of Limerick was presented to him
after his triumphal entry, he stood holding its special case in his
hand for a moment as if lost in thought. The design upon the
cover showed the treaty stone, that grey boulder mounted at
Limerick's bridge upon which Sarsfield, at the beginning of the
previous century, had been forced to sign terms with the British.
The President looked up from the gift he held and his eyes re-
kindled. "I will regard this as an omen and will take it as a warning that the English are capable of making treaties when it suits
them and of breaking them before the ink is dry."

The newspapers reaching Limerick on Tuesday morning
carried an indication that agreement of some kind had been
reached. To de Valera, this had only one meaning. The conditions
set forth by the Cabinet must have been accepted; external

association must have been forced down British throats. He had received no 'phone call, no message, from his chairman and was incredulous but told himself that the delegation would have referred to Dublin any proposal that fell short of the conditions set during the Cabinet meeting. By automobile he started for Dublin, reasoning that Griffith must have done better than had seemed conceivable. As his car neared the city early in the evening he grew anxious for more news but had to go directly to the Mansion House where he had been scheduled long before to participate in an academic programme commemorating Dante. There he found two of his Ministers, Brugha and Stack, but not Cosgrave, waiting for him. "Any news?" was his instant question.

"Yes," Stack replied slowly. The soberness of his voice was noticeable.

"Good or bad?" demanded the President.

Stack handed him the evening newspaper with one word, "Bad." De Valera concluded from the printed bulletin that what the delegates had promised would not be signed was, in fact, what had been signed in London and that Ireland's cause had been lost, not won, as he had begun to believe. He turned to put on the heavy, black Chancellor's robe that had been laid out for him. That he was confronted with a *fait accompli* he now suspected. Duggan entered at this juncture from London, carrying the text of the signed Articles of Agreement. He handed the President the envelope and asked him to open it.

"What should I read it for?" the President queried. There was a twist of grim jocosity about his mouth as he took what the envoy held out to him.

"Oh, it is arranged that the thing be published in London and Dublin simultaneously at eight o'clock" Duggan muttered, "and it is near that hour now."

"What, to be published whether I have seen it or not, whether I approve it or not?" His attempted indifference was overrun by angry irony.

"Oh, well," Duggan fumbled, "that's the arrangement." To his closest colleagues standing round, the President seemed all at once a broken man. He stood with the envelope between his fingers. Some in the ante-room thought they heard him say he would soon be back at teaching. The lines on either side of his mouth creased his cheeks. As he gazed around him at the scene of so many other gatherings, so many occasions of hope and enthusiasm, it seemed to him as if everything was lost. His plenipotentiaries had in one fateful moment lacked courage, had not been bold enough to make one heap of all their winnings and stake their chances on it, as he was to put it. Ireland had lost without trying; because Ireland had lost, he had lost. For all the safeguards he had set up to prevent precipitate decision, the deed was done. "There it was," he said in a calmer moment, "and I had to make the best of it."

CHAPTER IX

BROTHER AGAINST BROTHER (1921–1922)

DUBLIN was working itself into a holiday mood for the first peaceful Christmas many of the children had known. Yet in the first week of December 1921 the man who wore the people's crown as King of Ireland struck dismay into their hearts with the announcement that "The great test of our people has come." The people were tired of tests of their endurance and sick of the headlines which had covered the hoardings ever since the President's envoys had gone to England in the autumn. They were readier for the pantomimes in the Dublin theatres, for the balloons in the Grafton Street windows, for the bakeries full of iced cakes and plum-puddings. The children, barefoot though they might be, were running to see their fathers already being released by the British from the prison gates of Ballykinlar, Arbour Hill, Kilmainham and the Curragh in celebration of the Treaty that had been signed in London. The holly bushes glistening through the iron palings of Merrion Square took on a sheen. On the kerbs stood bright-eyed women in their black shawls selling bunches of holly and mistletoe, and carol singers clustered on the corners.

Why should there be more shootings from the hedges, more nocturnal knockings? the people old and young all asked. Why should their men pick up their guns to go back into the hills? The Articles of Agreement were festooned with shamrocks in green printer's ink on the front pages of the newspapers and it came as an anti-climax, when, a few days later, the Press followed up the Articles with ominous words from Dev, "My friends Irishmen, I feel it is my duty to inform you immediately that I cannot recommend the acceptance of the Treaty." And then he added, "There is a definite, constitutional way of resolving our political differences, let us not depart from it."

The day after the Dante celebration the President, having read the Articles as they had been signed, had summoned the Cabinet members who were in Dublin—Brugha, Stack and Cosgrave—to propose the dismissal from the Ministry of the signatories who were still in London. Cosgrave, while offering

146

no defence for the Articles, advised against such a step without giving them a chance to be heard. "It will be like releasing the west wind," spoke up Cosgrave's assistant, Kevin O'Higgins.

"Aye, the west wind," lamented the distraught President, striking his chest. Reluctantly, he agreed to wait. A secretary ventured to suggest altering the wording of his telegram summoning Griffith home. "It reads as if you were opposed to the settlement."

"And that is the way I intend it to read," was the reply. By noon of the same day that the envoys returned, Thursday, December 8, he called the Cabinet to order in the same room in the Mansion House where, less than a week before, it had been agreed that no terms except revised ones would be signed without communicating with Dublin. It was the dictum of the Chief that the delegates had settled for "dominion home rule," nothing more or less.

". . . but we have a united Ireland," Griffith burst out.

"You have neither this nor that," the President contradicted him, "neither unity nor sovereignty." What had happened in London since they had last confronted each other did not come out all at once, not for days and, in its entire purport, not for years. Childers had, with the help of Duffy and Barton, prepared the amendments adapting the oath which de Valera had verbally sketched, re-enunciating external association, deleting dominion status, and not mentioning Ulster. All this the British had summarily rejected when the Irish envoys had taken the amendments back to Downing Street. Collins, mindful of the British demand for a yes or no answer on the Articles as such, had not gone with his colleagues. The Prime Minister once again had urged a status parallel to Canada's at which Gavan Duffy, without thinking, had spoken up, ". . . our difficulty is coming into the Empire." At that, the British terminated the meeting and the Irishmen's resolve to break, if they had to break, on the unity of Ireland and not on the Crown had been forfeited.

Collins, summoned then alone by Lloyd George, had taken with him his own version of the oath and had received assurance that a boundary commission, in origin partly his idea, would restore substantial areas to the South. At a final negotiating session, the Prime Minister had produced the notes of the confidential talk at Park Lane during which Griffith had promised not to repudiate the proposition of a boundary commission. With that commitment from Griffith, Collins' wording of the oath had then been read into the Articles by Lloyd George, minor concessions on trade and defence incorporated, and an ultimatum delivered by the British. Lloyd George had had two missives with him both plainly addressed to Craig, one containing the Articles of Agreement, the other without them. If he had to send the latter, he had threatened the Dubliners with war in three days. Griffith, stunned anew at this harsh reminder of the seventy-two hours' notice for resumption of fighting, had responded on the spot that he personally would sign, but for Lloyd George this was not enough: each envoy would have to sign. Collins had convinced himself that to refer the decision to the people at home would mean a plebiscite and for that, the British would not wait. The deadline was upon them—Monday midnight. Barton and Gavan Duffy, till then against acceptance of the Articles, had been shocked by the threat of war and decided that, though the Articles did not match Dev's theory of external association, certain changes had been achieved since Saturday. At Downing Street, without attempting to telephone or communicate with Dublin, all the envoys had said yes and had signed.

At the aftermath meeting of the Cabinet in Dublin, the delegates tried to make the account of their ordeal comprehensible. Cosgrave saw in dominion status a working basis for future progress and declared himself on the side of the signatories. Barton, though indicating he had signed under duress, stood behind the document during the Cabinet discussion out of a sense of moral obligation, wanting it referred to the Dail. With Dev's view that they had gone further than they had a right to go, Ministers Stack and Brugha were quick to align themselves. The Cabinet had heretofore required unanimity for its decision, and not till late at night did the seven Cabinet members take a vote on the Articles of Agreement. Three stood staunchly opposed—de Valera, Brugha and Stack. Four—Griffith, Collins, Barton and Cosgrave—were in favour. The next step was to lay the Cabinet decision before Dail Eireann to accept or reject, and the deputies were summoned for December 14.

Before that date came, the Supreme Council of the Irish Republican Brotherhood met in secret. De Valera, though outside the Brotherhood, learned through sources of his own that

Collins as chairman of the Supreme Council suggested the Treaty
need not be considered as final but as a "stepping-stone" to
further independence. While Liam Lynch, the Army officer from
the south-west as well as member of the Brotherhood, took issue
with Collins, most of those present, discouraged about defeating
the English under prevailing conditions, convinced themselves
that the best thing was to accept the Treaty, to build up a standing
Army, and in a few years return to the idea of a Republic, and
Collins got the help of the Army's Chief of Staff, Mulcahy, who
was also in the Brotherhood, in urging those Army officers who
were *teachtai* to vote for the Treaty in the Dail. "Michael Collins,"
in de Valera's opinion, "got the I.R.B. machine working," but
Sean T. O'Kelly and a few others who so far had been Brotherhood stalwarts broke their connections over these moves and the
I.R.B. itself was split.

The attitude being manifested by the British was, Dev took
note, based on the assumption that the Articles of Agreement
were sure of adoption. Parliament lost no time in ratifying the
Treaty. In regard to the rights held for the Crown, Prime Minister
Lloyd George told the House of Commons that "The first thing
we provided for was that in case of war we should have full
access to all Irish harbours and creeks." On the subject of trade,
he confessed that only reluctantly had he consented to giving
Ireland the right to impose tariffs upon British goods, recognizing
that this was a dominion right. Churchill as the Secretary of State
for Colonies began to take over from Sir Hamar Greenwood the
direction of Irish affairs, since Southern Ireland as a dominion
would fall into the sphere of colonial affairs. "Should the
Dail ratify," Churchill conjectured, "the first step should be
to get an Irish delegation, comprising Mr. Griffith and Mr.
Collins, over here at the earliest moment." The incumbent of
the Presidency in Ireland already was being counted out of the
picture.

Matters neared a danger-point in Ireland when some of the
Army commandants proposed the use of violent measures to
preserve the Republic. Lynch was not at one with the Collins'
faction nor was Rory O'Connor, and it was urged that the Treaty
signers be arrested and tried on grounds of disloyalty. This the
Minister of Defence himself advocated. Though the President
considered himself legally entitled to do so, he refused on the

grounds that the Army was divided and that the country would not stand for such action on his part. "The Army, as such, is, of course, not affected by the political situation," he cautioned in a public announcement, "and continues under the same orders and control." The constitutional way must, as he had said, be observed. The best hope of getting the Dail to turn down the Treaty was to provide a counter-proposal for Anglo-Irish agreement. External association, not so far divulged to the deputies as a whole, remained his aim though he saw that if he was to reunite his Cabinet, he might have to go further in the direction of association.

The quarters in the Mansion House where the Dail usually met had been pre-empted before the emergency session was called for the *Aonach* or Christmas fair, so the deputies gathered across St. Stephen's Green at University College where two adjoining rooms were thrown together to form one long, narrow chamber. When the deputies began congregating, direction of traffic in the vicinity was taken over by the Irish Republican Army which could not, however, prevent unknown hands from marking on the walls and hoardings, "Down with the Free State." On the trains bringing deputies in from the country, some swore that they would not compromise, Sean McKeon the Blacksmith of Ballinalee among them. Cheers went up for Griffith as he arrived on an old-style "outside car," his short legs braced upon the shelf of the jaunting car. Bystanders shouted louder when Collins drove up in an automobile, clean-shaven again and insouciant, rid of the necessity of disguising himself. Brugha rode his bicycle, impervious to the people milling about him, a man with the pain of old wounds in his face.

The Irish Republican Army guards came to a quick salute when the saturnine-looking President stepped out of an automobile, his eyes fixed straight ahead, his expression forbidding applause. To those watching as he hurried up the few steps and disappeared under the portico of the University building, he looked thinner, almost ill. He was among the last to join the deputies inside the makeshift legislative chamber and without removing his overcoat, threw his attaché-case down beside Stack, Brugha and Childers to the left-hand side of Eoin MacNeill, the speaker, where the Government members belonged. Collins and Griffith had already seated themselves to MacNeill's right.

When the session was called to order, the envoys' instructions to submit any agreement to Dublin were, at de Valera's behest, read out. At the inference that the envoys had signed in disregard of their instructions to communicate with Dublin, and that they had meant to by-pass the Cabinet and enlist the nation's support for their action, Collins flared up and the Dail excluded spectators for a few days, hoping to clear the air. De Valera seized this as his chance to try out his new plan without any publicity, explaining that it was but a rough outline on which he and Childers were working.

/ Inasmuch as one document, the Treaty, lay before the Dail already, the new one was labelled Document Number 2. It represented, he said, the particular degree of concession from pure Republicanism which he was willing at this last moment to offer in the hope of preventing a serious mistake. He was proposing that Ireland be associated for purposes of common concern with the other states of the British Commonwealth. The King would be incorporated as head of the association but there would be no Governor-General in the capacity of royal representative such as there was in the Treaty. Document Number 1 identified Ireland with the dominions, which Document Number 2 did not do. The difference between the two documents was the difference between internal and external association. Document Number 1 postulated internal association with an oath to the King as head not only of the Empire but as head of Ireland specifically, so that Ireland would be associated with England in domestic matters as well as foreign affairs. External association on the other hand meant that the King would be recognized only for Ireland's international relations, not as King of Ireland. By this expedient he proposed to affix the Republican character of his government and yet induce neighbourly relations between England and Ireland. The envoys, casting their eyes over the new draft, saw what to them resembled Draft Treaty A that had been sent with them to London in October and there rejected, but to the deputies in general who had never seen Draft Treaty A or known of its existence, the concept of external association was entirely new in this or in any form.

The national crisis was forcing the President's hand and he gambled on securing the approval of the unswerving Republican as well as winning over any Treaty-minded deputies. The fine distinction he was trying to make for them between Document Number 1 and Document Number 2 seemed, however, like the distinction between Tweedledum and Tweedledee, what O'Higgins called the scheme of a professor turned politician. Document Number 2 did not appear to the deputies to give assurance of a real Republic, whereas Document Number 1 at least seemed to promise peace, and the President was forced to conclude that if the deputies themselves did not understand his proposition, it might be interpreted generally as an unworthy departure from the old idea of an isolated Republic. Political instinct made him wary of the taint of compromise. Deeming his substitute Document Number 2 not yet clearly enough developed to reconcile the factions, he requested when the Dail resumed in open session that it be regarded as confidential.

"Are my hands to be tied by this document being withheld," Griffith demanded, "after . . . discussing it for two days?" The world in general ought to know, Griffith protested, that it was not only he but the President who advocated something short of straight Republicanism whether it was Document Number 1 or Number 2, the Free State or external association. Griffith, having got the floor, moved that the Articles of Agreement be approved by Dail Eireann as a "bargain" he had made so that Ireland would be spared more bloodshed. "When I was going to London," Griffith emphasized, "I knew that neither I nor any other man could bring back a Republic and he [the President] admitted to me that it could not be done." Since part of the truth was being told, Dev thought to himself, better the whole of it. Griffith was still speaking of him, the President: ". . . he sent a Deputy here to America to prepare the country for——"

"For external association," interrupted de Valera, unable longer to restrain himself. He would not have his motives maligned about the private instructions he had given Harry Boland. The latter was still out of the country and unable to speak up in the Dail. ". . . for external association which was a united Cabinet policy." The time had come when these words, external association, must be said, the compromise named, for it was not a dishonourable compromise. De Valera was on his feet. These men, he said, pointing to Griffith and Collins sitting opposite, "are subverting the Republic. . . . This Treaty leads us to wars, and a period of internal strife." He was not done. "Parnell was asked to do something like this. . . ." He saw himself standing where his predecessor had stood decades before. "Parnell said practically, 'You have no right to ask me, because I have no right to say that any man can set boundaries to the march of a nation.' " His audience was struck into receptivity. They knew what was coming as he plunged the knife of history deeper. ". . . if you take this you are——"

"No!" shouted some from their benches, only to be drowned out by others crying, "Yes!"

Over the uproar the President lifted his voice, ". . . you are presuming to set bounds to the onward march of a nation." To the applause and outcries he had mercilessly exacted, he sat down without taking his eyes from the men across the room.

Collins, brushing aside the question as to why, before the Treaty was signed, no effort had been made to communicate with the President, insisted that the envoys had had to make a decision on the fateful Monday because Lloyd George had promised Sir James Craig an answer on Tuesday. But, thought de Valera as he looked back upon that night, "I could have been got on the 'phone if necessary." He had specifically left word how he could be reached in Limerick, and even if he had not been accessible, "The members of the Cabinet could have been got on the 'phone; a messenger could have been sent over."

The deputies listened as Collins continued his reply, "There was no opportunity of referring it to our people at home." That was true enough, if he was thinking of the people as a whole and not the President, not the Cabinet.

De Valera was curious as to how Barton, Minister as well as envoy, would explain the fact that he who had seemed the most hesitant of them all had signed. "I broke my oath of allegiance to the Republic because I believed it to be the lesser evil." Then, said Barton as he laid bare the envoys' dilemma, "Lloyd George . . . declared that the signature and recommendation of every member of our delegation was necessary or war would follow immediately."

This, de Valera felt, was the greatest of all the crimes that had been enacted. "To the utmost limit to which they could go, our delegates had gone to arrive at an agreement such as this nation could freely accept. . . . By the threat of war they were dragged beyond that limit." Many of the *teachtai* had come determined to keep the Republic, yet de Valera could feel them inclining now toward settlement. Sean McKeon, for instance, was talking in favour of the Treaty, as was the Army's Chief of Staff, Mulcahy. Three days before Christmas, de Valera, Brugha and Stack calculated that, if the vote could be taken then, they might win by a majority of one or two, but each day and each hour was making converts for the envoys. The President rose to say, "I am afraid that we will have to sit tomorrow night," but Collins was in no rush and on a motion from him, the Dail adjourned for the holiday period.

It was the dead of the Irish winter with farmwork at a standstill, and Irishmen had little to do but sit by the fire and debate politics. At Greystones the President's children forced him into snatches of merrymaking although he would not take his mind from the crisis. ". . . a grand peace could at this moment be had," he could not help saying, "and see the difference." All over the country, in the sparse and rainswept counties of the western seacoast, in the dairy-rich counties of the south-west, in the meadowed midlands, the people gathered to discuss the Treaty. The spirit of the season was turning their minds and hearts against further strife. The hierarchy of the Church tendered good offices to the Treaty-signers, and in local political circles the influence of the Minister of Local Government, Cosgrave, carried weight, as one after another the county councils forwarded resolutions endorsing the side that he had taken.

While the President waited for the holiday to pass, he found some comfort in analysing the situation for Joe McGarrity, asking that his letter be kept strictly confidential. "I have scarcely written any personal letters since I came home a year ago. You will know why. If I had written to you as often as I had thought of you and of the incidents of my time in America with which you were intimately associated, you would have had a letter daily at least." The Brotherhood's undercover campaign he described to McGarrity as "a case of Cohalan and his machine over again," an allusion which would show McGarrity how bad things were. "Though the rank and file of the army is right," Dev wrote, "the Headquarters staff is clean gone wrong—a part of the machine." He was referring to Dick Mulcahy, the I.R.A.'s Chief of Staff. "Curse secret societies!"

The deputies, reassembling in the first days of January with their constituents' pleas for peace ringing in their ears, found that the slogans chalked up on the walls of the University buildings in Earlsfort Terrace had changed. "Ratify or get out," was what appeared now. Most came back knowing how they were going to vote; it was merely a matter of letting everyone have his or her say. Mary MacSwiney was accused of rattling the bones of the dead by her four hours of imprecation against the Treaty in the name of the long-dead martyrs. "Michael Collins told his young friends—his young soldier friends in the Dail," she was sure, "that he would bring in a Republican constitution," if they would approve the Treaty, but she could not concur with the stepping-stone idea.

As the Dail wound up a day of interruptions on January 4, 1922, Dev distributed copies of the alternative he and Childers had over the recess completed, intending to introduce it formally the next day as an amendment to Griffith's motion for approval of the Articles of Agreement. He wanted the deputies to have a chance to study it ahead of time. He had transferred the section authorizing Ulster to retain separate status to the end, but he had made no substantial changes in Document Number 2. Griffith, suspecting that Dev was trying to fall back upon straight Republicanism and that he was going to deny his own willingness to compromise in order to recapture public favour, jumped to the conclusion that a new proposition was being substituted to cover up the compromise submitted without success before Christmas. "A document has been put into our hands this evening," Griffith exclaimed, "that is not Document Number 2." Not having violated the confidence of the private session while waiting for the President to bring forward the plan in public as pledged, Griffith felt he had been tricked and before the following morning gave the *Freeman's Journal* and the *Irish Independent* copies of the document just distributed and of the confidential version of Document Number 2.

"I didn't want the world or the Irish people confused and I didn't want the British to see it," de Valera said in stormy protest when the Dail sat the next day. To the tired deputies, still another document came as an added burden. Could it be, they wondered, that Dev was bound merely to have his own way, to draw over-fine distinctions? "I defy any person to point out where I have departed one tittle, or one iota, or one comma from the position of the Republic as established by the Irish people," de Valera threw out. "I stand definitely for the Irish Republic as it was proclaimed in 1916." Aspersions were being cast upon the thing on which he prided himself most, his integrity. The aspersions were coming from a source—the Brotherhood—that was guilty of the very thing of which he was accused, undercover methods of operation. "It is because I am straight that I meet crookedness with straight dealing always, and I have beaten crookedness with straight dealing. . . . I detest trickery." Seeing that his newest and his last proposal had no chance to succeed, he was driven to withdraw it and the duel of the documents was over. Collins, dismayed at the crumbling of the President's leadership, came forward with the idea of Dev's forming a coalition government. Though Dev listened to those sent to urge this upon him, they were asking, he considered, the impossible. When the Dail was finally called to order a day or two later, he rose, paused to get attention, then announced deliberately, ". . . as the Chief Executive authority, I resign and with it goes the Cabinet." He hesitated as the surprise took effect. "If you re-elect me——" he started.

"We will," came the ready answer from some of the members.

"If you re-elect me," the President picked up his statement of intent, "I will have to have the right to get a Cabinet that thinks with me . . . to have full use of all the resources of the Republic to defend the Republic." Clearly, he had no coalition in view. Upon the decision of Speaker MacNeill, Griffith's original motion on the Treaty became the order of the day, not de Valera's resignation.

"I knew nothing about political tactics until the question of this Treaty came up," de Valera defended himself. "I have seen too much of them, goodness knows, since, and I hope to heavens I will see no more of them, no matter how we finish this." His last card was played. "I am sick and tired of politics—so sick that no matter what happens I would go back to private life. I have only seen politics within the last three weeks or a month."

For the taking of the vote on Griffith's Treaty motion, de Valera would not stand by any means alone. Madame Markievicz could find no fault in the President but one. "He is too trusting and he believes too readily in the nobility of those with whom he is dealing." Mrs. Pearse drove up for the session in an old hack, the picture of dejection. Her shapeless black hat and old fur coat betokened mourning not for Padraic and Willie but for all Ireland. "I feel in my heart," she said, "the ghosts of my sons." Most of the women were staunch in the President's behalf and there was Childers, his lips moving, his face pale and drawn. Boland, hurrying back from America, landed just in time, ready to vote against the Treaty in spite of his membership in the Brotherhood. Liam Mellowes was in the chamber, inveighing against surrender. Brugha made the final speech repudiating the London terms. To take the vote on the Treaty, the roll of members was called in Irish: 64 answered "Ta," that is "Yes," in favour of the Treaty; 57 voted "Nil"—"No."

The President's hands, as he gathered together his documents and notes, were trembling and when he stood up his face had lost what colour it possessed. He was defeated, and in that moment spoke as a defeated man. "I would like my last word here to be this," he started. "We have had a glorious record for four years . . ." His voice choked but he had more he wanted to say. ". . . It has been four years of magnificent discipline in our nation. The world is looking at us now——" For once, his self-discipline was gone. He covered his face with his hands and sat back.

Dev's followers who had lost by so close a vote refused in the next few days to give up, even when the resignation which he had offered earlier was accepted. "If Eamon de Valera did not happen to be President," pressed Brugha, "who would have kept Arthur Griffith, Michael Collins and myself together?"

"He has exactly the same position in my heart," murmured the impulsive Collins, "as he always had."

Dev, admitting that ever since he had been released from his first imprisonment there had been friction between Griffith the moderate, and Brugha the extremist, termed the task he had had difficult. "In every Cabinet I formed I took care to have those two sides properly represented . . . to try . . . to hold the balance [and] until the sixth of December I succeeded in my task."

". . . no one here in this assembly or in Ireland wants to be put in the position of opposing President de Valera," interposed Collins.

"I do not want office at all," the losing leader broke in. "Go

and elect your President and all the rest of it. . . . I do not ask
you to elect me." His pride could not stand renewed buffeting.
"I am quite glad and anxious to get back to private life." Balloting
on his re-election commenced without any encouragement from
him. When his own turn to vote was called he exclaimed, "I will
not vote," and by a margin of two, 60 to 58, he was defeated.
Shouts of "Up de Valera" made themselves heard. With a sudden
smile he acknowledged his applause. "I hope that nobody will
talk about fratricidal strife. . . . You will want us yet." He, too,
was trying to be forgiving, to recapture the old spirit between
fellow Irishmen. ". . . it is not a question of persons because
where personality is concerned we are all the best friends. We
worked together as one team. Now we are divided funda-
mentally. . . ."

Next day, Collins nominated Griffith for the vacated office.
The candidate was being nominated as President of what, de
Valera inquired: of the Dail or of the Republic? He was not
satisfied when the nominee, himself somewhat at a loss at the
recurrence of this old conundrum, replied that he would occupy
the same position as his predecessor. As the vote on Griffith's
nomination became imminent, the ex-President sprang from his
seat—anger, hurt pride and a note of finality in his voice. "As a
protest against the election as President of the Irish Republic of
the Chairman of the Delegation, who is bound by the Treaty
conditions to set up a State which is to subvert the Republic . . .
I . . . am going to leave the House."

By late afternoon the Republicans were back in their seats,
Griffith having in the interim been elected unanimously to the
Presidency by those who had remained. "I cannot consistently
and sincerely congratulate the President on his election," de
Valera commented tersely, his mind racing ahead to other problems. As the person responsible for having brought the military
faction under civil control, he foresaw that the new head of the
Government could assert his authority over the Army and in so
doing could defeat the Army's initial objective—the Republic. "I
fear," he persisted, "that unless the Army is kept intact as the
Army of the Republic, the members of the Army will not have
the confidence which is necessary if we are to keep them as a
solid unit." Mulcahy, who was going to succeed Brugha in the
Ministry of Defence, asserted that the Army would occupy the

same position as it had before, but the ex-President was not satisfied.

He who had pledged himself to work against the Treaty in the constitutional way was offered a quicker method when senior commandants, knowing that the I.R.A. as a body was still uncommitted, hurried to Dublin early in the new year, 1922, to confer. They listened as the new Minister of Defence, Mulcahy, urged them to wait for the new constitution setting up the Free State before making up their minds. He authorized the scheduling of an Army convention for the spring, promising in the meantime to keep the Army as the Army of the Republic.

Dev, present at the sessions of the officers, was aware that some among them were missing—Rory O'Connor, Liam Mellowes, Cathal Brugha, for instance, their minds already being made up against the Treaty. Commandant Ernie O'Malley, scarred and toughened by hairbreadth escapes and British beatings, protested with thrusting chin that he would take no orders from Mulcahy. Backing this point of view was another officer, Sean MacBride, son of the Easter Week martyr. The Dublin Brigade, including its Third Battalion, Dev's Own, was reported by its commanding officer, Oscar Traynor, to be solid against the Treaty. The Treaty signers, some of those present muttered, ought to be shot as traitors. Commandant Liam Lynch, whose division in the south-west constituted one quarter of the Army's strength, declared that, in his eyes, Dev was still the President.

Such explosive fealty presented de Valera with a chance to strike at the new regime before it could get on its feet but he had never considered force as something to turn against fellow countrymen. Stony-visaged, he told the officers that the Republic was not yet disestablished and, God willing, never would be. Final acceptance of the agreement with England still depended upon a vote of the people, the date for which had yet to be set, and President Griffith had said that the new constitution, referred to by Mulcahy, would be ready for all to see before then. In de Valera's mind, the promised constitution would tell whether the Republic was going to be maintained or not, and till then it was his aim to keep the Republic intact and the Army undivided as the Army of the Republic.

It became evident to the officers that the ex-President meant to adhere to a course of political opposition, not military, but they did not hear in his voice the old zest, the old authority, the old timbre. Frank Aiken, the officer representing the key Northern division, recommended holding off violence but when de Valera asked that, for the time being, allegiance be given to Mulcahy as the new defence head, Lynch, O'Malley, MacBride, Traynor, Sean Russell and others refused. Dev ceased to associate himself with the militant-minded commandants, it being his plan to work toward a free election on the issue. "When," he had said, "I have done that and the decision is given, I shall have finished."

For the moment, he and the other Republicans could only stand by and watch the events transpiring. When Griffith convoked the Parliament of Southern Ireland in perfunctory observance of the Government of Ireland Act, that body put its stamp of approval upon the Treaty and upon the transition administration and then dispersed. Griffith himself, seeking to keep his role as President free of political implications, did not become a Cabinet Minister and Collins, while retaining the Ministry of Finance, assumed the chairmanship of the provisional government. The provisional government opened offices in Merrion Square as well as in the Mansion House. Cosgrave continued as Minister of Local Government; Gavan Duffy was Minister of Foreign Affairs; O'Higgins was Minister of Economic Affairs, a title later changed to Home Affairs; and Mulcahy, the Minister of Defence.

Dev was still head of Sinn Fein as well as the trustee of its funds, and the delegates to the *Ard Fheis* of that organization, assembling in Dublin's Rotunda in Feburary, lit their pipes and cigarettes impatiently while waiting to see if he would appear to preside over them. A half-hour late, the tall, forward-bending figure loomed out of the fog of tobacco smoke, shouldering his way from the back of the hall in the Rotunda up to the platform. The air was thick, the undercurrent noisy like a pub. Waiting for a pro-Griffith demonstration to work itself out, Dev deliberately removed his long, stiff-skirted overcoat and upon taking the chair abruptly ordered all smoking stopped; the fumes were British-manufactured. With this challenge, this plain mastery, the audience was his and applause succeeded an uncertain silence.

When President Griffith rose to address the *Ard Fheis*, he found himself on unsure ground. "I am the servant of the Irish people," Griffith commenced humbly and decorously, as he undertook to review the London negotiations. As for de Valera, he had come to interpose delay in the provisional government's course of action. Churchill seemed to be in a hurry to call for the Irish vote and Dev spoke against any "snatch election." Both Irish factions would, he suggested, gain by going slowly. Postponement would permit the provisional government's expert in constitutional law, Darrell Figgis, to draft the new constitution in plenty of time. Collins was heading the committee on drafting the constitution. Dev knew, furthermore, that delay would enable him to rally political backing of his own. At his initiative, the delegates agreed that the election should not be held for three months, and he adjourned the *Ard Fheis* without revealing his gratification at the time he was gaining.

CHAPTER X

STAMPEDE OF A NATION (1922)

IN the stress of the Dail's debate on the Treaty, de Valera had announced that he would return to private life, but with the encouragement of many of the men and most of the women who had come thus far on the road with him, he decided instead to form a political party of his own—Cumann na Poblachta, the party of the Republic—and Childers began to print a party paper called *Poblacht na hEireann*. Not only did the American Association for the Recognition of the Irish Republic, Dev's creation in another hour of need, empty its treasury in response to his request, but it undertook a new drive. On a raw, wintry afternoon early in the year 1922, the Republican Party's pre-election campaign was launched from a platform erected in O'Connell Street. There, under the shelter of Parnell's statue, de Valera, flanked by Stack, Brugha, Boland, O'Kelly, and guarded by I.R.A. soldiers loyal to him, issued his challenge to a street crowd. Under the Treaty, he said, the British Government could take over the harbours and make Ireland a belligerent in any war in which Britain engaged. As such Ireland would be subject to attack. Starting a tour in behalf of Cumann na Poblachta in Limerick, he said: "We are like a party set out to cross a desert. . . . We have reached a green oasis, and there are some would tell us to lie down and rest."

There in Limerick, the people were seeing how unsafe it was to lie down and rest. Both pro-Treaty and anti-Treaty Irish soldiers rushed to take over the local barracks evacuated by the British. A written appeal for mediation was dispatched by de Valera to the new Minister of Defence who, not many weeks before, had stood at his side in that city to take the salute of the soldiers. "You know the general human forces at work as well as I do," he wrote Mulcahy, "the natural discontent of men who took up arms for the Republic." The two Army factions were on the verge of open combat. Winston S. Churchill sent a note marked personal and secret to the Assistant Under-Secretary for Ireland in Dublin, Alfred W. Cope: "Do they [the members of the provisional government] intend to put down the Limerick revolt . . . ? Do you think there is any fighting quality in the Free State Government? Will anybody die for it or kill for it?" De Valera's appeal to Mulcahy went unacknowledged but Collins and Lynch entered into consultation with each other and O'Malley's men, acting in the name of the Republic, were persuaded to march out quietly. Churchill's fears, roused by the Limerick flare-up, halted the withdrawal of Crown forces from Ireland, and the British instead began supplying arms for the pro-Treaty units of the Irish Army. In the North, Sir Henry Wilson was named by Craig to be his military adviser, and a new corps known as the Ulster Specials was recruited from among the Orangemen.

De Valera, continuing his campaign for political action against the Treaty, appeared in towns like Wexford, standing in an open cart in the middle of the square. Bareheaded, his figure whipped and drenched by rain and wind off the sea, pointing with his finger, he looked to the people more preacher than politician. His journeys took him over black roads slippery with mud, awash under winter's downpours like the sea's own flats at low tide, and he told the crowds turning out to hear him that he was glad to see that the Republic was not dead, that the people did not want the British monarch as king of Ireland. Driving round the Kerry coast, he felt himself akin to all the storms and difficulties of the fishing and farming people. Their faces as they flocked round him showed the price of the struggle in the sacrifice of their husbands and sons and brothers. The question in his mind was how much more could they or would they stand in the cause?

Though he was neither President nor Minister nor any part of the provisional government, he had but to lift one finger to have a Republican underground come to life. On St. Patrick's Day, he told a large audience that if the Treaty were accepted the fight for freedom would continue and the Irish people, instead of fighting foreign soldiers, would have to fight Irish soldiers of an Irish government set up by Irishmen. For him it was the saddest St. Patrick's Day in five years, he said, this holiday that was meant to be the harbinger of everything good. On this day in the spring, according to the old saying, there was a nest in every wood, a trout in every pool, and a heifer calf in every paddock in Ireland. This was not the picture for the people in the year of 1922. Any outbreak precipitated by adoption of the Treaty, Dev warned in a speech at Thurles, would mean that the combatants would have "to wade through the blood of soldiers of the Irish government, and perhaps of some members of the Irish government, to meet their freedom."

This, interpreted by some as inciting the youth of the nation to revolt, was in his own mind merely syllogizing. He wanted to warn the people that if they voted to adopt the Treaty those opposed were sure to take up arms. But the day after he spoke of wading through blood, the *Irish Independent* accused him of encouraging and even preaching civil war. "Nothing, it seems to me, but deliberate, and in the tense circumstances of this moment, criminal malice," he replied to the newspaper, "could so distort the plain argument of my speeches, perfectly clear to all who listened to me. . . ." He was still intent upon the means of civil or political resistance.

When the Dail reconvened that spring, he sat as head of the opposition. The most important new business on the agenda was the election due at the end of the three-month interval to choose the deputies who would then, presumably, confirm arrangements for the Free State under the Treaty's terms. The Republicans' demand that the women's franchise be put on the same basis as the men's was opposed by Griffith not, he said, because he was against liberalizing women's suffrage but because of the further delay it would entail. De Valera next sought to insist upon the completion of the new electoral register, but this too was ruled out by President Griffith as intended to torpedo the Treaty. Collins' statement that external association would have perpetuated conflict touched its author to the quick. "Only that it is a sovereign assembly," Dev ejaculated angrily, "I would be the very first to ask the Army to sweep you and the like of you out."

Army men, waiting for their convention scheduled to take place in March, heard and took note. Into the pro-Treaty elements of the Army Collins was throwing his resources. Collins was, in addition, contriving to secure support on all sides, and authorized contact in London with Russian representatives, imbued as he was with the old hope of help from that quarter. At Beggars Bush Barracks, the General Headquarters of the provisional government forces, new uniforms of green with red and yellow service stripes and glossy leggings were issued to the men called the regulars. Officers were invited to come up from the rural districts to Beggars Bush to draw money, equipment and arms for their units. In spite of inducements in money and prestige from Collins personally, O'Connor spurned the offer of a top post, as did O'Malley and others. They did not regard themselves as mutineers; rather, as Republicans remaining loyal to their trust. Mellowes likened the existing government to a chameleon; one moment when you looked at it it was green, white and orange for the Republic and the next moment it was red, white and blue for the Empire. Anti-Treaty Volunteers who kept their old green uniforms from the days of the rising and the troubles had purple bands sewn on to their collars to distinguish themselves from the regulars. They were cut off financially by the provisional government and were without endorsement politically from the old government of de Valera but this did not alter their feeling.

De Valera's attitude on the question of the soldiers' allegiance was significant because he had remained non-committal and the Cabinet members, increasingly alarmed, asked the ageing nationalist, Timothy Healy, to solicit de Valera's support if they should cancel the scheduled Army convention. As the date set for it approached, Collins received a letter from Churchill: "An adverse decision by the convention of the Irish Republican Army [so called] would . . . be a very grave event at the present juncture. I presume you are quite sure there is no danger of this." Collins, who was by no means sure, consulted Mulcahy but the latter could give no promise as to what the Army might do. Griffith thought it not only possible but probable that the convention would, if it met, attempt to set up a military government.

Healy, dubious of his own influence with the one-time President, located him in the office into which he had moved at 23 Suffolk Street, a substantial old building surrounded by mercantile establishments in the centre of Dublin's shopping district. Separate suites of offices opened off the ground floor and landing of the dark, polished wood staircase, lit dimly by an ornamental torch on the newel post. Dev had his desk downstairs. He received his caller coolly and kept Boland by him while Healy warned that if he—Dev—lent himself to the use of force he would be a sorry man within a year.

"I don't think so," de Valera curtly replied. He had nothing to do with the Army, he emphasized to his visitor. In another room upstairs sat Rory O'Connor and fellow officers, but Dev had tried all along to make it clear that he and O'Connor had no connection with each other apart from sharing the same address, and his co-workers had observed that he had not liked it when O'Connor had arrived and taken over a room. What O'Connor was doing was reorganizing that section of the Army which had not recognized Mulcahy's authority, re-arming the flying columns and re-stringing the intelligence network that had fallen into disuse since the truce in the summer. Dev was conscious of all the hazards in any revival of an independent armed body, but at the same time he knew the strength it might lend. As the Irish proverb put it, "There's no crime in the blow that has not been struck." He let Healy out at the close of their brief meeting without any approval for the idea of cancelling the Army's convention. In private, nevertheless, he counselled O'Connor against defying a countermand. Frank Aiken added his confidential recommendation to brother officers that, for the sake of unity, the convention be put off. It was the existence of strength, not the show of it and not the use of it, that de Valera held valuable.

Without the desired news of Dev's sanction from Healy, the provisional government proceeded to ban the Army convention, and Mulcahy announced that any Volunteer attending would be considered suspended from the Army. This did not prevent several hundred Volunteers, uniformed in trench coats, from massing in Dublin at the Mansion House on the date set, Sunday, March 26, in defiance of the provisional government. De Valera did not join them nor did Frank Aiken. With Mellowes presiding, the extremists among the extremists proposed a dictatorship to overthrow the four governments in Ireland that were competing with the Republic: Dail Eireann, the provisional government, the British government, and the Northern government. A resolution was passed restoring the command function to the hands of an independent military executive, and those chosen to the Executive included O'Connor, Mellowes, O'Malley and Liam Deasy, with Lynch designated in secret to serve as Chief of Staff. Some on the new directorate were men who had entered the movement after the rising, among them Patrick J. Ruttledge, a deputy since 1920 from County Mayo and a lawyer who had worked in the Republican courts in the days of the Black and

Tans. To their Army command and to that only, these Republican fighters swore to be loyal, thereby absolving themselves of fealty to the Dail. Hundreds of them, armed with revolvers seized from a British ship in the harbour, marched out into the streets of Dublin while onlookers hooted at them as "Reds" and irregulars. Rory O'Connor led the marchers to Smithfield in the old region of the city where he and Mellowes presided over a new oath-taking ceremony.

By resolution of their convention, they offered to place their services at the disposal of a Republican government should one come into being, but O'Connor declared that the Army was no longer under the direction of the provisional government, no longer under the Dail, no longer subject to de Valera himself. De Valera had declined any suggestion that he serve as Commander-in-Chief. He did not, however, repudiate the action taken at Smithfield though he had reservations about it. It was only by straining his convictions about the subservience of military power to civil control that he decided to go along with O'Connor's overthrow of allegiance to the Dail, as he said later. His new party, Cumann na Poblachta, and the Republican Army were separate and distinct instrumentalities, neither being subordinate to the other, but on the question of objectives the two were agreed. In regard to means to reach these objectives, Dev as the political leader was not ready to do more than talk about military measures ". . . there are rights," he declared, "which a minority may justly uphold, even by arms, against a majority."

Originally, he had sought the Army's support for Mulcahy, but failure to keep the Republic intact was changing his attitude and Republicans he considered released from obedience to the provisional government. It was not, he charged, upholding the Republic though morally obligated so to do until the plebiscite. To the youth of the nation he issued, as had been his custom during his Presidency, an Easter manifesto: "Beyond all telling is the destiny God has in mind for Ireland, the fair, the peerless one. . . . Yours is the faith that moves mountains." And then, in words which the dissident Army men could not but take as meant for them, he proclaimed: "Ireland is yours for the taking! Take it!"

Rory O'Connor, intent upon reactivation of the Army, moved on Maundy Thursday out of the Suffolk Street offices and seized the Four Courts on the quay along the north bank of the Liffey. The judges, astounded and bewildered, departed in a hurry leaving their wigs and robes behind, and once the Republicans got the premises to themselves, they brought in Volunteers secretly each night to work on explosive devices. The Irish Republican Army, O'Connor explained to reporters whom he admitted under guard, was not associated with any political organization at the moment, although, he added, "I am safe in saying that if the army were ever to follow a political leader Mr. de Valera is the man."

Across the river in the Mansion House on that same day, Maundy Thursday, de Valera was calling by invitation to talk things over with the leaders of the provisional government. As he alighted from his car in the driveway, he had to push his way through impulsive bystanders. Dressed in his bulky, frieze overcoat and wide-brimmed, black hat, holding one arm slightly upraised as if to fend off interference, he moved straight ahead with the look of one unseeing, his head bent forward on his stem-like neck, no suggestion of a smile on his face, his lips pursed like those of a thirsty man. Women held out their arms toward him as if he held the answer to their cry for peace, and one old lady laid a restraining hand on his lapel to beseech a glance, if nothing more. Collins came in conservative and conventional attire, his shoes highly polished, a neat brief-case swinging from his left hand. He looked almost plump and stepped briskly across the pavement from his car with eyes lowered in dignified preoccupation, nothing of the desperado left in his manner. Fresh in his mind was the most recent letter he had received from Churchill: "I am glad to see that you have arranged a meeting with de Valera, but I hope you will understand that we cannot go further in any respect. Mr. de Valera may gradually come to personify not a cause but a catastrophe."

Easter came and went without results although the conferring continued intermittently. President Griffith's remarks to the sessions of the Dail during May were not conducive to *rapprochement*. His inference was that Dev, foreseeing a breakdown at the time of the negotiations, had sent those he deemed his political rivals to London to be tarred with failure, to be stigmatized with attempted compromise. "I say it is an infamous suggestion and I would not be fit to be alive if I had done that," the accused replied from the opposition side of the house. "My statement is on record."

"So is your Cuban statement," shot back Griffith, sticking to his contention that compromise had no more originated with him than with de Valera.

"Oh, you are mean!" de Valera winced. "You are vilely mean."

The general atmosphere did not augur well for peaceful conduct of the scheduled vote on the Treaty. Spring was coming in once more to a rain of shots. Dublin streets at night were laced with bullets when rebel machine-guns opened fire from roof-tops on the offices of the provisional government in Merrion Square. The Telephone Exchange, the City Hall, the Bank of Ireland, Beggars Bush Barracks became targets of the Republican snipers. Dev feared that an election would not be really representative of the people, and when newsmen pressed him to say whether the use of force was justified, slowly and hesitatingly he gave his answer, "The Army, as the last defence of the nation, is entitled to prevent elections such as those proposed. . . ." The men inside the Four Courts were waiting to hear that. "If the Army could save the nation from the calamities which are bound to follow the acceptance of these articles of agreement," Dev decided, "I think it justifiable for it to use its strength to do so."

Collins was also beginning to fear that to carry out the election as contemplated might precipitate strife in the South. "This state of things must be brought to an end," Collins declared. "The position is rapidly developing a state of civil war." In the seclusion of University College, confidential talks began between him as head of the provisional government and his former Chief. For both, the real enemy was in the North, not in the South. Orangemen were riding Belfast streets by night, preying on those deemed to be Republicans.

Craig remained obdurate against revising the boundary in the way Collins had hoped could be done, and behind Craig stood Sir Henry Wilson, on the alert with his Ulster armed force. Life in Belfast and its environs, de Valera asserted, was being made a hell for the nationalists who were, in turn, retaliating.

To forestall further Army friction in the South and to create a common front against the enemy in the North, Dublin's political and military heads followed the lead of de Valera and Collins and

sat down together. Liam Lynch for the one side and Richard
Mulcahy for the other undertook to work together on a plan of
attack upon the Crown forces in the six-county area, and Aiken
came to participate in the talks. O'Connor was not asked to
evacuate the Four Courts. The sporadic shooting from the guns
of the I.R.A. stopped, the thunder and the lightning ceased, and
the skies cleared as only Irish skies can. "I believe that peace can
be got," de Valera said as he stood up in the Dail to move for a
truce, a motion which Mulcahy seconded. Though Dev had rejected the suggestion of a coalition government the previous
January, he reopened the idea himself, forced by circumstances
to change his mind.

"If a Coalition Government is formed here," Collins told the
Dail, "we shall be on the road to a united Ireland." Not even the
letter he received from Churchill could daunt him. "May 15,
1922. . . . As far as we are concerned in this country," Churchill
wrote, "we should certainly not be able to regard any such
arrangement as a basis on which we could build." For his part,
de Valera felt that there was still a chance he and his former
companions might go along the same road together, and jointly
he and Collins submitted to the Dail on May 20 plans for a
coalition. Each side was to put up the number of candidates
required to maintain its existing strength in the legislature. The
date of the election was to be June 16 with proportional representation to protect minority interests. The Sinn Fein organization, once again common meeting-ground, was to draw up a
panel of candidates with a certain number nominated for the
pro-Treaty side and a slightly smaller number for the anti-Treaty
side, so that their *status quo* in the Dail would be accurately retained. To avoid the appearance of making the outcome arbitrary,
a clause was inserted in the pact to the effect that ". . . every and
any interest is free to go up and contest the election equally with
the National Sinn Fein Panel." This meant that groups other than
Sinn Fein like the Farmers and Labour were not prohibited from
putting up their own men, though the coalition would be ensured
only if the Irish people voted for the panel nominees. "As a
Republican," de Valera claimed afterward, "I was more afraid
of the Pact than anything I had ever done as far as the cause of
the Republic was concerned." It cast his side in a minority role,
but the danger of complete defeat at the polls required that he

make concessions. Griffith moved its adoption and without dissent the deputies agreed on the idea of a national coalition government.

Dev, still unchallenged as head of Sinn Fein, secured the action of that body in naming the panel of candidates. In spite of the fact that the intent of the plan would be undone by the nomination of independent candidates, Darrell Figgis of the pro-Treaty faction openly advocated this, and certain other names were entered in the lists by Labour and by the Farmers. On the platform of the Mansion House, however, the two old co-workers, de Valera and Collins, separated by a winter of disagreement, appeared side by side to speak for their pact, a feat which was in itself an achievement for both.

Anything seemed to Collins for the moment better than letting the South split just when some in the North most needed solid support and protection. Northern nationalists were arriving in Dublin with their babies and their bundled possessions, bringing tales of being set upon and stoned and shot at in the towns north of the border, a border for which he, Collins, felt partially responsible. Then he was summoned with Griffith and Cosgrave to Downing Street. Arriving there, Collins looked to Churchill half embarrassed, half defiant, when called upon to explain his dealings with the Republicans, and had to acknowledge that he had agreed "that they [the Republicans] should hold four out of the nine offices in the new Ministry, as well as their full number of seats which they held in the Dail."

"In the event a republic is set up," Churchill ominously informed him, "it is the intention of the British Government to hold Dublin as one of the preliminary and essential steps of military operations." No coalition government that included de Valera or any of his quondam Ministers could be considered, Churchill added with finality, and again war was threatened. Collins was given to understand before the interview ended that he had to go back and salvage the Treaty.

Dev was winding up his pre-election tour in County Mayo and only two days remained before the polling when Collins returned from London and went directly to Cork, home territory to him, to keep a campaign engagement there. "I am not," he said, "hampered now by being on a platform where there are Coalitionists. I can make a straight appeal to you . . . to vote for

the candidates you think best of. . . ." What he was telling the
people was to ignore the pact, to vote for the independent candidates that Figgis and others had managed to put up. "You understand fully what you have to do, and I depend on you to do it."
Dev, on the other hand, had gone so far as to persuade at least
one Labour nominee in Clare to withdraw his name on the grounds
that non-pact candidates would take votes away from the pact.

The next day, the last before the election, de Valera was still
in the West where he was to speak five times. No sun was shining
and the western sky was bruised with purple clouds as he drove
into the village of Kiltimagh and up to Murphy's Hall where the
First Brigade of East Mayo was on hand to welcome him. Farmers
gathered with the soldiers in a reception committee on the pavement and as their visiting speaker, obviously weary, climbed out
of his automobile someone handed him the newspaper which
had just reached Kiltimagh. It carried the report of Collins' speech
the day before in Cork. What had happened Dev guessed at first
glance, and he jumped to his own conclusion. "England," he
said afterward, "dictated the breaking of the Pact."

One other promise made by the provisional government remained unfulfilled as the hours crept on toward the polling. The
text of the new constitution which Collins had brought back
from London was not seen by the voters until the morning
papers on election day. Changes had been inserted so that the
document endowed the King with the formalities of executive
power, subjected judges to nomination by the Governor-General,
decreed that the King and the two chambers together should
constitute the legislature, and specified when and how the oath
to the Crown should be taken by every member of the new Irish
parliament. The changes made satisfied Churchill that no Republican would place himself in office under such a constitution
and that de Valera and his followers would be thereby precluded
from any share in the Government of Ireland. Any constitutional
provisions found to be in conflict with the Treaty were to be
voided by a repugnancy clause.

Republicans went to the polls with hearts that were already
heavy. Though Dev himself was returned, many of his stalwarts
lost—Childers, Mrs. Tom Clarke, Madame Markievicz, Mellowes
among them. In all, 58 pro-Treaty deputies were elected as compared with 36 anti-Treaty deputies; 17 Labour Party members,

7 Farmers Party, 4 Unionists, and 6 Independents. The Sinn Fein panel of candidates on which the coalition government was to have rested was disrupted by the election of others, which Dev attributed not so much to the instigation of his compatriots as to the old, the foreign enemy. "England's gain is for the moment only," was his comment. "England's difficulty will be prayed for as Ireland's opportunity."

Defeat or no defeat at the polls, he continued later in June to insist in public statements from his Party headquarters in Suffolk Street that the coalition government should be set up. Harry Boland, having been the go-between in preparation for the coalition and confident of an underlying fraternity between Dev and "Mick," still hoped to get a call from the latter as to the men from "our side" who would be required to fill the Cabinet posts in accordance with the pact. The new Dail was due to convene shortly, and Dev, committed to the use of constitutional means of opposition, continued to wait, remaining apart from the Four Courts even after the Army factions gave up their attempts at unity. Word went round that Rory O'Connor's men were commandeering motor vehicles for an attack upon the North and that they had seized a high Army officer from the provisional government forces and taken him inside the Four Courts as a hostage. Lynch, from a nearby hotel, was in touch with O'Connor regarding future action on their part. Underground activities were being resumed by elements with which de Valera would have nothing to do, the Irish Republican Brotherhood included.

The Brotherhood, not only ignored by Dev but blamed and cursed by him in private, was something to which Collins was clinging as the talisman of his old Republican loyalties. The arch malefactor against the Northern nationalists was, in Brotherhood eyes, Sir Henry Wilson, and Collins, unknown to his colleagues in the provisional government, contrived with a member of the Brotherhood's London branch named Reginald Dunne a plan to put a stop to the Wilson-inspired pogrom. On the afternoon of June 22, 1922, Dunne with a fellow Volunteer named Joseph Sullivan took up a position in London's secluded Eaton Place, not far from the dun-coloured Wilson residence. Sir Henry, returning home in full ceremonial uniform, his sword at his side, after unveiling a war memorial, fell to the pavement before he could turn his latch-key or draw his sword, fatally shot by Dunne and Sullivan. Griffith was quick to castigate this killing as anarchic, and Rory O'Connor repudiated any connection with it. De Valera, among the first against whom British accusations were directed, replied through the newsmen that he did not know who shot Ulster's military adviser or why; that he did not approve of it; that the killing of any human being was an awful thing; but that he could understand why the perpetrator of the deed had done it. The assassin or assassins were motivated, he told the Press, by indignation over the persecutions in Ulster for which they had no legal redress. British fury over Sir Henry Wilson's death, a fury not directed at Collins, demanded action from Downing Street and secret orders were dispatched from London to General Macready to seize the Four Courts as a nest of treason. Macready, fearing that the assault, if started by him, would drive Collins to the side of the Republicans, was in favour of waiting. Prime Minister Lloyd George saw the advantage if the provisional government would, upon its own initiative, take action against the irregulars, and the orders were altered. Macready, instead, arranged secretly to loan Collins a battery of eighteen-pound guns.

A few days later, as de Valera left his family to drive as usual into Suffolk Street, his thoughts were fixed upon the impending legislative sessions as the proper battleground on which to defend the Republic. Since the ending of the election campaign, he had spent his days in Suffolk Street at his office, but he was living at home in Greystones where his wife remained as always apart from the strife and strain. Earlier that month she had given birth to their seventh child, a boy named Terry. Newspapers at the time reported that twins had been born, of whom only one survived, but so little personal information did the parents reveal that even the baby's name was at first incorrectly reported. Dev's own name and reputation had reached such proportions that David Dwane's biography of him, *The Early Life of Eamon de Valera*, just completed after interruptions from British raiding parties, was selling a hundred copies a day. His role as a man of mystery had survived numerous vicissitudes already.

It was Wednesday morning, June 28, and he had not driven far on his way to his office when a stranger stepped from the side to stop his car. "I wouldn't go to Dublin," the man warned. "The Free Staters are shelling the Four Courts."

"Nonsense," Dev replied. "I cannot believe it." But on the outskirts, the sound of bombardment across the Liffey River struck his ears. He saw lorries, drab-coloured and heavily loaded, rolling with accelerating commotion through the narrow defile of Grafton Street down toward the Pillar and the quays, their guns at the ready.

At the Party office he found Stack, Brugha and Brennan waiting for him with news of what had happened. Soon after midnight, Rory O'Connor had received a note from the provisional government demanding that the Four Courts be evacuated. Oscar Traynor had advised compliance but had also begun to mobilize the Dublin Brigade. At four o'clock that morning with O'Connor and his men refusing to come out, the provisional government forces had opened fire from the south side of the Liffey with the guns loaned by Macready. Dev was handed a message O'Connor had sent out at daybreak: "The boys are glorious and will fight for the Republic to the end." Lynch, assuming his active role as Chief of Staff with Liam Deasy as deputy, was on the point of leaving Dublin to rally Republican forces in the South.

"Well," Dev said, "will we try to stop it?"

"Stop it!" exclaimed Brugha. "What do you mean by stop it?" and he left the room, bent upon joining the fight. Stack concurred that it was too late to prevent the fighting. The British, Dev was thinking, not Griffith and not Collins, were the real aggressors and it would be a war of defence; Churchill had squeezed those Irishmen whom he had in his grip until they had been driven to attack their own countrymen. It was Churchill who could not let them wait the few days till the legislature should meet. If he himself took up arms again, it would be only to defend the constitution that Sinn Fein had cherished, the constitution which was largely of his own making. "It was they [the British] that swept away the Constitution," he reflected later.

The soldier in him reasserted itself as he made his way to a house in Mercer's Street where, he was told, the Dublin Brigade's Third Battalion, his own, was mobilizing. There, a young commandant, busy with incoming recruits, paid no more attention to him than anyone else, as with severe decorum he administered the Republican oath to all-comers. By nightfall Dev had to take

care on the street lest he be apprehended by provisional government sentries, and he took shelter in a big house near the centre
of Dublin where he occupied himself with drawing up possible
peace terms.

Late on Friday, the Four Courts caught fire, its pillars toppled,
the statues of Mercy and Justice surmounting its pediment
were engulfed in flames, and plumes of black smoke rose
high in the sky. Traynor, watching the conflagration from the
Gresham Hotel in O'Connell Street where he had established
Dublin Brigade headquarters, decided to exert his authority as
senior officer in the city, and sent O'Connor an order to surrender.
When the men came out of the inferno, O'Malley made his escape,
but most of the garrison was captured including Mellowes and
O'Connor himself. All that was left of the imposing façade was a
charred screen perforated with paneless windows beneath a
top-heavy, blackened dome.

De Valera managed to bicycle through the streets to Traynor
in the Gresham Hotel, carrying the terms which he had drafted.
There he found Stack, Brugha and Madame Markievicz, the latter
no longer a young woman but incorrigible in her will to bear
arms if the men were doing so. He noted among those coming in
from the maze of lanes at the back of the hotel the slight figure
of Barton, his signature upon the Treaty branded upon his heart.
Childers was printing stop-press editions of *Poblacht na hEireann*
on green and orange paper. "Eamon de Valera," announced the
June 30 copy, "is on active service with the Dublin Brigade,
fighting for the Republic." A pall of passivity came over the
Chief, however, as he roamed through the deserted hotel corridors and lounges, watching the efforts of the men to fortify the
Brigade stronghold. He seemed to comrades in his old outfit
shaken and shocked. From the windows he looked out with
stricken eyes upon the familiar thoroughfare as traffic dwindled
and then ceased entirely. He took the revolver which was issued
to him as if, for the first time in his life, not knowing what to
do with one. "A gun to fire on my own countrymen," someone
heard him say.

"Aim high, Chief," a young recruit called out but the man
bridled, then sank back into zestlessness. More sought after as
negotiator than soldier, he was designated as the Republican
spokesman when the elderly Archbishop of Dublin entered the

Gresham to counsel surrender. The Archbishop, when face to face with de Valera, saw instead of the once imperturbable countenance a face flushed and eyes staring balefully. The man had not slept for several days or nights, and he agreed readily with the Archbishop that it was a terrible thing to see Irishmen fighting each other. De Valera, in consultation with Traynor, informed the intermediary that their O'Connell Street positions would be evacuated if two conditions were granted: first, Republicans must be allowed to keep their arms and ammunition; second, the Dail must meet at once as planned.

"Let them lay down their arms and then we'll talk to them," was the answer President Griffith and Collins sent to the Republican proposition. When the reply from the provisional government reached Brigade headquarters, Dev despaired of averting further warfare. Griffith held him responsible for "this, for all of it." Collins had the big guns moved from the Liffey quay where they were no longer needed and trained them on the Gresham Hotel. Only urchins dared to cross the enclave of O'Connell Street, a narrow no man's land of tram tracks, shattered glass and débris. Inside the beleaguered building, the men gouged openings in the interior walls of the adjacent Hamman and Granville Hotels and took them over as well, dragging mattresses, bedsteads and garden settees across the windows, hoping to hold on till Lynch might send a relief column from the south-west. It was the fratricidal strife of which the Chief had warned. The danger he had feared most, civil war, had come. On July 1, President Griffith ordered proroguement of the scheduled meeting of the Dail, terminating de Valera's persistent hope of the coalition and depriving him of his only constitutional channel for opposition.

After a week's siege in O'Connell Street the Republicans were driven to the back of the line of hotels, and on July 4 Commandant Traynor ordered gradual evacuation. As the fire from exploding shells spread through the battered buildings, de Valera, Stack, Brugha, Traynor and their followers waited at the rear of the wreckage for a lull in the shooting. De Valera was offered a white coat as a disguise by the Brigade's doctor but refused it, opened the door of the shed where they stood, and then, overwhelmed with the sense of the occasion and heedless of the risk attached to every moment, turned back to shake hands with each of those standing round. "Good-bye, lads, and good luck." He followed Stack in a dash across the alley. Brugha, spurning surrender, refused to go with them and when finally he emerged from the burning hotel it was not to escape, for his own gun was blazing. Ignoring the shouts of the provisional government soldiers fast surrounding him, he fell under their fire, to die within a few days from his wounds.

With Traynor, Dev succeeded in walking across one of the Liffey's bridges back to the south side of the city. As he escaped through the cordon thrown around Dublin, he left behind in the ruins for ever not only his frenzied follower, Brugha, but he left behind him also the Presidency, political methods, the hope of settling Ireland's future by peaceful means, and his reputation for invincibility. Somewhere in the fresh ruins lay the publisher's stock of Dwane's biography of him. British booksellers who had placed an order for a thousand copies had abruptly cancelled it. Now, when search-parties came upon a supply of the new volumes in the Dublin bookstores, each bearing a picture of him on its cover, they destroyed them on the spot.

His own home was the last place to which he could go. In the middle of the night, his wife and children were roused from their beds to find their house in its lonely country district surrounded. Armed men entered and searched every room, cupboard and drawer, smashing open a box when the key to it was not at hand. Mrs. de Valera declined to answer when asked where her husband was or to speak at all except in Irish, and this was the first of similar raids in the course of which her letters were scrutinized and the children questioned. All replied in Irish and this the raiders found unintelligible.

For days, Dev's family had no news of him. At Cathal Brugha's burial, there were furtive looks for him by the graveside. The de Valera children, except for the baby, were big enough to sense their mother's anxiety, and the dark-haired Vivion, aged twelve, entered into the situation with the intensity of boyish convictions. Finally, the bearded Father Dominic in the brown robes of his order, himself an ex-prisoner of the British and Terence MacSwiney's last comforter, came to Greystones through the military lines round Dublin in a car flying the Red Cross pennant. Trusted by the Republicans, Father Dominic had been inside the Four Courts and to the de Valera family he brought word of the father's safety.

Places of refuge Dev had used on the run before, being well known to Collins, were not now safe for him, and no disguise could conceal his height or distinctive features entirely. Dressed in the garb of a priest, he opened a garden gate one evening early in July in the suburb of Rathgar and went up to the door of a professor's house which he knew had been Stack's hideout for a year before the truce. When he was admitted, the young woman acting as his lookout left but returned shortly to say he had been recognized in the vicinity. As soon as it was dark, the professor escorted him to the house of a neighbour, a Protestant and non-Republican who was away on a vacation. There the Chief spent the night till next morning when he could continue on his way. There was only one place in the country not under the military control of the provisional government, the south-west, and that was the place for him to go. He left behind him along the coast the Dublin mountains like a tidal wave transfixed at its crest. A contingent of Lynch's men, hearing before the middle of July that the ex-President was in their vicinity, marched out to escort him into the Clonmel barracks where they had established Republican field headquarters.

"The Chief is at General Headquarters," Boland got word to friends in America, "hale and well, the same gentle, honest, straightforward, unpurchasable man that you knew in the States. . . ." He was assigned as adjutant to Commandant-General Sean Moylan, the director of operations, but it was his own plan to fight a propaganda war and he sent for those most able to help him along that line. Childers, Brennan and his secretary, Kathleen O'Connell, joined him, and Childers was soon getting out *Poblacht na hEireann* on a hand press. While Lynch studied his maps, Dev talked of negotiating. The intricacies of the proposals he expounded as he paced the floor were incomprehensible to the fighters coming and going at the field headquarters.

Militant action was easy compared to the road of politics. His knowledge of firearms stood him in good stead as he slung a rifle across his shoulders. He put on horn-rimmed glasses and grew a beard, wearing habitually a trench-coat and a cap pulled over his face. For a while he and his party quartered themselves in County Tipperary, choosing a large country house surrounded by its own grounds, Cahir Park. The owner, Colonel Charteris, an aristocrat belonging to the Anglo-Irish Ascendancy, was at Cowes for the regatta, and the Republican soldiers, stepping into another world in Cahir Park, lifted the lace-fringed blinds from the french windows to look at the sweep of greensward along the private reaches of the River Suir. From the housekeeper's suite on the ground level at the back which Dev used, there was a quick getaway over the Colonel's own footbridge crossing the river. In the hall, the men set up an indoor practice target, spraying the white panelling under the window with small bullet holes in the course of their stay. When Dev heard that the Colonel was on his way back to Ireland, he opened the guest book lying on the desk, and under the column headed Names he wrote with heavy strokes: "July 29. Eamon de Valera," and under the column for Addresses he put a thick, black question mark. Underlining his entry, he took his departure. For the moment, Lynch was in control of the city of Cork and Dev let his son, Vivion, come down to stay near him in the home of a friend. This was the time, Dev insisted, while they were in possession of the counties of Kerry, Cork, Waterford, parts of Tipperary and Limerick, the country south of a defence line running between the cities of Limerick and Waterford, to seek a truce, but he was not a member of the Army Executive. Lynch was not ready to ask for peace terms and as the Free State forces grew stronger, all the less would he do so. Commandant Aiken had come down to see Lynch, urging upon him as he did upon Mulcahy a truce, while trying to hold his own men back from action.

Collins as Commander-in-Chief of the regulars appointed Cosgrave as deputy chairman of the provisional government and set up a war council so that he could take to the field himself. In sympathy and encouragement Churchill wrote him, "I feel that this has been a terrible ordeal for you and your colleagues, having regard to all that has happened in the past." Then he added: "P.S. I hope you are taking good care of yourself and your colleagues. The times are very dangerous." In Dublin, Cosgrave had to act not only for Collins but for President Griffith as well when the latter entered a nursing home, exhausted. At the age of fifty, this man, from the start a believer in peace, had climaxed his career by the Treaty on the peaceful operation of which he had pinned all hope, but instead of peace he saw his provisional government engaged in a civil war. Collins was thinking primarily in military, not political, terms and by early August he succeeded in bringing his men down around the coast by sea to recapture Cork from the Republicans.

Lynch, retreating inland, was being driven out of the towns into the bogs and hills and thickets. The older Irish fighters had placed their reliance upon battalion strengths and chessboard campaigning, but in this summer of 1922 there was no massing at salient points for a decisive stand. A few in the ranks agreed with Dev that they should all come together instead of remaining in their own areas to be defeated piecemeal, but the retreating men did not coalesce. Lynch had walked out of Fermoy into the wilderness of guerrilla campaigning where he and Dev were separated from each other.

De Valera became just another Republican in hiding as summer wore on, moving about by night in the dark country-side, foraging for food and shelter, slaughtering cattle in the fields to eat when it became too dangerous to go near the towns. People in the south-west who spotted him as he drove rapidly here and there in cars that were commandeered thought him some gaunt ghost of his former self. When he heard that Harry Boland, trailed by provisional government soldiers to a hotel in Skerries, had been fatally wounded in a night-time raid, some of the last words this friend had spoken to him seemed more than ever true. "There is no glory," Boland had said, "in civil war." There never could be glory in it, Dev had acknowledged to him, no glory such as they had known in war against the outside enemy. The direst affliction for any human being, he realized afresh, was taking arms against brothers.

Bruree, his own home town where his uncle and cousins still were living, fell to Collins and Dev reached Mallow on the Blackwater twenty miles or more north of Cork. Those following him were in full retreat and at Childers' instigation they set to work to blow up the Ten Arch Bridge carrying the Dublin-Cork rail line over the river. They were trying to reach Kerry and this would halt their pursuers. The assistant county surveyor at whose home Dev quartered himself tried to get him to prevent such destruction but met only obduracy. "It will save thousands of lives," was the reply. He sent Brennan back to Dublin to carry on the propaganda war with Stack who had gone underground there, and the young Vivion travelled back with Brennan.

Before Dev himself left Mallow, his driver, a lad from a local Republican family, the Bolsters, showed him where old William O'Brien was living in retirement with his wife at their home called "Bellevue." Dev directed Bolster to turn in at the gate in the high wall, to continue past the little lodge and thick screen of foliage, and round the short drive up to the front of the yellow stucco house with its jutting entry. It faced up the river with gardens at the side stretching down toward the Blackwater. O'Brien's wife, opening the door, looked as if she recognized the caller but did not ask his name and hastily ushered him in, assuring him that her husband was at home.

When the two men were left alone in the drawing-room with its Victorian furniture and atmosphere of an earlier generation, the younger man candidly confessed to worries long pent-up. O'Brien seemed at once to understand when Dev, speaking of himself as having been a constitutionalist from beginning to end, said in perplexity that he did not know what step to take next. "In the London negotiations," he began, "I should have preferred to make our first stand upon the integrity of Ireland, and the inclusion of the six counties." Why, O'Brien wanted to know, had he not attended those negotiations?

As if a nerve had been touched, Dev said he had remained in Ireland as a reserve in case the English behaved badly. Had the envoys only held out for unity, "All the world," he insisted, "would have understood our stand against partition and would have been with us." Even the obdurate Ulsterman, Craig, he was convinced, could have been brought into a united Ireland if the envoys had not given in. But, the elder statesman remarked, things had not worked out that way. Dissension among colleagues was nothing new to de Valera or to O'Brien, who had lived through the Parnell period. For years, the visitor confessed, he had tried to keep the peace between Brugha and Griffith, between the councils of desperation and of moderation, as he referred to them. Nodding in the direction of the windows from which could plainly be seen the foundations of the breached bridge standing in the water amidst tumbled rocks, Dev volunteered that his was the most hated Party in Ireland but a Party that intended to go on fighting. Surrender, O'Brien suggested, would mean the return to civil opposition through the channel of the Dail; it would mean taking the oath to the King as set forth in the Treaty. But de Valera evinced his adamancy not only against the new pledge but explained that he had never approved the idea of any oath at all. Now that it was war, he was only a soldier again and the military men were in command. Two hours passed for Dev like minutes and then, refusing the offer of tea or anything at all to eat, he resumed his retreat.

As O'Brien and de Valera had sat talking in the quiet of "Bellevue" on August 12, 1922, the fate of their country was passing into other hands in Dublin. President Griffith, strained and nerve-worn but seemingly better for his rest, collapsed as he got up in the morning to leave the nursing home and return to his office. The doctor was summoned and then a priest, but he died before noon. By a *communiqué* the people were informed that Cosgrave would continue to act as head of the provisional government. The story was told that de Valera first learned of Griffith's death when he stopped and saw a newspaper. When the woman in the house where he was hiding brought him some food, she found him sobbing so that he could not eat, and he left without any good-bye to continue his unknown way. "For Griffith as for me," he was to own, "the securing of a united Ireland—a single state—was of first importance."

Collins, unlike de Valera, had at least the assuagement of paying final homage to the founder of Sinn Fein. The provisional government's Commander-in-Chief returned from the field for the funeral and, garbed in a new green uniform trimmed with gold, he walked with Mulcahy behind Griffith's coffin the long way to Glasnevin Cemetery. As to the choice of a successor, Collins said of himself: "I shall not retire from my military duties until the trouble is ended. Afterwards, who knows?" From the obsequies he drove back to County Cork to take up his military campaign. At the end of a day's inspection, as he detoured from Bandon over roads he knew inch by inch from his boyhood there, his motor-cars ran into an ambush. It was his driver's instinct to speed past but Collins ordered him to stop. Jumping out to do battle, Collins was shot in the head and died as he lay in the road. When de Valera heard, he grieved again as he had ten days before for Griffith. These were the men who had been his intimate associates, once his closest allies against a foreign foe which was, to him, the only real foe still.

After two months in the field Dev saw nothing but defeat in arms for the Republicans. The constitutional method, not bloodshed, was what he had originally urged as the means to freedom. He looked at the men retreating with him, their faces all features, hollowed and starkly delineated. The wind and rain, filled with the coming of colder weather, flapped their mufflers up around them. Some were mere boys who had joined his tatterdemalion train. On his own resolution he took a decision and urged all who wanted to go home to do so. By the continuation of armed warfare none would gain, all would lose, he saw, for the resources of manpower and equipment on both sides were being diverted from the national reconstruction. The objective of the Treaty signatories had been a united, peaceful Ireland and thereto both Irish and English had made dangerous concessions. Had this objective been achieved, he would have been proved wrong in his unrecanting opposition, but peace and unity had not been attained nor had his own hopes been realized. Griffith was dead. Collins was dead. Only Cosgrave of his original co-workers remained in command. He, de Valera, though on the run again, was left with his life at least, and something more in his undiminished sense of leadership.

CHAPTER XI

NO TIME FOR EPITAPHS (1922–1923)

SEPARATED as he was from the Republican Chief of Staff, Liam Lynch, there was little left for de Valera to do in the field. His advice on military tactics had not been adopted and his opinions on future strategy went unsolicited. He had time to ponder as he sat over the slow, acrid fires of smouldering turf and as he ate his stirabout or the potato cakes given him with his tea in the remote cottages where he took refuge at the end of the summer of 1922. A long letter reached him that had been smuggled out of Mountjoy Jail. It was from Liam Mellowes. "I am strongly of the opinion that the Republican political and military outlook be co-ordinated," de Valera read. "We have suffered badly because responsible officers, in their desire to act as soldiers, and because of an attitude towards politicians . . . could only judge of situation in terms of guns and men." This was corroboration of his own fears. By means of couriers, he was in touch with his wife and sent her a message to forward to Mellowes. The two men were in agreement that Republican policy should be re-formulated.

News from Dublin intensified de Valera's sense of responsibility for giving a new lead when the deputies elected the previous June were finally summoned by President Cosgrave after five proroguements to assemble on the date of September 9, 1922. Any resumption of political opposition looked futile without the fighters' endorsement, so de Valera wrote Lynch requesting the chance to talk with each member of the Army Executive individually, but the time came and went when the Executive was due to meet at the end of August. Members of the Republican Party, Cumann na Poblachta, in Dublin, showed impatience for some kind of action; Dev decided to wait no longer with all initiative on his part suspended, and he set out to return to the capital. Scouts arranged relays of transportation for him by motor-cars, horses, carts, and set a watch on the roads he would have to travel. Up through County Tipperary he threaded his way, garbed in trench-coat, visored cap and leggings, his pistol strapped in a holster to his leg. The fields were scarlet with poppies and yellow with autumn asters. As he rode through County Carlow in a pony cart, a lorry-load of regular troops bore down the road and, only a few yards from him, the driver turned off at a cross-road. Approaching Hacketstown in an automobile, he spied a detachment of government soldiers ahead, halted his driver, and slid out of the car into the ditch. The soldiers who interrogated his driver from the road did not suspect who lay at arm's reach.

Once the Chief reached Dublin, Republicans opened their doors to him though he dared not remain long under the roof of any one of them. To go home would have been to invite discovery. While newspapers reported that he was a prisoner, sick, deranged or dying, he gave evidence of his vigour and sanguinity in a secret interview with a correspondent from the *Manchester Evening News*: "I still maintain that the straight bold course is the best. . . ." Through notes and through a Party worker named Cathal O'Murchadha he re-established contact with his old office in Suffolk Street which had been kept open by Kathleen O'Connell. Some among the Republicans coming and going in Suffolk Street held that the provisional government had overturned the Republic and therefore had no power to convene the Dail and these, including O'Kelly, Madame Markievicz, Mrs. Pearse and Barton, wanted Dev to call a meeting of all those who had been deputies prior to the June election as the only true Dail. They received a message from the Chief advising them that the provisional government might be an illegal junta, but reminding them that they had attended the Dail summoned by the same Government the preceding spring and he declined to call a separate session for the Republican *teachtai*. A public statement from him might serve to clear up doubts as to where he and his supporters stood in relation to the imminent convening of the legislature, but he wanted to go slowly. "I do not know," he wrote in a note of instructions to O'Murchadha, "whether anything which may happen at tonight's interview will change my mind in the matter. . . . Will let you know early tomorrow."

Under escort of guards, Dev went after dark to an undisclosed rendezvous where the provisional government's Minister of Defence, Mulcahy, was waiting for him, looking tighter-lipped and straighter-faced than when they had last seen each other across the controversy-riddled Dail. Impelled by the memory of Collins' wish for peace but fearful of his own Cabinet colleagues' disapproval, Mulcahy had come on the guarantee of secrecy. No one was gaining by the war, Dev began; all were, in fact, losing and the Treaty as it stood would mean agitation in one form or another for years. His unaltered suggestion was to seek new terms from the British based on external association. Mulcahy interrupted to tell Dev that he must first compel the irregulars to lay down their arms. This, said the Republican leader, he could not do; he was only a humble soldier subordinate to the Republican Army leaders. Realizing that he was being held to account for the policy Lynch was pursuing, his face grew stiff with unspoken contention. Dick Mulcahy, he concluded, expected him to throw up the sponge.

Late as it was when he and his escorts reached his place of refuge for the night, he sat down at a typewriter to send O'Murchadha the promised word. The Republicans would be justified, he wrote, in refusing to attend the assembly of deputies next day because it would not be the real Dail, and because those who attended would be required eventually to give an oath to the King in fulfilment of the Treaty. He did not ignore the fact that resumption of political activity on his part might mean entering Dail Eireann eventually. "If we issue a statement it will tie our hands and if at a future time a course other than non-attendance should seem wise we might find ourselves precluded from taking it." Tired and hurried, he noticed that he had put the carbon paper in the machine the wrong way and added a postscript, "I cursed naturally." Then, punctilious about keeping a record of his recommendations yet careful not to tie himself up in knots by stating policies that might embarrass him later, he wrote, "Could you have a carbon made of this letter and send it to me. . . ."

The provisional government made no claim when the parliament convened that it was the Dail of the Republic, and declaration of a *de facto* Republican Government was proposed by the organization of Sinn Fein which remained in existence. The idea was taken up by Oscar Traynor of the Republican Army's Dublin Brigade, but de Valera did not know whether the Army as a whole would heed any such shadow regime. He doubted that Lynch had the power to defend any *de facto* administration even if he should want to do so, and there was still no way of knowing the attitude of the Republican forces in the field. He had received no answer from his letter to Lynch. "The present position is that we have all the public responsibility, and no voice and no authority," Dev at first replied to the suggestion of declaring a *de facto* government.

The middle of September, a brief letter signed by Liam Lynch, Chief of Staff, that had been delayed *en route*, arrived. The Army Executive had not met and was not likely to meet for some time, Lynch wrote, because of the risk for the officers in moving about the countryside. After noting that there was some improvement in the military prospects, Lynch concluded his note by saying, "I would, however, be only too pleased to have your views at any time on the general situation, and matters arising out of it, and they will receive my earnest consideration."

"This is too good a thing and won't do," Dev commented in exasperation to O'Murchadha. He was in a dilemma between the Army's autonomy and the Party's pressure upon him in Dublin. "If I do not get the position made quite clear," he wrote for the information of Suffolk Street, "I shall resign publicly." By resigning he would save himself and his family from hardship and physical danger of which they had already had their share. To be so near and yet so far from his own home was tantalizing. His wife had moved from Greystones after the raids during the summer to a rented house in a suburb closer to Dublin at 18 Claremont Road. Here, she was not far from Church Schools for the children and small shops—a cobbler, a newsagent and stationer's, a provisions store—facing on the small, unkept green of Sandymount and not far from the showgrounds of the Royal Dublin Society which lay along the main road to the city.

Dev asked O'Murchadha to see that his wife represented him at Glasnevin for the interment of one of Emmet's descendants, stipulating that she receive "timely notice". The memory of Robert Emmet he had always revered and he could repeat the words Emmet had uttered in the dock just before being hanged: "Let no man write my epitaph: for as no man who knows my motives dares now vindicate them, let not prejudice or ignorance asperse them. When my country takes her place among the nations of the earth, then, and not till then, let my epitaph be written." "When Emmet's epitaph can be written," Dev wrote in a letter from his place of enforced isolation, "coupled with his loved name will be the names of all who gave their lives . . . that Ireland may not be false to herself."

If the Republican movement was to survive, a controlling agency was becoming essential, as he told a few members of the Army Executive who came to see him in the autumn. "If it is the policy of the party to leave it all to the army, well, then, the obvious thing for members of the party to do is to resign their position as public representatives." Commandant O'Malley was keeping Lynch informed of developments. Dev directed O'Murchadha to ascertain how many of the members of Cumann na Poblachta were available for a meeting and though he knew it would not be safe for him to appear personally he set to work on an agenda. To each member of the Army Executive including Lynch and to each Party member he addressed a memorandum.

What he sent was a series of alternatives designed to put the situation to them as sharply as possible. First, the Party— Cumann na Poblachta—could take control. The fact that the Army had withdrawn its recognition of all political authority was the stumbling block here, he pointed out. As he said in his letter to Party headquarters, "Rory O'Connor's unfortunate repudiation of the Dail which I was so foolish as to defend even to a straining of my own view in order to avoid the appearance of a split, is now the greatest barrier that we have."

As a second alternative, the Army Executive could take control. This would have the advantage of dispelling the charge that he was inciting the Army, but it would mean that he and the other members of the Republican Party would have to give up political activity. They would have to resign. "This is the course I have long been tempted to take myself," he wrote frankly, "and were it not that my action might prejudice the cause of the Republic, I'd have taken it long since."

Thirdly, a joint committee of the Army and of the Party could take charge, though riding two horses—the Party and the Army—would, he thought, prove too much for anyone. Once the burden of decision had been transferred from his shoulders to the other Republicans in Dublin and in the field, he waited for matters to take their course.

The increasing curbs imposed by the Cosgrave administration on guerrilla action could not be ignored by Lynch any more than by de Valera. When Dev's memorandum setting forth the alternatives for future action reached Lynch in the middle of October, the latter summoned the members of the Army Executive to a house in Ballybacon near the Glen of Aherlow. The havoc wrought by the loss of manhood was, he admitted, sinking into his very bones. All present were convinced they could no longer carry entire responsibility for the Republic. Several hundred Republicans had been killed already in the fighting and several thousand captured. A Republican military dictatorship, Lynch read in what Dev had written, was open to a host of objections but alternatively any Government which Dev might proclaim would be a mockery if they—the military—did not give it their allegiance. The Chief was pleading with them for reunion of all Republicans on the ground that their ultimate objectives depended upon solidarity, "whilst divided we can scarcely make a success of any." Specifically, Dev's message proposed that the Army Executive call upon the Republican members of the Dail to set up a government. Lynch was finally persuaded by his comrades at Ballybacon to do this and the Army Executive, reserving to itself the right to make the final decision on any terms with the Free State, authorized de Valera to seek arrangements that would keep the country out of the British Empire. Lynch set out on foot for Dublin, taking with him word that the soldiers were prepared to recognize Eamon de Valera as "President of the Republic and Chief Executive of the State."

Before the end of October, the Republican deputies from the old Dail convened in Dublin in the semblance of a legislature and formally requested Dev to resume the Presidency, and the man who had not ever really wanted to give up the struggle in order to go back to teaching accepted the assignment without further hesitation. The first of his alternatives had, with modifications, been accepted and he took the steps to reassert his civil jurisdiction, declaring that a new Council of Deputies was in existence, the *Comhairle na deTeachtai*.

After re-declaring the Republic, de Valera as President undertook to sign jointly with Lynch decisions to be issued on defence matters. In strict concealment, Lynch set up new Army headquarters in a private home, Tower House, in Santry outside Dublin. The two men did not risk a personal meeting, but the President, backing by word as well as deed his Chief of Staff, accepted responsibility for pursuance of the military campaign against what he called the Draconian order of the Free Staters. He and Lynch, through couriers, continuously interchanged reports, orders and *communiqués*. "Since June," Dev announced, still in strict hiding himself, "the republican army, has been engaged in defending by arms the republican position against the unlawful exercise of force by the Free State Executive." Though he knew in his heart and said to some that the civil war was a forlorn hope, he became an avowed protector of the fighting units in return for their support. "The Government of which I am the head is temporary—an emergency Government," he explained through the Press.

To thrash out the new relations between the military and the political sides of the movement, Ernie O'Malley and other military men, heavily armed, succeeded in joining Dev at a house in Ailesbury Road, the home of the sister of The O'Rahilly, Mrs. Humphries. It was agreed that there should be an announcement denying the desire for peace negotiations. Late into the night they worked, till outside in the quiet, residential neighbourhood footfalls were heard.

In a matter of seconds, soldiers of the provisional government were forcing their way through Mrs. Humphries' door. Everyone at the meeting was a wanted man but the Chief, the others knew, was the most wanted of them all. He managed to reach a rear exit, while O'Malley in the hall drew the fire. Cornered, he shouted, "You'll get no surrender here," and returning shot for shot, fell with seven bullet wounds. When the raid was over the regulars thought him dead. A few days afterward, from an unknown spot, the newly acclaimed Republican President issued a statement of defiance to offset persistent rumours of peace: "Victory for the Republic or utter defeat are now the alternatives."

The organization of a Cabinet and a Council of State he soon completed from old associates, but included other Republicans who had made names for themselves in the civil war like Ruttledge who, being also on Lynch's staff at Tower House, provided a link between the military and civilian sides of the re-established Republic. The coffers in Suffolk Street were still solvent because McGarrity remained a loyal provider, but they would have to be replenished. The funds Dev had raised for the Republic in the United States had been frozen in American banks under an injunction sworn out by Collins shortly before his death on the claim that the money belonged to the government in office, and the provisional government was trying at the moment to name new trustees.

Dev was supporting the efforts of an American lawyer, John F. Finerty, to prevent anyone else from using the bonds. His followers were proud of the fact that he had not taken a penny since entering public life for what they called "outside work". They boasted that Dev had never owned a house or property except for the furniture in the home rented by his wife and children. The annual sum of £1,000 had been voted him the year before as head of the Republican Party, but of that amount his wife returned to Suffolk Street the last quarterly payment covering his new term of office as President, and his new Presidential salary was set at £500.

In need of an executive secretary for his newly formed Ministry, de Valera sent for Childers whose trained mind had provided him with rare partnership over the past months. Childers, on his way from the south-west, got as far as County Wicklow where, at the home of his cousin, Barton, regulars lying in wait arrested him. "If it is not the people's will," de Valera protested through the newspapers, after Childers' release on *habeas corpus* was denied, "that a faithful and loyal servant should be sacrificed to any of Churchill's hate, then within an hour you will rise up and fling from the positions they have usurped and dishonoured those who dare to blacken forever the fair name of this nation." As it grew light on the morning of November 24, 1922, Childers' slight figure limped toward a firing squad in the courtyard of Beggars Bush Barracks. He shook hands with each soldier in it, then walked back and faced his executioners. Chief of Staff Lynch served a warning through the Press on every deputy in the provisional government's parliament who had voted for the kind of military tribunal by which Childers was condemned—the murder bill, Lynch labelled it, and no contradiction of the warning was issued by the Republican President.

Under the low-hanging cloud of internal disorder, President Cosgrave formally proclaimed the Irish Free State—Saorstat Eireann—on December 6, 1922, a day selected as the first anniversary of the Treaty. Kevin O'Higgins as Minister of Home Affairs had secured adoption of the Free State Constitution. The British Parliament had passed the necessary enabling legislation preparing the way for the Saorstat to replace the provisional government, and as Ireland's first Governor-General the King designated the old nationalist, Timothy Healy. It mattered little as far as Ireland was concerned that Lloyd George had, that autumn, been succeeded as Prime Minister by the Conservative, Bonar Law. Cosgrave and his Ministers had secured from the Royal Dublin Society permanent quarters for the Free State at Leinster House, once the seat of the Duke of Leinster. This eighteenth-century ducal mansion with its sooted, grey-black façade was approached from Kildare Street by a circular drive around a large, seated statue of the stern-visaged Queen Victoria, so unwinning of mien that it was known as "Ireland's Revenge." In the sky-lighted chamber of Leinster House the deputies stepped up to swear "true faith and allegiance to the Constitution of the Irish Free State" and to be "faithful to his Majesty, King George V, his heirs and successors by law. . . ." Labour Party members said that they took the oath under protest as the formality which was a condition of membership in the legislature and nothing more. Organization of an upper chamber, the senate or *Seanad*, was completed and the two houses together were named the *Oireachtas* or bicameral parliament. The *Oireachtas* contained no representatives from constituencies in the North as had the original Dail. Missing from the solemn function were the men best known in the movement. Of the five Treaty signers, only Duggan was at Cosgrave's side. One, Gavan Duffy, had left the Treaty Cabinet in protest over its abolition of the court system set up by Sinn Fein before the split. Another, Robert Barton, had rejoined the Republicans. The two who had been foremost in the negotiations lay in Glasnevin.

Though December 6, 1922, was a silent day, overcast and gloomy, December 7 was a day reddened and reverberating with blood and gunfire. On a Dublin street corner, assailants presumed to be Republicans shot down two newly sworn deputies, wounding one fatally, the other seriously. From his hiding-place, de Valera nursed his own sorrow. Within a matter of hours, reprisal was taken by the Free State Cabinet and the Free State Army Council. From Mountjoy Jail, Rory O'Connor, Liam Mellowes and two other Republican prisoners were taken before an Irish firing-squad and shot. When, in shocked surprise, the deputies learned from the evening papers of the summary executions, they demanded an explanation. President Cosgrave at first refused to discuss the situation. The Labour leader, Thomas Johnson, protested that the Government had killed the new state at its birth. O'Higgins, taking responsibility for the decision as the Minister of Home Affairs, told his fellow deputies heartbrokenly that the executions had been ordered as deterrents. But all the might of all the empires on earth, de Valera asserted, could not have made him kill fellow Irishmen like Brugha, Boland, Childers and now Liam Mellowes, Rory O'Connor and the others, men in each of whose little finger there was more love for the Irish people, he said, than in all their executioners.

No sooner was the Irish Free State inaugurated under these omens of violence than the North exercised the option accorded in the Treaty of remaining apart from the South. In the ensuing elections announced by Craig, Northern nationalists were instructed by de Valera to take no part on the grounds they were called by virtue of English authority. "Ask not the permission of the foreigner," he advised, "to do that which we have a right to do and which we can do ourselves." After the vote in the North had affixed the Craig Government in power, the only hope held out by the Free Staters in the South was for getting the border redrawn to take the Northern nationalists out from under his control.

De Valera had no such hope. The English politicians seemed to be running away from their pledges about revision of the border, betraying the Irish envoys who had trusted them. "Mr. Griffith was," as he said later, "led away by the chimera of the Boundary Commission, which he had hoped would take Fermanagh, Tyrone, and other areas from the Northern territory, and so bring partition to an end later automatically." The reason why Griffith and Collins had not protested, he concluded, was because they had become too deeply committed to the British and could not make effective resistance to what was perpetrated upon them. He was seeing the bitter reality that Griffith had not lived to see. That dogged little founder of Sinn Fein had wanted above all peace, a wish he had had to forfeit before his death. Companion to his wish for peace had been his wish for the historic unity of his country; and that too was now lost. Griffith's survivor, de Valera, though again possessed of the title of President of the Republic, took scant comfort in having foreseen all that was coming to pass.

As Christmas time returned in 1922, he found himself near old haunts in St. Stephen's Green where he was drawn irresistibly toward two low pillars arching the entrance to University Chapel. Increasingly he depended on the Church and on the Bible, being cut off from friends and from his family at Sandymount. His children would have their share of holiday celebration. His wife, he knew, would see to that. Her life was devoted the more exclusively to them because he, though not far away, could not come home. "Christmas is their time," she was to write. "The love of the Christ-child encircles and surrounds them and . . . they can enter into the festive spirit with a zest and enjoyment that cannot be experienced in later years." Like a ghost in disguise, de Valera stepped quickly through the Chapel entrance-way, then down into the thick shadows cast by the columns that supported the low ceiling of the crypt itself. Mass was being said and the soft intonation of the ritual seemed to muffle the forces of destruction at work outside. As the service ended, he saw that he had attracted suspicion and, losing himself in the throng of dispersing communicants, he got into the street and away as the authorities were summoned.

"As we consecrate ourselves anew to the achievement of the independence of our country," he wrote over the holidays to the Republican fighters still at the way stations and cross-roads far from Dublin, "let us humbly beg God so to direct us that we shall obtain His Blessing." In the fastnesses of the south-west the men lacked food and weapons. The weather had worsened as the days shortened, with darkness setting in at mid-afternoon. Dev could count, within the three months past, fifty-five "drum-head court-martial murders" and, exercising the prerogative of the Presidency he had assumed, he decreed an interval of national mourning. The harsher the measures adopted by the Free Staters the more every rebel would, he warned, tighten his Parabellum in his pocket. It was now brother against brother and best friends became bitterest foes. Dev felt as if he were separated by a glass wall, he wrote one woman sympathizer in England, from all that was transpiring around him, being powerless to stop it. That defeat impended he was sure, for the people as a whole were losing heart and the desire for peace was overwhelming, but he could not turn his back on Lynch.

His Chief of Staff, importuned by the officers in the field to call the Army Executive into consultation, left Tower House in Dublin early in the new year of 1923 to return to the south-west. Lynch's deputy Chief of Staff, Liam Deasy, was taken prisoner and sentenced to death. For the fact that thousands were still up in arms, the Free State's Defence Minister Mulcahy held de Valera personally responsible; de Valera who, the deputies were told in Leinster House, was being goaded on by hysterical women; who had, it was said, actually forsworn the Republic in conversation with Griffith and Collins before those two ever went to London; for whom the only question had been the price at which to sell the cow.

President Cosgrave and his Ministers, trying not only to stamp out an insurrection but to convert a provisional government into the fabric of separate statehood, felt, they said, as if they were working with wild men screaming through their keyholes. Somehow they had at the same time to retain British support. The way had been left open in the Treaty for financial settlement and President Cosgrave undertook in a secret, handwritten agreement to turn over to the British Government the payments he collected from the Irish farmers to redeem their lands from British control. This document Cosgrave did not submit to the Dail for ratification but kept it to himself and a few of his Ministers. Few learned what was taking place between London and Dublin. The Free Staters were at the same time bringing overt pressure to bear in their individual approaches to the Republicans.

By special messenger, Dev received early in February 1923 a note from the Free State's key prisoner, Liam Deasy, recommending that the Republicans surrender unconditionally. Lynch, when informed, termed his deputy's action a blow to the heart, and Mary MacSwiney castigated it as abject. De Valera himself called it "the biggest blow since we started", but did not give compliance a second's consideration. "It must be death or glory now." The Government, pressing its advantage, gave Deasy a stay of execution and made his letter public with an offer of amnesty to all who would surrender. Some of the men in the field at that gave themselves up but Dev, writing to McGarrity in an appeal for more resources, maintained that there could be no turning back. "One big effort from our friends everywhere and I think we would finally smash the Free State." Lynch, he knew, was hoping to direct a new offensive against England. "Our people have a hard time and suffering before them . . . but God is good."

From the south-west came unmistakable indication that the Republican Army was disintegrating, possibly cracking up, Dev bluntly put it. Reports of the officers from Cork and Kerry sounded desperate: "We are fought to a standstill." "If we cannot carry on successfully, we should not waste lives." "We are flattened out." Looking for political instead of military solution, the President tentatively advanced an idea for putting the choice between Free State and Republic up to the people. A "Court of the People," was the way he described his plan to the Council of State he had formed. He had always had faith in plebiscites provided they were fairly conducted. Mary Mac-Swiney, known among Republicans as the sea-green incorruptible, argued that a plebiscite would be ruinous. "Forgive me," she added to the Chief, "if I have hurt you but Ireland comes first."

When the reaction of others proved scarcely more favourable, he did not pursue this idea but did not drop his conviction that something had to be done, a settlement of some kind secured. To a correspondent who was brought in a closed car to see him at a private home, he stressed that the terms of the peace he would seek were not unconditional. His own conditions would not, he insisted, make Ireland an Esau among nations; external association would not mean selling the national birthright. Though aware that some of his associates might not be satisfied with the proposals for external association, he was willing at any time, personally, he informed the newsman, to sponsor these proposals as the basis of an honourable peace. When the Republican Adjutant-General, Derrig, asked Dev what his minimum terms from the Free State would be, he got a reply in writing. "The obvious answer," Dev wrote, "is our minimum will be the maximum that the conditions of the moment enable us to obtain." He spared no illusions. "Under conditions which it is possible to conceive, this maximum might be as low as zero."

Lynch, unable to postpone a meeting of the Army Executive any longer, agreed by early spring with his discouraged officers that the Republican President should, for the first time, be invited to attend. To make the trip back to the combat area, Dev grew a beard, removed his glasses, and put on the clothes of an

American tourist. Aiken and Stack, also dressed as Americans, accompanied him and at his instructions all travelled unarmed. Weapons would, if they were caught, bring sure indictment and death. The party left the city in a big automobile. Signs of returning life were visible upon the countryside, the cowslips showing yellow in the marshes near the sea and green tingeing the fields which were still crisped with frost. Streams rushed with freshet noise down the Wexford hills as, between showers, the clouds' shadows raced from slope to slope. When the car brushed the thickets along the back roads, blackbirds winged upwards. "Peter," as the Chief was called, and his party spent the first night in the cottage of an old couple near Kilkenny where they slept in chairs by the fire ready to be on the move. They continued their journey southwards across County Waterford's turf bogs beyond Clonmel till they turned into the Monavullagh foothills to follow the valley of the Nier River. Past the village of Ballymacabry at a remote farmhouse, Dev found awaiting him on March 23, 1923, his Chief of Staff, Liam Lynch, Adjutant-General Derrig, and other senior officers, making a group of a dozen altogether. Some of them he had not seen for weeks. Their faces were raw from the cold and wet. Their physiques were weary, their expressions harried. Others whom he looked for were not there, being either under arrest or unable to reach the destination because of regular troops in their divisional areas.

Lynch, dressed in nondescript tweed breeches with puttees and a worsted jacket, much thinner since he had left Dublin, was ready to face facts but not to accept defeat. The tenacious belief he voiced in the fight he was waging struck de Valera as evidence of his lion-heartedness. But coming to terms was inevitable, the Republican President tried to make clear to him; it could only be a matter of time, and the best thing they could do was to bargain for terms. On the second day of their meeting, Free Staters were reported approaching and the conferees moved farther up the Nier valley. There in another Republican household the discussions recommenced, Lynch arguing for continued resistance. A few expressed readiness to give up. Some, including Stack and Aiken, were willing that de Valera should negotiate with the Free State, but on the explicit condition that the Republicans be allowed to participate in politics without taking any oath. Peace terms would, de Valera affirmed, have to be contingent upon recognition of sovereignty and abolition of the oath, but he saw in the course of several more days' talk that his Chief of Staff needed time to consider. No agreement was immediately forthcoming, so plans were made for another meeting in a fortnight's time. The whole Executive was to try to assemble then at Araglin farther to the west where they had, as Dev remembered, not far from there a blind hide-out built into the rear of a farmer's cowshed. This was called "Katmandu" and it had bunks enough to sleep them all. He would go back to Dublin to work on specific peace proposals for the Executive's consideration. The morning that he and Aiken started their journey out on foot, rain lashed the untracked reaches of the countryside, and the March wind beat so fiercely upon them that they had to get down on their hands and knees to cross the open rises of the mountains.

On the day set for the re-convening of the Army Executive, April 10, 1923, the Chief waited in Dublin for a decision from his Chief of Staff. The latter, heading for the second meeting, had set out from the South with Aiken and a small party carrying the proposals drafted for surrender, and they got as far as the Knockmealdown Mountains which they had to walk across before reaching the Galtees. In the vicinity, the Free Staters were starting a round-up. As Lynch with his companions headed into the hills, the mists of daybreak lifted and there was little cover from the gunfire they heard around them. The Chief of Staff was shot down by a single bullet. He thought of the documents they had with them, and made Aiken and the others, who were half-carrying, half-dragging him along, leave him to keep ahead of the oncoming regulars. When de Valera learned of Lynch's death by nightfall of the same day in a hospital at Clonmel, he tried to comfort the surviving soldiers in a eulogy of the man they had lost. "You have to fling yourselves across the path of the stampede of a nation."

Plans for the second rendezvous were suspended. Like the men in the field, the Chief in the city found himself in daily, hourly jeopardy. O'Higgins informed the Dail that a man with a brown beard had been seen entering Gavan Duffy's house, that a wanted man was believed to be in hiding there, though he had not so far been caught. Before the middle of April, a whole group of Republican Army men was seized in the Glen of Aherlow. Derrig, trying to escape from a moving lorry, was wounded in the head and captured. Stack was apprehended alone and unarmed in a field not far from Clonmel, and from his person Free State troops took the document prepared for the meeting. It authorized the President of the Republic to order an immediate cessation of hostilities. When a few members of the Army Executive managed to come together on April 20 at Poulacappal, they first chose Frank Aiken as successor to Liam Lynch, and on the night of April 26 in Dublin he—Aiken—presented to the Republican President and Cabinet the Army's unanimous decision to cease resistance.

"The Government of the Republic . . . proclaims its readiness to negotiate an immediate cessation of hostilities," announced de Valera for the Press next day. "The war so far as we are concerned is finished." He ordered all commands to suspend aggressive action as of noon, April 30, 1923. He was not submitting unconditionally, for he had undertaken to get whatever terms he could from the Free State. When President Cosgrave declined to meet him or any of his "collaborators in destruction, male or female," de Valera outlined his terms to two Free State senators who were designated: Andrew Jameson, the former unionist with whom he had worked already, and James Douglas, one of the drafters of the Free State Constitution, known for his belief in terminating the civil strife. If the oath could be abolished and Republican funds unfrozen the Republicans would, Dev offered, store their arms in sealed barracks. But Cosgrave sent back the ultimatum, "No truck, no negotations unless there is a surrender of arms." If de Valera's party complied, they would be given every opportunity, Cosgrave added, to take part in an election. The Republicans consequently went one step farther in the process of submission, and Chief of Staff Aiken issued an order directing them to "dump arms". This was different from surrendering them. "You will arrange accordingly that all arms and munitions be checked and carefully dumped under the supervision of an officer." To this blunt military directive, the Republican President attached a compassionate farewell addressed to all ranks in the "Legion of the Rearguard," in which he entreated them to bear the suffering and the indignities that would lie ahead in a manner worthy of them. They would be cut off without any source of income, unable to get jobs. "If they [the people] have turned away and have not given you the active support which alone could bring you victory this last year it is because they are weary and need a rest."

By his enemies, de Valera was discounted and reviled as a mountebank and megalomanic. The Government secured the passage of another safety bill like the one authorizing military tribunals which would, its opponents said, not only out-Herod Herod but out-Higgins O'Higgins. The former Chief awaited opportunity for renewed action on his part, and when it came it lay, as he hoped it would, in the political sphere. "There will be an election this year," announced O'Higgins in the Dail, and a date in late summer was named. "Mr. de Valera's people may, if they choose . . . return de Valera's party with an effective majority." There was a note of cynical challenge to a discredited minority. Mulcahy dared de Valera to go back to Clare and see what the people would say to him this time.

Without emerging from concealment, Dev called a score of Republican Army leaders together in a well-guarded house on Adelaide Road to decide what to do. Contesting the election would mean using the machinery set up by a Government they did not recognize, and some present feared it would imply the validity of the Treaty. His own approach was the pragmatic one. Not by any enthusiasm for the prospects but by insistence upon his concept of duty did he influence his colleagues, and in the early morning hours they agreed to participation.

"We are ready," the Republican leader answered the challenge, "to accept a free decision of the people at any time." To finance the campaign, he put in a request to the American Association for Recognition of the Irish Republic, mustering all the hopefulness he could and requesting a hundred thousand dollars. He turned also to Sinn Fein which, through his efforts and Stack's, had been reconstituted and the old offices in Harcourt Street re-opened. Sinn Fein nominated eighty-seven candidates including Aiken, Mary MacSwiney, Cathal Brugha's widow, Stack, Ruttledge and Madame Markievicz. The Chief, standing for his original constituency in Clare as well as for his other constituencies, issued word that whatever the outcome might be, hostilities would not be renewed; that neither the Republican Government nor the Army Executive intended to re-open the war, but: "We will never swear an oath of allegiance to a foreign king, whether he be a symbol or a reality."

"Clare has ever been true to Ireland," his constituents notified him, "and because you have been true to Ireland, Clare will be true to you." His opponent in the electoral contest was the man who had once campaigned by his side, Eoin MacNeill, now Minister of Education for the Free State and member of the Boundary Commission that had been set up in pursuance of the Treaty. The forces turned against Dev were powerful and Cohalan, propelled by old grievances, arrived from America to join Cosgrave's campaign team. In not being free to speak or attend rallies, Dev was at a serious disadvantage. Word reached him through informants that he would be shot at sight and he was compelled to cancel attempts to see the American lawyer, Finerty, who had come to Ireland in connection with the continuing litigation over the Republican bonds. Though he was campaigning not through a glass wall but through a barrier that rendered him invisible, Kathleen O'Connell in an open letter to the Press denied Free State allegations that he was out of touch with affairs, insisting her Chief was in contact with advisers, correspondents and outside observers.

One midnight, on the third floor of a Dublin residence, he received an American clergyman who wanted to carry back some word of the Republican cause, the Reverend Edgar DeWitt Jones. This visitor, who had been picked up in Dun Laoghaire, as Kingstown had been renamed, and driven over a roundabout route, found the Republican leader hard at work at a desk, the curtains drawn behind him. He looked more like some distinguished European than a rebel, in a well-tailored brown suit, matching silk tie and white shirt. "I wasn't expecting to find you wearing a beard, Mr. de Valera," the caller began. "Your American friends would scarcely recognize you."

Dev brushed aside the personal reference, uninterested in the trappings of mystery. "It is a mere incident, and not important." He was readier to talk about what he called the currents of history.

"You are interested . . . , Mr. de Valera, in Ireland's unity?"

"I am more interested in seeing a united Ireland than I am in complete severance from England." Weariness dropped away from his manner. When a maid entered with glasses of milk and a plate of cakes he did not stop for it. "To divide a country so small as ours into two nations is a calamity and ridiculous besides.

When Ireland is united and free, she will become the Switzerland of the Sea." His eyes flashed as if he were making a speech; he clasped and unclasped his white hands. "I am for peace and have never willingly advocated anything else."

His Clare backers were both thrilled and alarmed when they heard that he intended to make his appearance there before the election on Lady Day in August. More than a year had passed since he had dared to come out in public. Direct word came from the Chief that "nothing but a bullet will stop me" and that it mattered little whether he got a bullet or a jail term. "In either or any event, I shall be at Ennis." Having made this decision, he announced that he would also make a public appearance in Dublin on the Sunday before election day.

"You see by the posters that Mr. de Valera is announced as speaking in Dublin on Sunday and in Ennis today," said a pro-Treaty campaigner. "He may speak in Ennis but he won't speak in Dublin . . . it is our duty to arrest him." The Ministers of the Free State, still nursing the infancy of their regime, foresaw in the prospect of open political opposition new complications. They were beginning to anticipate that Republicanism might gain a foothold as the legitimate opposition with a free voice and open facilities for congregating. Armed sorties they had countered; flying columns of gunmen; bicycle brigades wheeling over dark hills and dales; bands descending from cave hide-outs upon the villages; all these had been successfully put down by the regular Army. A shadow-box Republic could be ignored, but could the Free Staters tolerate political rivalry?

On Lady Day, Irishmen set out from all over the counties of Limerick and Clare for Ennis. Those trudging along the stone-pocked roads, up hill and down, were overtaken by motors, side-cars, carts, horses and bicycles. Donkeys laden with wicker baskets of turf waited in the brown bogs while the girls of the Gaeltacht with their strong, bare feet and straight, black hair stopped to watch and gossip about the event to which everyone was heading. The air was warm with August sunshine and sweet with cut clover. In the fields the unharvested rye looked golden under a silvered sky.

" 'Tis for Clare, ye are?" said those who were walking to those who offered rides.

"It is, please God," the drivers replied.

"Then Up de Valera—Up the Republic!" all sang out as they resumed their journey together. The donkeys jog-trotted gaily on their trip to town and addled flocks of geese made for their mud ponds to be safe from the traffic. Farmers left their potatoes. Fishermen along the Connemara coast beached their curraghs. On the outskirts of Ennis, electioneering posters and slogans plastered the fences and the hoardings. "Who looted your shops, robbed your banks, destroyed your bridges, murdered your sons?" screamed one. On the other side of the street appeared the placard: "Damn your concessions, England. We want our country. Up de Valera." Together with the Free State flags there floated out banners bearing the initials of the Irish Republic in black.

At the high point of the town where the narrow streets intersected before angling down to the centre, the speaker's stand was ready. The Crusheen Pipers, at the announced hour of two o'clock, struck up *The Soldier's Song*. Those in the waiting throng whose fingers had been passing the Rosary back and forth clutched their beads now. De Valera, clean-shaven, wearing no disguise, was driven slowly through the crowd in an open car. His overcoat, his suit, his tie, his hat, were black. The loose-fitting collar of his white shirt emphasized the thinness of his long neck and his mouth was margined with lines.

"There he is!" the shout went up.

"My God! 'Tis himself——" The air became a cyclone of waving caps and sticks. His oldest son, Vivion, now thirteen and intensely alive to his father's sense of mission, had ridden with him to Clare as the year before he had gone to Cork. Cheers followed Dev up the steps of the platform, and a Christian Brother stayed at his side. The Chief stood up tall and stark against the background of uneven roof-tops and rough stone walls of Ennis.

"Shake hands, my darling, that I suffered so much for," cried an old woman in the front, and grasping the rough railing he leaned over to do so. His gaze seemed troubled behind the eye-glasses he was wearing, but in a moment he straightened up to acknowledge his welcome in words of Irish.

"Clare says that never," interrupted a high, singing voice from the crowd, "will our enemies hound to the death another Irish patriot." Then the President of their Republic, taking off

his top-coat in the oppressive August afternoon, commenced to
speak in English.

"I have come to tell you that . . . I have never stood for
brother's hand being raised against brother. . . ."

A whisper stirred below him, and the whisper turned to a cry
of warning. "The soldiers are coming." Dev looked over their
heads and saw moving in from the outskirts an armoured car
mounted with a Lewis gun.

"They are coming for me," he told his audience, unperturbed.
"I am glad it was in Clare I was taken." It was not a bullet which
was going to be used to stop him, he saw, but the shackle again.
Two columns of Free State soldiers marched into the throng,
firing their rifles into the air as the people threw themselves to
the ground. As friends tried to encircle him, Dev freed himself
and stepped down, hatless and coatless, to the soldiers waiting
for him with fixed bayonets.

"Good-bye now, boys," he turned to say. "Whatever about
me, maintain the Republic." He was gone. The afternoon's
enthusiasm and excitement vanished and with it the terrified
spectators. Throughout the rest of the day the local hospital was
taxed to treat all those injured in the *mêlée*.

" 'Tis cruel, clever, strong men they are, President Cosgrave
and O'Higgins," muttered one old Republican. With his arrest,
de Valera's campaign rested. In Dublin, his election headquarters
were entered by the police, his workers searched, and his election
director taken away. The Sunday before polling day, spectators
gathered on the pavements and streets in College Green for the
mass meeting the candidate had scheduled before his arrest. At
the centre of things were two boys. One, seventeen years old, was
the son of the late Erskine Childers, and the younger was Vivion
de Valera, dressed in a rough, woollen jacket, his eyes alert behind
round, rimmed glasses, his dark hair combed straight across the
top of his wide forehead. He began to speak from the platform in
staccato Gaelic. Then, so that everyone might understand, he
repeated in English, "My father promised that he would speak to
you here today," the high, boyish voice reached out to the still
crowd, "and he is a man who would keep his word if he could."
That knowledge the family and the nation shared in common.
He was a man of his word surely. "But he cannot speak to you
today, for *giollai nan Gall* (the foreigners, the boy said) seized him

in County Clare the other day. . . ." Vivion clutched his paper in front of him, got his breath, and went on at a tense pitch, "I know not what they will do with him . . . but they cannot kill the spirit of freedom in Ireland."

From Sandymount, Vivion's mother tried by telephone and telegraph to get information from the Government as to the whereabouts of her husband. "It is not the practice," Mulcahy had explained when others had been summarily seized, "nor is it the intention to address communications to the relatives of men who are arrested, with the exception that, in the cases of men executed, formal notification is after execution at once sent to the next-of-kin. . . ." The only statement issued by the Government was to the effect that de Valera was responsible for the civil war. ". . . he must take his place with his associates and other dupes until such time as he and others can be released without injury to the public safety." This was all; there was no warrant; there were no specific charges; there was no trial.

In desperation de Valera's wife wrote to the Free State's Adjutant-General: "Sir,—I demand from you information as to the place of detention of my husband. I have already on Tuesday, 21st inst., and again on Wednesday, 22nd inst., sent you a wire demanding the information, and have received no reply. I have also on one occasion on yesterday, and on three occasions today, by appointment, got in touch by telephone with your office at Parkgate Street and have failed to obtain the information. Sinead de Valera." All she had received was a brief note her husband had been permitted to send her from the Limerick jail where he had been taken the night of his arrest. With public concern and indignation mounting, and with the election only a few days away, the Free State authorities then wired Mrs. de Valera: "Eamonn de Valera detained Arbour Hill Barracks. Adjt.-General."

The effect of the Free State's action upon the election was not what Cosgrave and his advisers calculated. The prisoner in Arbour Hill received from his old constituency in County Clare more than twice as many votes as his rival, Minister MacNeill. Though the Free State Government secured 63 of the new total of 153 seats in the Dail, the Republicans won 44 of them, thus retaining 28 per cent of the seats, the same proportion they had held since the pre-civil war election. The Treaty forces declined from 45 per cent to 40 per cent, with the Farmers and Labour representatives and the Independents gaining the difference. Of the Republican candidates, Mary MacSwiney and Madame Markievicz were returned and the widow of Cathal Brugha who had been personally commended to the voters by the Chief as Cathal's faithful companion and confidante. Stack won his seat from County Kerry, Aiken from County Louth, Ruttledge from County Mayo, and Ruttledge was designated to act for the *de facto* Republican Government because of the Chief's removal from the scene of action. In Arbour Hill, the prisoner took note of the results of the balloting. "Those who talk about democracy cannot say, I think, that democracy in the 1923 election got very much of a chance."

CHAPTER XII

THE GREY WISDOM OF THE WORLD
(1923–1927)

THE slow, suspenseless rhythm of prison life settled back upon de Valera, with the difference this time it was not the English but those he considered their agents, the Ministers of the Free State, who held him in solitary confinement. During exercise periods in the cindered yard the guards would play handball with him, and except for them he felt like the lone inhabitant of an unpeopled universe of blank walls and unsunned air. The one window in his cell was high and small and the artificial light served only to cast shadows across the pages he tried to read. Newspapers were forbidden and he asked for books by Einstein. "I don't object to solitude," was his comment in speaking later of this time, and he went so far as to say that he had never spent a happier time in his life, being convinced that he and all the Republicans had done right.

He had permission to write word home once a week, but when it was delayed by the censoring authorities, fear for his safety and for his life beset his wife, fear which the officials did little to assuage. To the messages of friends she replied with the same serenity she had expressed to her husband's election manager in Ennis, "We must now spread the doctrine of quiet, determined, individual effort." This was what she was trying to do single-handed at home. "No one need be a slave in heart, no matter what forces are arrayed against him." Her signature was in Gaelic: "*Le meas mor. Sinead Bean de Valera.*"

Public opinion rallied not only about her husband after he was imprisoned, but about the hundreds of other Republicans who were rounded up by Free State troops in that autumn of 1923. Thomas Derrig in Mountjoy Jail and others in Kilmainham, Hare Park, Tintown and Newbridge started a hunger strike, vowing they would fast till they got their freedom or the grave, and Austin Stack, after forty days without food, weakened dangerously. Ernie O'Malley, scarcely recovered from the wounds received in Ailesbury Road, a scar branching from the centre of his upper lip across his cheek to his eye, soon could not rise from his mattress on the prison floor. By early November 1923, several died of starvation. The hunger strikers, as their suffering increased, wondered if their Chief was sharing their ordeal, some remembering that in the past he had frowned on hunger strikes. For de Valera, the dim passageways of Arbour Hill were frequented by the kindred spirits of those who had begun in the hope of freedom and who had got, instead, the grave. Ruttledge as Acting President of the Republic issued a message stating that the Chief, on strict orders of the Republican Cabinet and in the best interests of the cause, was not on hunger strike, and before the end of November the other prisoners lost heart in their campaign and Derrig called it off.

The Arbour Hill solitude was broken for the first time in the middle of the winter when de Valera was led from his cell into a small, unfurnished ante-room at the Barracks. He found awaiting him the American lawyer, Finerty, who had with difficulty secured permission to take his deposition regarding the Republican bonds. In the unsteady murk of the gaslit gloom Dev turned his head, straining to catch every word and every glance as the lawyer reviewed President Cosgrave's claims to the money banked in America. His face took on colour and his toneless voice kindled as he recounted his own part in floating these bonds, and when the time allotted them had expired, he bade farewell to Finerty with all the aplomb he had once evinced in America.

It was June before Mrs. de Valera and the children were allowed to visit the prisoner, and the following month without prior announcement he and most of the Republicans were released. Public opinion in Ireland, in America and even in England had convinced Cosgrave that de Valera in jail was a greater threat than he would be at large. The Chief, emerging from the dark portals of Arbour Hill after eleven months, was surrounded by an exuberant crowd but he stood sober-faced, his hair rumpled, dazzled like a man coming into strong sunshine, while hands reached out to stroke his coat, just to touch him. In Sandymount, his children were eager to tell him about all they had done while he was away. He could see that Vivion was developing a serious turn of mind. The boy owned that he hated Euclid like poison but was dutiful, nevertheless, in studying him. At thirteen, Mairin seemed to have inherited a scientific aptitude from her father but she looked like her mother with a round face, down-tilted glance, and quick smile.

So far as the schools were concerned, the father suspected a tendency toward indiscipline and laxness. In English, for instance, grammar and spelling were being, he thought, slighted. In arithmetic, the children were being given a nodding acquaintance with the whole field of mathematics, whereas in the old days such essentials as the multiplication tables had been prescribed out of a textbook. It was due to his wife's efforts that Irish was being spoken at home, and his second son, Eamon Junior, ten years old, displayed with pride his vocabulary. Brian, at eight, and the three smallest children—Ruairi, Emer and Terry —were beginning to talk it. Dev went with his wife just as they had done in the first years of their life together to the annual meeting of the Gaelic League's branch, *Ard Croabh*, of which he had been head for a decade. It was the first time in two years that he had been free to return home to his family or to engage publicly in national activities.

Because of the general amnesty, the spirits of Republicans soared throughout the country and a gala reception was held for the released men. The Republican President, sitting on the stage of the Round Room in the Mansion House, smiling and content, watched the audience pouring in and listened to a new song, more martial-sounding and less plaintive than the old ones like *Wrap a Green Flag Round Me*. When he caught the words, he recognized them as those he himself had written in farewell at the end of the civil war to "the Legion of the Rearguard." No longer, he turned to say to those close by, were Republicans in the rearguard. "If you ask me where we are to begin," he said when he rose to speak, "I will say to you we will have to begin with the moral stiffening that we had when we began in 1917. . . ." The civil war he spoke of with regret as he said must all, moderates and extremists alike. He prided himself on being a genuine moderate but declared that the Republican flag was still at the masthead where he had nailed it. "I did not intend really to say so much but when one is silent for a long time I suppose one lets go." The night's celebrations were just beginning. Bonfires glowed like great jewels atop the coronet of mountains encircling the country. This was the old way of spreading good news and the indigo sky of the summer night reddened with the refulgence.

Dev was out, the word went round the West; the heather would
be on fire again.

At the old headquarters in Suffolk Street, the man himself
soon sat down with the working committee of Sinn Fein around
a conference-table strewn with ink-pots, papers and congratu-
latory messages. Among the cables from America was one from
his mother and another from the McGarrity family. His first
desire as the President of the Republic was to draw from the man
who had acted for him, Ruttledge, the details on all that had
happened. The Irish Republican Army had been decimated but
Aiken, still the Republican Chief of Staff, urged his men to remain
organized and disciplined, even though inactive. While certain
of the Republicans just released were picking up their guns again,
Dev opposed further use of force against the Free Staters. "You
cannot," he said, "win Irish freedom by moving men as on a
chessboard."

Constitutional means were what he laid down for himself,
and with by-elections due in the autumn of 1924 he resolved to
take up the political campaign exactly where he had been forced
to drop it a year earlier. As he crossed by train to the West,
companies of Volunteers lined up on the railway platforms to give
him a salute. Farmers came on their carts to shout a salutation
in Irish—"*Cead mile failte*"—a "hundred thousand welcomes."
When his train arrived in Ennis it was getting dark, but he found
waiting to meet him in the blaze of torches and of crackling tar
barrels the Clare men and women who had given him his first
start in politics, and he was driven from the station in a waving,
cheering, dancing procession of townspeople. The cottage windows were banked with candles burning beneath his picture. "Up
Dev" was the reverberating shout, and "Up Dev every whole
time." Next day, from the platform that had been re-erected on
a well-remembered spot, he looked out over a crowd even larger
than it had been the summer before. The men in their patched
homespuns and the women in their thick, red, woollen skirts and
black shawls looked different from the Dublin people, but Clare
with its hardy patriots and granite land meant home to him
politically. Irish could still be heard as the natural tongue. Here
in Clare, the children had found a kind of butterfly striped in
green, white and orange and had named it the Republican butterfly. On the platform, those chosen to introduce him did not

conceal the Banner County's pride of possession. He had been faithful, said one, to his nation's call in spite of the ties of a devoted wife and darling children. The women had made a gift of lace he was to take to Mrs. de Valera. He rose to speak. "People of Clare——"

"And Limerick," came the eager audience as still others chimed in with the names of their counties; all wanted to claim him.

"People of Ireland," he acknowledged smilingly, "as I was saying to you when we were interrupted. . . ." The crowd went wild over this joke at the expense of the Free State troops of a year before. Freedom was sure to come, said he in quoting a revered bishop, "as long as grass grows or water runs."

The words he spoke in Clare became sharper as he faced meeting after meeting in other parts of the West. Thousands assembled on the Grand Parade in Cork to listen to what he had to say about the boundary, knowing that Craig had reiterated to Cosgrave his determination not to yield an inch. Whether or not revisions were going to be proposed by the Boundary Commission, Dev made it clear that there could be no boundary at all for Republicans. Though the Free State Government had named Eoin MacNeill as its representative on the three-man Boundary Commission, Craig had refused to designate his appointee and Britain had had to name not only its own representative but Ulster's as well. Birkenhead and Lloyd George were cautioning that the Commission was not a free agent, that the boundary had been set once and for all by the Government of Ireland Act, which constituted a prior commitment. De Valera in Cork read aloud from Griffith's letters written during the Treaty negotiations, letters till then kept secret, expressing confidence that part of the six counties would be given to the South, and de Valera contrasted Griffith's expectations in 1921 with the actual situation in this year of 1924. He blamed the situation "on the despicable, mean, low trick by which the British Ministers have been carrying on their game."

Just a few days before the by-election at the end of October, he went across the border to Newry to address the electors there as their incumbent and their candidate for re-election from that constituency. Belfast newspapers had warned that the town lay in County Down, a Northern area prohibited to him. It was true that the Northern deputies, sitting in their own parliament, had passed an order forbidding de Valera to enter parts of the six partitioned counties. No sooner had he commenced to speak in Newry than the Ulster Specials seized him and, after holding him overnight in the local jail, escorted him back to the boundary line. Next day, undeterred, he set out again to re-invade the North, this time without announcing his destination. By dodging across country roads, his car succeeded in reaching Derry where the people, predominantly Catholic and nationalist as in Newry, did not hesitate to give him a welcome. England—and he said he would quote England's greatest poet—was grappling Ireland to her with hoops of steel. Hamlet's mood of ineffectuality against overwhelming forces struck a chord in his heart. Apprehended again by the constabulary, he was this time taken to Belfast. On the day of his trial at the beginning of November 1924, he was led from the jail to the courtroom through a glass-covered arcade in the centre of the city.

"There he is, God love him," sighed an old lady on the kerb. "If I could only touch his hand——" Police pushed her back.

"Which is he?" demanded someone in her ear. "Is it the very tall one?" and the old lady nodded. He was walking in long, even steps between files of guards with drawn carbines. The spectators to whom the very name of de Valera was anathema had conceived of him as a sinister, evil-eyed individual of unknown extraction. After the formal charge that he had violated the exclusion order, the magistrate turned to him. "Have you anything to say in your defence?"

Promptly he stood. "I refuse to recognize this court because it was set up by an alien power and——"

"You may make any statement you like in your own defence but we can have no political speeches, and on no account can we listen to any statement showing contempt of this court."

"In that case," the prisoner resumed, "I have only to say that I do not recognize the court."

News that County Down had re-elected him arrived while he was serving a one-month sentence in the Belfast jail. His wardens allowed him a few books, among them Francis Thompson's poetry, and as the autumn days dragged on he read, thought, prayed and planned, this being, according to his own calculations, his fourteenth prison experience.

The people at home felt more in common with him than with the Free Staters when he reappeared after his return in the same crumpled frieze coat and the same rain-drenched felt hat. Referring to the formal attire of the Free State Ministers, he mocked "this wonderful tall hat, this most capacious and highly respectable tall hat." It would be no tall hat for him. There was a look of constriction on his features, pulled and peaked, a look that came of hunger, if not of the body certainly of the spirit. His cheeks, after he returned from Belfast, sagged, and his lips were set straight, unsoftened by the old emotions.

The population was falling steadily. Jobs were scarce and for Republicans non-existent. For every two youths who had left Ireland in 1924, three were sailing in 1925, and many who had been indifferent to politics were stirred into opposition to Cosgrave's Party, Cumann na Gaedheal. De Valera told himself that the Irish who went to the United States, to Canada, or elsewhere were successful because they were treated there as equals. Boys and girls were emigrating as in the generations before them while others, idle and disillusioned since the Treaty and the civil war, were spending their time in the village pubs. Those who drank, he reflected, would not have the backbone to make their dreams come true. Cosgrave was making progress in administration; the system of local government had been revised and the teaching of Irish had been made compulsory. But criticism of general conditions existed within the Government's own circles. Some who had accepted the Treaty as a stepping-stone were becoming impatient. Agitation among members of the Free State Army for further independence led to a mutiny within the ranks, whereupon Defence Minister Mulcahy, suspected of being active again in the Irish Republican Brotherhood, was blamed by his fellow Minister O'Higgins, who had no use for that organization. Mulcahy abruptly resigned from the Government.

Though the number of Republican deputies increased as a result of the by-elections in the spring of 1925, this heightened Dev's sense of frustration because they had no voice in the Dail. He would not, he asserted, spend the rest of his life in any sleepy hollow. "Do you realize," someone wrote him after the by-election, "that if you don't go into the Dail you will have barriers against you even when you get a majority." The political way was the way he had staked out for himself at the end of the civil war, but pressures to move in the other direction were equally strong and it seemed politic to put a quietus upon reports that a wedge was being driven between blue-eyed Republicans and brown-eyed Republicans. He called Father Flanagan, Sinn Fein's vice-president, home from America for a confidential review of the abstention policy with Sinn Fein's executive committee. This included Stack, O'Kelly, Cathal O'Murchadha and Madame Markievicz. Newcomers to this group like Sean Lemass, who was influential with the Republican Army, were alarmed at the possible effects from any softening of their attitude and it was decided to stand by their refusal to enter the Dail. No decent Republican, the Chief then replied to the letter which had come in his mail, no one with personal or national self-respect, could ever enter the Dail if it meant swearing allegiance to a foreign king. It would be like the fly fighting in the spider's web.

Told when he went to Cavan that the town was expecting some "lava" from him, he reiterated that he was a moderate, that he would not go any farther in what he said than he could make good by what he did. Militant action was over, finished, although those who had fallen in it would never be forgotten and should, he urged, be for ever honoured. ". . . who among us," he asked, "in our earlier years, before the grey wisdom of the world bade us repress the warm instincts of our hearts but would have thought that was the way to die?"

It had been a point of honour with him as Republican President to refrain from violence after the cease-fire, but paid organizers were going round the country re-grouping the underground fighters. Though public consciousness of the *de facto* Republican Government he headed was weakening, the Cabinet continued to meet with him, to receive communications from the Republican Army, and to share with the Army the small funds that were available. Secret Republican Army headquarters had been re-opened in the midlands at Dunboden House and in Dublin at Roebuck House, the home of Sean MacBride and his mother, Madame Maud Gonne MacBride.

A proposal to get Russian guns was discussed by Aiken and other Army men, who then recommended it though Sean Lemass, head of defence in the Republican Cabinet, to the Chief. Contact with the Russians was established by Sean Russell, quartermaster general on the Republican Army Executive Council, and in 1925

Russell and Gerald Boland, brother of the slain Harry Boland, set forth for Moscow. De Valera himself, though wary of foreign entanglements, acceded to a request that he talk with a man considered by some of his co-workers as a go-between with Russia, a Montenegrin who called himself Marino, but Dev after one meeting declined further contact with him. In Moscow, the two emissaries found the Soviet authorites engrossed in their own concerns. When news of the journey leaked out after their return home, Boland defended it, pointing out that other missions had previously been sent to Russia, that it was not because they were pro-Bolshevist that they had gone, but because they would take help wherever they could get it. Sean Russell, being re-imprisoned by the Free State Government after he came back from Russia, was rescued from Mountjoy Jail, Lemass taking a hand in the break.

Though Dev personally had renounced the tactics of force and violence, he was at a dead-end of political influence. That autumn he was taken ill, very ill, he was to admit, and Ruttledge again took over his speech-making, the Sinn Fein *Ard Fheis* being put off. He was still not completely recovered by the time he learned that the Republican Army, its toleration of passive resistance being at an end, had called a secret convention. Sick or well, the Chief was determined to put in an appearance on the date fixed. What he heard when he joined the Army leaders at their undisclosed meeting-place on November 14, 1925, was a proposal that a military group be designated to operate under the Brotherhood's Supreme Council, one of the members of this group to be in the "position of Dictator to direct military policy." Dismayed, he exclaimed that it was that body—the Brotherhood—which had put over the Treaty. "Are you going to have the same sort of thing started again?" He induced the Army men to reject the Brotherhood's bid for control but they decided, having turned one bid down, to rid themselves of any political control whatsoever and they formally withdrew their allegiance from him as President of the Republic.

On the political front that month, a crisis simultaneously loomed because Eoin MacNeill resigned from the Boundary Commission, denouncing as he did so the failure of the other two commissioners to consider the wishes of the Northern nationalists. As Cosgrave was conferring in London with Churchill and

Craig, Dev's own sources of information led him to warn that the Northerners were going to be sold by one of the most disgraceful acts in history. President Cosgrave, announcing that he had got a big bargain, "a great nought," brought back and submitted to the Dail for ratification an agreement in which the British promised to cancel their financial claims against the Free State provided the Irish agreed to leave the boundary as it was. This sounded bad enough on the face of it but Dev did not know, nor did anyone except Cosgrave's most intimate advisers know, that the land annuities had already been pledged to England and that this agreement for wiping the slate clean was over and above the payment of the annuities. Whatever the financial advantages were or were not, leaving the boundary alone meant that the city of Derry, for instance, would belong to Northern Ireland though it was the marketing centre for County Donegal, which was under the jurisdiction of the South. There would be no All-Ireland Parliament, since the Northern representatives would sit in Westminster and in their own Belfast parliament.

Against this de Valera pronounced instant judgment as a "second treaty." It was the "sinister proposal" of which he had tried to speak, the consummation of the "sale" which he had mentioned, a piece of gerrymandering pure and simple. Approval or disapproval of the second treaty rested with the Dail and since the Labour Party opposed it, the thought struck de Valera that if the forty-eight Republican deputies could take the seats to which they had been elected, they could pool their votes to defeat Cosgrave. Yet he saw himself condemned to stand impotent, and one-third of the elected representatives of the country exercised no vote whatsoever when the Dail moved to ratify Cosgrave's agreement, voluntarily making partition the law of the land. For the meanest of all considerations, de Valera declared at a protest meeting in the Rotunda, for a money consideration, the Free Staters had sold their countrymen.

One stormy night later in the winter after he had addressed a protest meeting in the North, Dev reached the small hotel in the town of Sligo, having come down over icy roads from County Donegal. A country youth got back into his waiter's livery and stirred up the peat fire in the dining-room. As the leader sat warming himself with a cup of tea and recounting to a handful of local Republicans his experiences earlier in the day, the Sligo police entered, ordered him from the table, pulled papers and letters from his pockets, only to withdraw after half an hour without making any arrest. In the face of such treatment at the hands of the Free State, indignant supporters urged him to reassert his old position somehow, and Gerald Boland suggested that they ought to become part of the governing crew and get a say in running things.

De Valera thought of assembling the Republican deputies outside Leinster House so they would not have to take the oath. When he got them together in the Shelbourne Hotel in Dublin, the Labour deputies agreed to come also and Dev then proposed that they join forces against partition. The Shelbourne Hotel parliament, as Cosgrave termed it, produced no immediate results but a contact had been established with the Labour leader, Thomas Johnson. A new toughness entered into Dev's fibre: "I believe that when you go out for something you ought to try to win it. I do not believe in giving up before I have to." Taking stock of what he stood to gain and lose by legislative participation instead of abstention, he announced early in 1926 that, provided he did not have to take the oath, he was going into the legislature.

As the political vehicle to carry out his new policy he undertook to get the co-operation of Sinn Fein though its officers had within the year reaffirmed Sinn Fein's long tradition of abstention. This organization had since 1917 elected and re-elected him as its president. "Dev, I say like a wise man, has announced that he will go into the Free State Parliament if there is no oath," Madame Markievicz wrote her sister, "and this has caused an unholy row." Entering the legislature would not, Dev tried to tell a special Sinn Fein *Ard Fheis*, imply recognition of that junta. He made a motion which Ruttledge seconded that, if the oath were removed, entering the Dail would not be regarded as a question of principle but a question of policy only. Principles were difficult to put into practice, Dev admonished. "We are not all Thomas Aquinases. We are not all able to judge of the application of principles. . . ."

Father Flanagan moved to amend de Valera's motion to the effect that it would be incompatible with Sinn Fein principles to send representatives into a usurping legislature and Stack stood up, implacable, his face and figure still ravaged by his last, long hunger strike, to declare himself in favour of the amendment. So far as going into Leinster House was concerned, Mary MacSwiney commented, once the first step was taken the descent into hell would be easy. When the *Ard Fheis* was ready for the question, Father Flanagan's amendment was put first and carried 223 to 218. With a mystifying calm, Dev announced that he was resigning the presidency of the organization. He went even further in severing old political connections and submitted to the Council of Deputies his resignation as President of the Republic. His old friend, Austin Stack, moved its acceptance there.

"The fact is," he told newsmen in April 1926, "we are ourselves forming a new organization." Plans were being rushed to completion under a committee headed by Ruttledge. Lemass, Boland, MacEntee and a doctor named James Ryan from County Wexford were working with Ruttledge, as were Madame Markievicz and Aiken. Since the name of Dev's earlier party, Cumann na Poblachta, was associated in people's minds with the civil war, Fianna Fail, meaning Soldiers of Destiny, was the new designation. Ruttledge's committee moved out of Suffolk Street to open new offices at 33 Lower O'Connell Street opposite the General Post Office. "We believe that Republicans ought not to stand aside and allow the country to be utterly ruined," read the Chief's first manifesto from O'Connell Street. When Mary MacSwiney, more hostile every day, called upon him to define the limits of his so-called "new departure," suspecting that if he was bent upon getting inside the Dail he would do so with the oath if he could not do so without it, he said only that he would lead the people down the path at their own gait but that he intended to bring them out eventually at the destination of his original choosing, nothing short of sovereignty and unity.

The prospect of a general election in a year's time gave the Fianna Fail Party workers a chance in which to organize, and the response to his reinvigorated leadership was evident by the time the first convention of the new Party was summoned. Five hundred Fianna Fail delegates from almost as many newly created branches assembled on November 26, 1926, in Dublin on the anniversary of Erskine Childers' execution. Death, Dev said in opening the convention, sanctified the work which they were left to do but Fianna Fail had to abjure bloodshed now that the road of peaceful progress had been chosen. "I have never said, and am not going to say now," he was quick to add, "that force is not a legitimate weapon."

To contest the election set for June 1927, with Cosgrave's Cumann na Gaedheal Party, Dev knew he would need funds. Lying in American banks was close to three million dollars, by his estimate, from the Irish Republican bonds, and the Supreme Court of the State of New York was about to hear the suit brought by the Free State for title to this money. Reports that he might be held liable for legal costs in the case did not alarm him. "I have no personal estate, they cannot do anything, but they are going to proceed," he owned with vexation. In a sudden move, he applied to the Free State authorities for a passport and before indignation at this technical recognition of an unrecognizable regime could make itself heard, he had arrived in New York, travelling with an ease he had not enjoyed on his crossing six years earlier. He took the witness stand, but the New York court awarded the money back to those who had contributed it. Dev then appealed to Americans for new backing in the name of his Party.

His mother looked slight and frail in her sombre black. His arrival in Rochester coincided with his stepfather's funeral. The family priest had received Charles E. Wheelwright into the Catholic Church just before his death, and over his grave in the new, bare section of Rochester's Cemetery of the Holy Sepulchre, Father Thomas Wheelwright, his own son, spoke the final prayers. Left a widow, Mrs. Wheelwright, as sure-minded as when, many years before, she had decided to make a life for herself in America, was going to stay on in her own house in Brighton Street with nieces and nephews living close by. Neither of her sons was free to spend long with her.

By the time de Valera got back to Ireland, the election campaign was on in full force. Fianna Fail leaders were condemning Cumann na Gaedheal for giving away the North; for setting up a senate weighted against Republicans; for participating in imperial conferences in London; for sponsoring public safety acts and treasonable offences legislation; for subjecting teachers, doctors, agricultural inspectors to political tests; for drawing exorbitant Ministerial salaries. The Government found itself saddled with the burden of five years of authority. Fianna Fail had the advantage of being untainted with any responsibility for the immediate past, and at the end of its first electoral campaign it won 44 seats in the Dail. Cosgrave's Party fell to 46 with Labour, the Farmers, the National League, and other minority groups filling the rest of the chamber. De Valera repeated that under no circumstances would his deputies take any oath to get into Leinster House, though the day the legislature was to convene he set out from his home with a fixed purpose. From Sandymount he drove down the long, curving street bordered with suburban villas from 84 Serpentine Avenue where he and his family were living, and he joined the newly elected Fianna Fail deputies at a prearranged rendezvous. With him at their head they formed into a column and marched off to take Leinster House by storm.

The streets leading to their destination were under police guard and traffic was barred. On through the protective cordon and into Kildare Street the Chief strode and around the gravelled drive, followed closely by his two score and more Party members. He mounted the shallow stone steps under the pediment of the long façade of the *Oireachtas'* home, but as soon as they got inside guards demanded identification papers. Dev brushed them aside, insisting upon access to the inner part of the building where the other elected representatives were assembling. He moved on down the wide corridor but found the doors of the chamber itself locked. It was three o'clock, and within the Clerk of the Dail read out the names of those who had complied with Article 14, the oath article, of the Constitution, while those whose names were not included continued to clamour outside for admittance. President Cosgrave was re-elected as head of the Government though the vote was close because of Labour's objections, and Cosgrave then nominated the presiding chairman or *Ceann Comhairle*, the man who would have the deciding vote in case of a tie. For several hours more de Valera stalked the corridors of Leinster House and then withdrew with his companions to Party headquarters, there to plan their next move.

President Cosgrave was needling him for using the oath as an escape from taking responsibility. Only too ready to prove that he was not, de Valera set Fianna Fail to securing the 75,000 signatures which were required to force the Dail to submit the oath question to the people. The Free State's Constitution had provided for the popular initiative and referendum in Articles 47 and 48. At this juncture, just as Constitutional wheels seemed to be turning, tragedy struck both de Valera's Party and Cosgrave's. Illness ended the life of Madame Markievicz, the woman who had kept closest through all political vicissitudes to the Chief. "Madame, the friend of the toiler," he said in tribute at her grave in Glasnevin, "the lover of the poor." In the same week of July 1927, Kevin O'Higgins, the Free State vice-president, who was serving also as Minister of Justice and Minister of External Affairs, while walking to Mass near his home, was fatally shot on the street corner. The whole of Ireland was shocked. De Valera instantly denied any knowledge of the killer. Sean MacBride was accused but proved he had been out of the country. Suspicion flew to the Irish Republican Brotherhood, since O'Higgins had baulked its influence in the Free State Army, and then to the Irish Republican Army, but its members were quick to repudiate such private vengeance.

Consumed with grief, President Cosgrave submitted to the Dail simultaneously and without the customary advance notice three measures, each purposefully designed. First, another public safety act was brought in, the provisions of which included suspension of jury trial, sentence of death for such crimes as possession of firearms, expulsion from Ireland of dangerous persons whose guilt could not be proved in court. Then an act was introduced requiring that all seeking nomination in parliamentary elections declare in advance their willingness to take the oath. The third proposition was intended to limit use of the Constitution's initiative and referendum to the deputies inside the Dail. Of these three measures introduced as the antidote to O'Higgins' murder, the first two were passed into law within a few days but the third, since it required a Constitutional amendment, advanced only to its second reading before the Dail rose.

Cosgrave's battery of laws would, Dev saw, wipe out Fianna Fail unless they yielded on the oath because they would be unable even to nominate candidates. Henceforth, it would be impossible for Republicans so much as to run for office without swearing allegiance. Some at the meeting of Fianna Fail deputies which he called were convinced that they could never get rid of the oath by standing on the outside looking in, and these declared themselves in favour of going in though it might mean taking the oath to get there. De Valera had not forgotten all the times that he had said neither he nor any decent Republican would swear royal allegiance. If, however, the oath was as others professed a mere formality, would subscribing to it be, in fact, perjury? To the statement giving notice that Party members had made up their minds to take their seats the Chief appended his name, followed by the names of all the rest. Not for a long time did he confess that he felt the necessity for this reversal humiliating.

The day before the Dail was scheduled to sit again in August 1927, the Fianna Fail deputies returned to Leinster House and were met at the entrance by the friendly minority leaders, Thomas Johnson and Captain Redmond of the second generation of Redmonds, who led them up a stone staircase and down a long hall to a side-room. As Dev looked around him, the place seemed dim and bare, as if hidden away so that the public would not know what took place there, not at all the setting for a ceremony regarded by anyone as significant, and quite unlike the other handsome apartments they had passed with Adams ceilings and marble mantels. Going over to the table, Dev closed the Bible lying there and put it out of sight. Then he turned to the Clerk who was in charge of swearing in new legislators. "You must remember I am not taking any oath," and he handed over a statement he had pencilled in Irish to the effect that the Republicans were not prepared to take an oath. The Clerk seemed to be inclined to interpret the Government's regulations liberally, and the rank and file of the Republican deputies began the quiet, methodical process of subscribing their names in a ledger under the required formula: "I"—and then the deputy's own name—"do solemnly swear true faith and allegiance to the Constitution of the Free State as by law established and that I will be faithful to His Majesty George V, his heirs and successors by law. . . ." "I am prepared," de Valera said when his own turn came, "to put my name down here in this book in order to get permission to get into the Dail, and it has no other significance." It was, he assured himself, only blazing the trail for all the others standing on the outside of constitutional government—the militant Republicans.

Though he did not expect to form a Government himself at once, he expected to join forces with Thomas Johnson and Captain Redmond to turn Cumann na Gaedheal out of power, and soon after the Dail opened Johnson introduced a prepared motion of no confidence in the Cosgrave regime. Members new and old

heard it with an air of manifest indifference but the casual atmosphere concealed a ferocity of interest. Through the swinging
doors on either side behind the speaker's raised chair deputies
hastened in, their footsteps hushed by the thick carpeting woven
in rich Celtic colouring and bordered with scrollery. Fianna Fail's
members were in their places and each of them on the front bench
of the opposition side was to handle a specific area in debate,
mostly the same each had covered in the Republican Cabinet from
the time of the civil war. Aiken would bring his experience to
bear upon military matters. Derrig, who had once taught school,
was to watch for educational legislation. Ryan, farmer as well as
doctor, was to speak on agriculture. Lemass was equipped on
economic grounds to attack the interdependence with Britain,
"the Merseyside mentality." Sean T. O'Kelly, sitting close to the
Chief, was the Party's orator, already an elder statesman. Ranged
behind these leaders were the old guard, Mrs. Clarke, Frank
Fahy, Donal Buckley and the others.

President Cosgrave commented that they all seemed "to have
blown in here . . . from an outer world like little winged angels."
Overhead, the steep, screened balcony was filled to the roof with
spectators waiting to see Fianna Fail in action. Without prolonged discussion and without any speech from Deputy de
Valera, the Labour Party's no-confidence motion was put to
a vote, the deputies trooping up the steps at the rear and turning
right or left to pass through the Yes or the No lobby into the
balcony, then back down to their places. When the tally was
announced it proved to be a tie vote which, when the *Ceann
Comhairle* cast the deciding ballot, was broken in Cosgrave's
favour. Cosgrave, not satisfied with so slim a majority, decided
to dissolve the Dail and call another general election. Fianna
Fail, having just come through its first trial at the polls, was
indignant at being rushed into another campaign, especially in the
middle of the harvest season.

Political sentiment polarized rapidly around the two main
factions now diametrically opposed, and in the autumn de
Valera came back to Leinster House with 57 seats as compared
with his previous 44 and Cumann na Gaedheal with 61 instead
of 46. Both he and Cosgrave had gained at the expense of the
smaller groups. It would, in the normal course of events, be five
years before another general election and Dev saw that his Party

might be cast for that entire period in the opposition role, so he settled back into his seat on the *Ceann Comhairle's* right to wait, putting out of his mind his first plans for forming a coalition government between his Party, Labour and the others. The clogs on public action, he philosophized, were great. ". . . our people are conservative and the barriers . . . to progress are many. . . . One should not be in a hurry."

CHAPTER XIII

NOT THE PURPLE HILLS AND GREEN
FIELDS MERELY (1927–1933)

EACH afternoon about five or six o'clock, Deputy Eamon de Valera, leader of the legal opposition, would leave Leinster House to walk through Merrion Square to his own office. Returning for the evening debate in Dail Eireann, he would describe the "little children" whom he saw, "their hands stuck down in the bins . . . put out the side doors, in some cases looking for scraps of food and in others looking for coal," small scavengers coming up at twilight from the purlieus of Pearse Street behind the handsome square. In the Dail's debates, de Valera harped upon the needs of the poor, reminding the Government of the dole lines forming in the depression, of the men walking the country in search of jobs, of the paupers cutting thistles in the rain to earn a pittance. "Ireland must mean not the purple hills and the green fields merely but . . . the men and women of the Nation—the souls that can agonize and suffer," he told the deputies.

His own Party members he set to studying the inner workings of factories and farms, perusing trade and commerce reports, investigating the hardships of their rural and urban constituents alike. His remedy for the farmers' dilemma was that they should diversify their crops instead of sticking to potatoes. Why should they not raise their own wheat? Britain was dumping goods which the Irish people could manufacture for themselves, food and clothing, for instance. Ridiculed for his Robinson Crusoe economics by President Cosgrave, Dev kept right on suggesting that they look at Ireland as if there were a wall around it, the way he said a pure mathematician would deal with physical problems.

Being in the house gave him, in the months that followed and then the years, his opportunity to teach again, though it was a change and adjustment from the period he had spent on the run. Not all the deputies understood the guttural-sounding Gaelic with which he would begin his speeches and he had to revert to English. Beginning in a courteous, deferential tone he

would veer into questioning the Ministers sitting opposite him.
As emotion bore through his statistics and his statements, his
voice rose, his long dark hair fell over his forehead and, pressing
the tips of his long fingers on the desk in front of him like a pivot,
he swayed forwards and backwards. Interrupted often from the
Government benches by references to his past when he was
outside the pale of legal opposition, and by attacks upon his
patriotism, he would reply: "In any country wherever there has
been, between two parties, a conflict such as there has been in this
country, you always find one party trying to use treason as a means
of overcoming their opponents. . . ."

He drove his old Ford car back and forth from home to work
ten, twelve or more hours every day. Though his income as
opposition leader brought to an end years of uncertainty, the
de Valera family continued to live simply and the children shared
in the chores of the household. Mrs. de Valera required that the
one maid they employed should know Irish. Vivion, aged seventeen, could not help noticing as he listened to the discussions at
home of the arguments in the Dail, how often his father repeated
that, in legal matters, he was only a layman and the boy saw where
he could train himself to do his part for the country—in the field
of law, a field he liked and one which promised a good living as
well. Mairin at fifteen was a keen pupil, interested particularly in
nature study at the Loreto Convent which she attended. Eamon,
the second son, though only fourteen, was also scientifically
inclined, and Brian, a curly headed twelve-year-old with dark
eyes under arched brows, had an eagerness resembling his father's.
Ruairi was eleven years of age; Emer, the younger daughter,
nine; and Terry, the baby of the family, was still at home with his
mother. The father thought that starting school before the age
of seven put children "into the wrong state of mind."

His wife, still in her thirties though he was now forty-five,
did not accompany him in public any more after he went into the
Dail than before. She did not have time. Only at occasional
Gaelic-speaking fêtes for children to which she was drawn by her
own family interests did she customarily appear. To the gossip
circulated about their private life by political detractors, she and
her husband appeared impervious. While in America, as Dev told
fellow deputies scornfully, "I was supposed to be living with
two or three women." From the opposite side of the house came

the interjection that nobody looking at Deputy de Valera could mistake him for a Don Juan.

As the children grew older the family moved again, this time to Cross Avenue, a broad street paralleling the Dun Laoghaire-to-Dublin road, but lying inland and connecting the quiet suburb of Blackrock at one end and the closer-built area of Booterstown at the other. To live in Blackrock connoted eminent respectability. Although there were fine residences behind their own walls at Blackrock and across the avenue, "Springville" stood near the pavement and comparatively alone, a double sort of grey, cement house that was two storeys high on one end and low on the other. The wall separating it from the pavement was topped with an iron railing behind which were some bushes and a narrow, gravel plot. It was a simple, roomy home for a large family, not beautiful, but close to a cluster of shops and the bus line to the city.

Dev liked to get home for his mid-day meal. A look into some of the children's textbooks roused his ire. "I have had the humiliation," he was to relate, "of seeing my own children reading what purported to be Irish history books, but what were really villainous lies and nothing else." Over the whole educational process he believed there should be a religious guardianship and for his children he selected Catholic schools. Assignments that entailed rote memorization also made him critical; lessons should, in his opinion, be confined to school hours. One of the boys was credited with special ability at the piano and the father enjoyed the moments of music in the house. He urged his sons out on to the playing field for sports like Gaelic football and hurling.

The Booterstown Church round the corner from "Springville" on an asphalt courtyard became the family church and Dev attended Mass as many mornings of the week as he could, here or wherever he happened to be. With his religion went a puritanical morality which made him indifferent to taunts for airing his views. In Leinster House, for instance, a bar was connected with the members' dining-room, and he raised the question soon after entering the chamber as to whether the bar could be separated or else abolished altogether. He himself, it was said, neither drank nor smoked. "We do not wish to encourage the drinking of either beer or stout, but," he could not help adding, "we think that if beer or stout are being drunk, it should be either Irish beer or stout." His strictures extended beyond the evils of drink to the evils of jazz, the evils of betting on the races, the dangers from indecent books, and he concurred in the Government's bill to censor publications. The literary censorship, he urged, should be aimed at sexual immorality and should apply not only to books and moving-pictures but to the Sunday papers as well because they reached so many people.

Although Leinster House gave him one sounding-board, the Press did not satisfy him in its treatment of the ideas he expressed as his experience in parliamentary opposition increased. There seemed to him to be full coverage for the Government's achievements like the engineering scheme to dam up the Shannon River for electric power; like the decision of the League of Nations to register the 1921 Treaty against British protests; like the participation in imperial conferences out of which came a declaration of autonomy for the dominions. With the idea of getting funds for a newspaper that Fianna Fail could use as its own mouthpiece, he embarked upon another American pilgrimage, crossing the Atlantic in time to spend part of the Christmas season of 1927 with his widowed mother. Instead of speaking publicly on his journalistic business, he worked quietly, interesting specific Americans in the prospectus calling for 10,000 shareholders for his newspaper. Back in Dublin with substantial financial encouragement, he put Frank Gallagher, once an associate of Childers, to work as editor-designate of the *Irish Press*. One young man, applying for a job as journalist, was asked by Dev if he was qualified to write editorials. The applicant answered that he was not much interested in politics. "Good," was the Chief's reply. "Neither am I." Politics, though now becoming his necessary business, lacked for him the sense of sacrifice and attainment he had known while up in arms.

The daily round month in and month out of a deputy's duties was not enough to content a man who was accustomed to hazarding much for his objectives, and upon being invited early in 1929 to open a Gaelic League bazaar in Belfast, he decided to disregard the ban still in effect against him and took the train to the North. Without seeming surprise when his compartment was entered at the border stop by members of the Royal Irish Constabulary, he took his hat and bag from the luggage rack and got off with them as directed. Given to understand that he was under arrest, he was conveyed to Belfast by car

and at his trial there, his second in that city, the magistrate interrupted the stream of Gaelic which he uttered: "You might as well
be speaking Greek." The prisoner had shown no difficulty in
speaking English, testified one of the arresting officers, when he
was apprehended at Goraghwood. Again, he was sentenced to
one month in prison, though this time he was an official member
of the parliamentary opposition in the Free State. President
Cosgrave took it as his responsibility to ask Sir James Craig for
the prisoner's release as an act of grace, whereupon Sean T.
O'Kelly upbraided the President in the Dail for his "crawling,
creeping, begging letter" to the head of a subordinate state of the
British Empire. Craig's reply to Cosgrave was that Eamon de
Valera would be set free if he would not again cross the border
without applying personally for permission. Dev preferred to
remain in the Belfast Jail cell. "I am able," he emphasized later,
"to live alone when I want to. . . ."

Upon his release, he found himself almost as much out of
sympathy with what was going on in the South as he had been in
the North. For over a year he had been devoting himself to civil
opposition, but neither it nor the persisting tactics of force were
producing the results he had anticipated. The Government's
anti-Republican measures had not squelched the violent kind of
agitation. Banks and money-lenders were being raided, jurors
intimidated, picture theatres blown up, trap mines sown for the
police and soldiery, while the marauders proudly brandished their
I.R.A. credentials. Under the public safety laws, Sean MacBride,
Adjutant-General of the Republican Army, was re-arrested by
the Free State Government and Sean Russell, Quartermaster-
General, was seized after inspecting dumps of arms around the
country. Mary MacSwiney was reported to be urging the legislature of the Republic, which had remained extant in spite of
Dev's resignation as its President, to establish contact with the
"revolutionary body," by which she meant the I.R.A., and to
launch another uprising. The ailing Stack, meeting with the
shadow legislature, abused Fianna Fail for entering Leinster
House. However, the number of political leaders who remained
aloof from Dev's "new departure" declined, and gradually the
underground deputies lost their old leadership.

From the floor of the Dail, de Valera took it upon himself to
defend the men and women put in prison as Republican agitators,

some of them not much more than boys and girls. Young Sheila
Humphries, in whose family home in Ailesbury Road the Republican Cabinet used to meet, went on hunger strike and Dev
pleaded for her release. When Stack whose health had been irre-
parably impaired died, de Valera attended his funeral in spite of
their rift as Fianna Fail's official mourner. He demanded an
explanation from the Minister of Justice as to why a Clare
Republican named T. J. Ryan had been attacked and beaten, and
on the week-end drove to Clare to get the facts for himself. As he
approached the remote farm where Ryan lived with his mother,
police accosted de Valera. He found Ryan lying in bed, bandaged,
his face bruised and his eye blackened, and listened as the man
told how he had been roused one night from his sleep and set
upon in his own farmyard. By the time Dev succeeded in laying
the story before the Dail, the Government had its own explanation: Ryan, described as a leader of violence in Clare, was only
being held under surveillance. As for the black eye, Cosgrave's
Minister of Justice announced that the injuries had not been
received at the hands of the police at all, but from Ryan's own
cow which kicked him while he was milking her. Ballads about
the kicking cow in the County Clare promptly sprang up all over
Connaught.

Fianna Fail's anti-Government attacks did not abate, even
though the Chief departed once again for America in the spring
of 1930. With his mother, who was in declining health, he spent
as much time as he could take from the drive to collect a million
dollars for his projected newspaper. The suggestion arose in the
United States that those who held Republican bonds might
transfer their title to him as one means of ensuring capital for the
newspaper, and he had a form drawn up whereby this transferral
of title was accomplished in a number of instances by willing
bondholders. Enabled by this transaction to calculate when the
payments would fall due, he and Gallagher proceeded to order the
equipment and machinery needed to start publication.

At home he had left the Party in the hands of his front
benchers and was himself in the Mid-west when he got the news
that the Cosgrave Government had failed to secure a majority
during a routine division. The reported vote was not a landslide
but it showed the Government's hold upon the minority parties
was weakening. Immediately thereafter, Dev was informed,

President Cosgrave resigned. His own name was then placed in nomination for the office by O'Kelly as that of the man who had brought Ireland closer to her ideals than anyone since Owen Roe O'Neill. Fianna Fail leaders were appealing to the deputies to show whether they wanted the Crown with them and the British Navy in their harbours for ever. At this, Labour and the National League took alarm lest the obvious emphasis on Republicanism take precedence over internal needs. The minority groups wanted peace and prosperity above all and Dev, they recalled, had once said that there could be neither till the Treaty was revised. Cosgrave capitalized upon such fears and Fianna Fail's brief hopes were dashed by lack of support from the minority blocs. Cosgrave was re-elected but Lemass, noting that Labour did not concur, predicted that the Government's days were numbered.

The Chief, upon his return, surmised that the less he said for the time about breaking ties with Britain the wiser it would be, and the more he might say about improving living conditions at home the better he would be received. Ireland, he contended, should stick to a policy of neutrality. He found little to protest when the British Parliament proposed in the autumn of 1931 what was to be known as the Statute of Westminster. The purpose of the British was to write into statutory law the autonomous status of the dominions that had already been initiated by imperial conferences. Under the proposal, each dominion was to be free to determine its connection with the Crown, and the assent of the dominions was to be required in the event of succession to the throne.

De Valera could not believe the British were capable of making such advances as the act proposed, and was therefore not surprised when Churchill warned that it would give the Irish Free State the power to abrogate the Treaty. Churchill urged Parliament to amend it so that Ireland could not repeal or alter the Treaty, the Constitution, or the Government of Ireland Act. But Ramsay MacDonald was in office as Prime Minister and his Secretary of State for the Dominions, J. H. Thomas, answered Churchill that it would be unfair to distinguish one dominion from the other. When the Statute of Westminster was passed by Parliament without the special limitations Churchill sought in regard to Ireland, Dev owned to himself that the position of external association had been achieved with two exceptions: the advances applied only to the twenty-six counties, and Ireland was still a monarchy and not a Republic.

Dissatisfaction with Anglo-Irish relations continued, and the ranks of the I.R.A. offered an outlet for the grievances of the restless, workless men. When, as a possible inducement to reconciliation, the public safety legislation was allowed by the Cosgrave Government to lapse, it produced no remission in the episodes of violence. The Fianna Fail Chief realized that no means seemed to the Republicans impossible because they had nothing to lose. Dublin's statue of King William of Orange was found blown up, and not long afterward police came upon the head near a remote ravine high up in the Dublin Mountains. In the same vicinity, they discovered by an overhanging bank the entrance to a dug-out, lined inside with concrete and packed with rifles, German automatics, revolvers, Lewis machine-guns, ammunition and high explosives. Taken into custody from a hut nearby were two brothers named Gilmore, known to be Republicans. The Government decoded a captured document showing that six revolutionary leaders had been students at "Lenin College" in Moscow. The Russians were at this juncture exerting an influence upon the I.R.A., as Aiken and others silently sensed.

Dev, when held responsible in the Dail for the underground situation, acknowledged that vicious methods were coming in and he insisted to the deputies that, though his sympathies might remain with the I.R.A., he would not let those sympathies run away with him. He had a specific proposal to offer, for him a drastic one. It was time, he told the house, to call in all arms throughout the country if that were possible. Surely, he averred, the I.R.A. could not be so foolish as to think that the legitimate forces backed by the majority of the people could be overthrown in favour of secret devices? What he meant was that the Irish Republican Brotherhood was regaining control and no good would come from its orders. ". . . if there is to be any progress in this country and freedom is again to be achieved it will . . . be through . . . the leadership given by the elected representatives of the majority of the people."

By October 1931, a new public safety act more severe than any that preceded it was brought into the Dail. While the vote on it was impending, gunmen paid midnight visits to deputies' homes to warn them against approving it. Dev, though opposing the bill, intended that what he said during the debate should reach the ears of the Republicans. "They have," he declared, "done terrible things recently but let us appeal to them and ask them in God's name not to do it." The new public safety act, passed over the objections of Fianna Fail and Labour, deepened the cleavage between the Government and the opposition. De Valera, during the course of several days of vitriolic debate, attributed to Cosgrave cowardice for running away from Ireland during the Black and Tan days, but in a calmer moment he withdrew the remark, explaining that he had been stung by imputations that he himself had avoided danger by staying in America. "I am ashamed," said the downcast, stern-faced de Valera, "that I said anything about cowardice to anybody."

The Government barely kept its head above water in various divisions and President Cosgrave decided early in the new year of 1932 to dissolve the Dail and go to the people without waiting till his full term expired. "You are not going to stop the blades of grass from growing as they grow," Dev reminded the opposition. The people who, ten years before, had tired of him and his diehard determination were weary in 1932 of the Cumann na Gaedheal Party and its static policies. Deputy de Valera, in pre-election campaigning, asked only for a mandate limited to two things: to keep the land annuities at home and to abolish the oath to the King. There was no longer any hope of getting rid of the oath by the popular initiative because Cosgrave had struck that provision from the Constitution. At a rally in Dublin's College Green, Cosgrave was heckled, booed and jeered. Chants of "Up Dev" drowned out everything else. "We are either in a prison house with the doors locked on us," he challenged the voters, "or those doors are wide open." Either he was to remain powerless or the people were going to make him the head of the Government.

Into the county seats east, west and south in Ireland, he drove on his campaign, escorted by a volunteer cavalry, the manes of the horses braided with Republican colours. At the sound of the local drum and fife bands, children rushed to the cottage windows while their parents dashed off to the market-square. Standing up in a cart, the middle-aged Chief, unsmiling, dressed in seedy black, seemingly oblivious to the flamboyant electioneering, recited statistics to show that England was not only draining off the annuities from the farmers but was using the Irish market for her own ends. All the blood and tears that had been shed, he lamented in the piercing phrase first used by the poet Byron, could have been saved if British statesmen had in 1921 acted wisely. The pro-British policy was blamed by him for making their economy lop-sided. For almost five years he had been able to do no more than protest as the voice of the opposition. When he proclaimed that Ireland was virgin soil for her own industries, followers of the Labour Pary opened their ears and he pointed out the similarity of Labour's interests with Fianna Fail's, recalling the influence James Connolly had had upon him personally as a young man. The actual turnout at the polls was not heavy and did not give him a controlling majority, but Fianna Fail won more seats in Dail Eireann than any other party: 72 as compared with the 44 held previously. Cosgrave's Party fell from 61 to 57 seats, but the Independents' 9 seats and the Farmers' 5 were known to be on his—Cosgrave's—side. The balance of power lay with Labour's seven uncommitted members. De Valera waited to see what they would do.

When the legislature convened in March 1932, the roll was called, the prayer recited, and quickly the incumbent speaker was voted down in favour of the Gaelic Leaguer, Frank Fahy, an associate of de Valera's. With the votes of the Labour deputies thrown to his side, de Valera was then named for the Presidency. As tradition decreed, the Dail adjourned briefly so that he might call upon the man who was Governor-General, James MacNeill, brother to Professor Eoin MacNeill. At the Viceregal lodge, de Valera was formally appointed as President of the Executive Council of the Irish Free State, or, as he preferred to call his title, *An Uachtaran*. Twice before he had been President, from 1919 to 1922 when he had resigned because of the Treaty, and, after a few months' interval, from 1922 to 1926 when again he had resigned as head of a hopeless, *de facto* regime in order to pursue the path of constitutionalism. On each previous occasion when named to the Presidency, it had been by a *de facto*, unrecognized administration. Now, in 1932, after a career that had moved from armed leadership in rebellion to prison insurrection to self-proclaimed governmental headship to civil war and, most recently, to leadership of the constitutional opposition, de Valera stood where his own convictions and nationalist aspirations had led him. He was, at last, the duly chosen leader of the majority bloc in the Irish legislature, the chief executive of a *de jure* Government. As such, he approached his responsibilities with intense seriousness.

Assigning to himself the portfolio of external affairs, he selected for Vice-president and Minister of Local Government the veteran Sean T. O'Kelly; for Finance, MacEntee; for Defence, Aiken; for Industry and Commerce, Lemass; for Agriculture, Ryan; for Education, Derrig; for Lands and Fisheries, Ruttledge. All bore the marks of battle. All had been with the Chief for a decade at least, and some since 1916 and before. Each had rehearsed for years his part in the governing team and displayed little outward sign of jubilation upon the long-awaited accession to office. Ex-President Cosgrave, having moved to the speaker's right, commented wryly that it was the sole desire of the party opposite to wrap the green flag round them.

"And you," retorted Gerald Boland, acting as chief whip for Fianna Fail, "the Union Jack." At the head of the Government bench sat the Chief, shoulders dropped, head bent forward, his eyes staring speculatively from behind the large, round lenses of his spectacles. In fulfilment of his campaign pledges, he proceeded to release the Republicans who were still in jail, among them the Gilmore brothers. Public safety legislation, though not abolished, was suspended by him and immediately the liberated leaders resumed their recruiting for the I.R.A. which, so long as it should be for political and not military purposes, the President defended. He denied that he was ashamed of his sympathy for the extremists. That he was acting on the strength of feeling as well as reason he knew. ". . . the really strong man," he asserted, "is the man who conquers himself, and no one who imagines he conquers himself when he freezes every decent emotion and turns himself into a machine. You do not become strong simply by freezing all those natural instincts that will be in human beings made in the image of God."

Within short order, he introduced a bill to remove the oath from the Constitution, as the first part of his election mandate, and went to the upper house in order to lay his measure before that body. In the *Seanad*, Cosgrave still had a majority, and if that chamber demurred the measure could not without another general election become law for eighteen months. The three score senators sat in a slender, oblong chamber redolent of the ducal days of Leinster House, their blue leather armchairs arranged in a shallow semi-circle lengthwise of the room. The two marble mantels, the high windows, and the medallions sculptured in plaster on the walls befitted the balls and soirées they had once graced. The new President, a stark contrast in his usual black, took up his place before the austere assemblage that included the Earl of Granard, one the Guinnesses, Douglas and Jameson, George Moore's brother, Colonel Maurice Moore, Countess Desart, The McGillicuddy of the Reeks. "I am very glad," the unaccustomed visitor began stiffly, "to have this opportunity of addressing the House." There was momentary decorum.

As soon as the oath was gone, he ventured, the Republicans operating outside the law were sure to enter into participation with them all. With sceptical murmurs the senators objected that removal of the oath would be a violation of the Treaty. But Ireland, the President continued, had been placed by the Statute of Westminster on a par with Great Britain and with each dominion. Whatever the situation had been before that Statute, they could certainly free themselves of the oath now. The senators suggested submitting the matter to negotiation with the British. Senator Oliver St. John Gogarty, as he waited to speak, sharpened his tongue and then, in malevolent denunciation, ascribed to anyone who set out to lead Republicans certain peculiar responsibilities. Such a one, for instance, had to dress like "the manager of the Cats' Home; he had to look grave; he had to be filled with the milk of human kindness but touched withal by a gentle melancholy on account of the dope he must administer in the end." The senators would, the President fumed, wait to act till Tibb's Eve; the *Seanad* itself would have to go if it was bent upon perpetuating the imperial ties. "*Fan go foill*"—we shall see—he said.

De Valera's intent to do away with the oath as that intolerable burden, that relic of mediaevalism, that test imposed from without under the threat of immediate and terrible war, brought official British disapproval in a note sent by J. H. Thomas as the British Secretary of State for Dominion Affairs to "His Majesty's Government in the Irish Free State." Thomas had also heard, he wrote, that Ireland was not going to pay the land annuities in spite of "explicit undertakings" on this subject. What would Britain think, Dev replied, if Britain was expected to remit abroad a fourth of her tax reserve which in Ireland's case amounted to

£5,000,000, the sum due annually in land annuities? Thomas' reference to "explicit undertakings" regarding the payment non-plussed him, and he wrote that the Government of the Free State was not aware of any such undertaking. Thomas, for his part, could not understand the bewilderment his reference had caused. "On 12th February, 1923," he enlightened de Valera, "a Financial Agreement was signed on behalf of the British Government and on behalf of the Government of the Irish Free State." Further, his letter continued, "This undertaking was confirmed in the 'Heads of the Ultimate Financial Settlement' . . . 19th March, 1926. . . ."

De Valera was incredulous the morning he received this word, but set his aides to searching the archives of Government Buildings for corroboration. By late afternoon, a sheaf of battered pages was discovered partly typed, partly written in hand, interlined with corrections and substitutions, and bearing the date February 12, 1923. "Honestly, I never saw such a contract of any kind," the President exclaimed in the Dail as he waved the papers in front of Cosgrave. Therein the Irish Free State had agreed, through Cosgrave's representative, to collect the land annuities and to turn them over in full to Great Britain. The Cumann na Gaedheal Ministers had told the country in 1926 that they had made a great bargain in cancelling all indebtedness, a "big nought," de Valera parodied, but it was turning out that there had been five other noughts and in front of them a five. Being at the moment in correspondence with the British, he declined to discuss further what he termed "this thing of shreds and patches."

President de Valera was, as a matter of fact, initiating discussions on Anglo-Irish relations in general. He considered it his duty as the new President to invite to Dublin the British Secretary of State for Dominion Affairs in the interests of future neighbour-liness. The Fianna Fail Government was ready to negotiate trade treaties. In Dev's view, ties with England of an economic and geographic nature were inevitable and Thomas seemed to be a new kind of Dominions Secretary, being a leader of Labour. When Thomas arrived in Dublin to spend the day early in June, 1932, he was escorted at once to the President's office in Government Buildings, a dignified room, darkened by books which lined the walls. There was a marble fireplace with Doric columns and ornamented mantel, on top of which was a large clock, and in a corner stood a revolving globe of the world. Rising from his swivel armchair behind the panelled, mahogany desk, the President of the Irish Free State greeted the visitor from across the Irish Sea with a warm, firm handclasp. For all the immutability of historic facts, he had never conceded that the way to conciliation could not be found, some *modus vivendi*, and he proceeded to outline what he had in mind. Ireland would have to be reunited, and reunited as a Republic, but that need not mean the country would abandon all association with the Commonwealth. Though abolition of the oath he deemed to be entirely Ireland's own business, he acknowledged in regard to the annuities that Britain might have legitimate grounds for dispute.

Within a few days, he himself took the evening mail-boat at Thomas' invitation to repay the visit. Coming roundabout to the two points at immediate issue, de Valera said to Prime Minister Ramsay MacDonald that the oath could not be made mandatory by the Treaty which had been forced upon his people at the point of a gun. As for the land annuities, he would not honour the 1923 agreement because it had been arranged behind the backs of his people, and the express terms had been ratified neither by the Dail nor the British Parliament.

"Look," broke in Thomas, "there ought to be some Empire tribunal . . . to adjust this difference." Such an arbitration panel should, Thomas went on, be chosen from within the Commonwealth. But the dice, de Valera objected, would then be loaded against his country. Before leaving to catch the evening mail-boat, he consented nevertheless to send immediate word after consulting at home about the arbitration idea. Debate was pending on the Anglo-Irish situation in the House of Commons.

After conferring with his Executive Council in Dublin, he dispatched a confirmation of his position on the oath and the annuities. A tribunal to arbitrate the latter would have to be international in character. Fulminations resounded in Parliament against the new Irish intransigence, but Sir Stafford Cripps pointed out that the Statute of Westminster did indeed entitle Ireland to abolish the oath. Mere mention of the name de Valera re-aroused the ageing Lloyd George. "Quite frankly," ejaculated the ex-Prime Minister, "I have never found anyone like him; he is perfectly unique." He banged his brief-case down in front of him. "I think the poor distracted world has a good right to be profoundly thankful that he is unique." The man had not, according to the Welsh Wizard, changed one iota since 1921. ". . . he will never change right to the end; he has always turned back to the past like a pillar of salt." Thomas, insisting that the Irish were repudiating the explicit undertakings on the annuities, proved himself as unyielding as de Valera and announced that Britain need not renew tariff preferences on the importation of Irish goods.

So ominous a shift in economic prospects was reported at once in Dublin, but the news found the President for the moment personally preoccupied. His half-brother cabled that their seventy-six-year-old mother, for some time under the care of Dr. Katherine Daly, a physician of Irish antecedents and a friend, had died peacefully in her own home on the morning of June 12, 1932. Father Wheelwright had arrived in time to administer the last rites of the Church to his mother, and the Irish Minister in Washington represented her older son when she was buried beside her husband in the small plot in the unwooded, new section of Rochester's Cemetery of the Holy Sepulchre. Under the name of Wheelwright engraved in the polished granite of the double headstone were put the dates of her birth and death, and her other name of "de Valera," with the one word "Mother." To her two "beloved sons," Eamon and Thomas, her will bequeathed equal shares in the small house that had been her home and the sum of $500.

In Ireland, the President, solaced by the family's pervasive reliance upon the will of God, hid his bereavement underneath an accumulation of official obligations. The British imposed the threatened duties on imports from Ireland when the Irish Government put the land annuities into a suspense account in Dublin. No time was lost by the *Oireachtas* in passing retaliatory legislation levying duties on British goods, and sharply trade between the two countries declined. Economic war, though not declared by either side, commenced. De Valera with official sanguinity asserted that, if the Irish people would make a virtue of the necessity, the Sinn Fein ideal of self-sufficiency could at last be realized.

Senator Gogarty, scornful of the privation and denials which self-sufficiency entailed, ridiculed the President for his economic theories as a sixpenny Savanarola in a world of Woolworths, and said that never in his life had he heard such ideas—"a voice from a mathematical madhouse, from some algebraical world of minus values where everything is upside down and all the quantities are negatives." Gogarty asked if self-sufficiency would make it necessary to extradite the potato which Raleigh had introduced to Ireland? Was smoking going to be taxed as a foreign game? As far as tea was concerned, were Lipton and Assam to be considered sources of national humiliation? Goods customarily imported from England became scarce and prices climbed for the substitutes manufactured at home. The market for Irish farm produce in England shrank to nothing.

Resistance to the Fianna Fail regime grew because of the economic war. It had never been Dev's intention that the farmers should keep the annuities themselves, and their talk of this roused his impatience. The Government needed the money to pay subsidies and the dole. The attitude of those in the Farmers Party was deprecated as something formulated on the beam of a plough, but in a gesture of compromise to them he reduced the amounts they owed on their lands. In the stringent budget which MacEntee introduced the income-tax was raised and levies were imposed upon all the things that Fianna Fail, with its streak of puritanism, deemed least essential to the public welfare like racing, betting, gramophone records, tobacco, foreign magazines.

The opposition made fun of the President's theory of an Irish-Ireland as exemplified by his recommendation that coal, which had to be imported, be replaced: "You can get quite nice and warm with turf, too." Jeers arose from the Cumann na Gaedheal benches: "Get back to the bogs." He was mocked, too, for advocating the hair shirt. Unabashed, he picked up the taunt. All right, he retorted sarcastically: "That is the policy that is going to reduce us to the hair shirt and *bainin*. If we did come in here in *bainini*, we would not be a bit colder than we are and we might look just as well." When an acquaintance complained because it was no longer possible to afford a holiday or keep a car, Dev informed him that there were people without their daily bread and without fires to warm their homes. He gave up the chauffeur assigned to the Presidential Office and cut in half the allotment for official entertaining.

Though he and his wife had never embarked upon a social round as part of their obligations, they felt the pinch. "I had, myself, been living comfortably on a much smaller salary," he said. "I found it was quite a different thing when I took office.

I saw my expenses increase." Nevertheless, he cut his own salary from £2,500 to £1,500 when he reduced all Ministerial salaries. "I thought," he said in retrospect, "that we could . . . bring down the scales in the Civil Service. . . ." But pay reductions for civil servants, teachers and police evoked concerted political resistance. In politics as in military tactics, there was a point beyond which people could not be pushed.

The annual sum of £28,000 required to maintain the Governor-General was, for Dev, being spent on a "useless office." He blamed the Governor-General for creating a new kind of court life at Phoenix Park, and silk hats symbolized all that Fianna Fail detested in public deportment. The first change de Valera made in this quarter was to transfer some of the Governor-General's functions to the Executive Council, and then he replaced MacNeill with an inconspicuous Fianna Fail man, Donal Buckley, the proprietor of a Maynooth shop. Buckley, entitled to draw a £10,000 salary, took only £2,000, did not move into the Viceregal lodge, and declined all social invitations, so that he was compared by one wit to the Dalai Lama, confined to his holy city and allowed to see nobody but his monks.

To keep his hard-pressed electorate aware of the reasons for the economic war and for their resultant hardships, the President undertook a summer speaking-tour, in the course of which he joined thousands of devout pilgrims to celebrate the fifteen-hundredth anniversary of St. Patrick. With one of his younger sons he left Limerick in a car at midnight, and after driving over wet roads running between the stone walls of Connemara and around black-faced lakes, they entered County Mayo before daylight. It was raining, but for two hours father and son climbed the grey, cone-shaped mountain in a file with the other silent, hard-breathing pilgrims, up slopes of loose stones and scree amidst the matted heather on the holy mountain—Croagh Patrick. The rain sifted down heavily as the boy pushed ahead with his father following, and they were soaked when they reached the summit. Through sheer curtains of rain lay Clew Bay, dark islands mottling the pale water far below. De Valera's identity in his trench-coat tightly belted, his black felt hat pulled down, was discovered and the crowds escorted him to the chapel so he might serve at one of the Masses in progress.

As he moved about the country on his tour, Dev picked up

rumours that the Republican extremists were growing, that their friends and their enemies both were coalescing. In the summer of 1932, the Irish Republican Army seized the deserted Donamore Castle, stocked it with supplies, and sent in a contingent of recruits for manœuvres. Ryan, the Clare Republican, and one of the Gilmore brothers, being caught in a gun battle with the police, had to be arrested, this time under de Valera's regime. The danger from secret organizations continued, the President said, because certain individuals were still operating outside the Government. It was only a matter of time, he argued, till the motives which held the I.R.A. together would vanish. The young people, and Dev counted especially upon his hold over them, would see that their rights could be achieved better through their elected representatives than through gunmen. Once the oath was gone, violence would cease.

A counter force to the I.R.A. announced its existence in the middle of August, calling itself the White Army or National Guard, and stating that it was going to protect persons from secret bodies and from communistic influences. Its members appeared in blue shirts and berets, suggesting that they were patterning themselves upon the shirt organizations in Germany and Italy, and as talk about them spread they were called the Blueshirts. Dev's old fear of internecine factions returned to haunt him when he realized that Ireland had two militant bodies, each ready to use the other as an excuse for its own activities.

Though his mind was far from free about internal affairs, he had to leave the country in the autumn of 1932 to attend the Council of the League of Nations in Switzerland. It was the turn of Ireland's representative to preside over the sessions, and immediately upon his arrival he had to take the chair amidst a company of expert international statesmen. The opening speech which the League Secretariat had prepared as was customary for the presiding officer was put aside by de Valera, and he chose his own words. Unless the delegates there assembled were ready to pledge the use of force against any violation of world peace, the very existence of the League, he predicted, was at stake. The delegates listened as they had not expected to listen to this gauche-looking man, this insular, black-suited messiah. His fearsome reputation as a revolutionary was belied by his measured logic, by his practical assessment of the future.

From his experiences in Geneva and from his impression that chaos was threatening the outside world, the need for internal harmony and for the re-unification of his own country pressed in upon him. His political hold, maintained only by Labour's co-operation with Fianna Fail, was so precarious that he could not lose as much as one deputy's vote. If he went to the people for a firmer basis of support he would be taking a long chance, but only by another election could he hasten the oath's demise, so far stalled by the *Seanad*. If that was dispensed with, he could expect the militant Republicans to join in his programme of peaceful emancipation. This, in turn, would deprive the White Army of its reason for existence. His Party had been in office less than one of its five allotted years when, at the beginning of 1933, he called a general election. At his rallies, he repeated his earlier promise to get rid of the oath and to withhold the annuities, and went farther to announce that he would do away with the Governor-General and would either abolish or revise the *Seanad*.

When it came to the key question of declaring a Republic, however, Dev said only that he would leave that to the Irish people. "I never had any special interest in forms of government as such," he made clear. "If they [the people] were free and if they chose to have a Monarch instead of a President, I for one would not attempt to interfere. . . . I do not care a *thraneen*." The majority in the six counties did not seem to him ready for a Republic, and Ireland in his estimation could afford to wait. No final settlement with Britain could be contemplated, even though the economic war might be won, until partition was solved. "You might as well talk of the freedom of the prow of a vessel, the stern of which [and he was referring to the North] is anchored to the shore." Though the general election took place in the throes of the economic struggle, it brought out a heavier vote than the year before and it proved to be a greater victory for him and for Fianna Fail. The Party was returned with five more seats than it had before, a total of 77, giving Dev a clear majority of one. Cumann na Gaedheal lost 9 seats, being returned in only 48. Labour got 8 seats, the Independents 9, and a new conservative group called the Centre Party won 11. De Valera, upon being re-named President, set to work to carry out his new and ex-panded mandate in the face of difficulties and dangers he had not exaggerated.

CHAPTER XIV

NEITHER RIGHT NOR LEFT BUT CENTRE
(1934–1938)

TWO unofficial armies were waiting to leap at each other as the month of August in 1934 approached with its triple anniversaries of the deaths of Griffith, Collins and O'Higgins, and President de Valera banned any parade. When the White Army's commander, Eoin O'Duffy, proclaiming that party politics had outlived their usefulness and advocating a corporative state like Mussolini's, refused to cancel plans for a mass demonstration, de Valera removed him as Police Commissioner of the Free State. Mulcahy then spoke out about the Blueshirts, daring the Government to prevent them from marching as their sacred duty to the dead. An alliance of sorts was in process between the Blueshirts and Cumann na Gaedheal, and Cumann na Gaedheal itself was amalgamating with the Centre Party to form the new United Ireland Party. With the rightist faction, combining in itself political and military elements, poised against its counterpart to the left, the Irish Republican Army, the President issued strict warning against the emergence of Irish fascists.

He was fearful that the Republican gunmen and the Blueshirts would start fresh blood flowing in the streets on the crucial memorial Sunday, August 20, 1934. So Government troops were ordered to take over all routes leading to the cenotaph of bronze and stone that stood on Leinster Lawn for the three who had died for the Treaty Government. "They were my comrades for longer than they were my opponents," Dev chided a visiting newsman who attempted to query him about his personal feelings. He meant that an outsider had to know the history of Irishmen to understand; that at one time or another they had all been together: "so our differences have the intimacy and emotional exaggeration of family differences." On the anniversary, no wreath was laid at the cenotaph and no sound of marching was heard in the alerted city of Dublin, but elsewhere farmers and their friends, lapping trench-coats over the blue of their shirts, mobilized in little squads and marched off to meetings held far and wide in spite of the Government's order.

President de Valera, noting the day's developments, concluded by nightfall that tolerance on his part had been mistaken for cowardice. The Blueshirts might use their force to set up in Ireland a dictatorship of the kind which he had seen on the Continent. Immediately available to him was only one recourse, inherited from his predecessor, the public safety legislation he had held in abeyance but had not abolished. His Ministers, meeting in the aftermath of the Blueshirts' defiance of them, agreed that their authority was in jeopardy and the public safety act was invoked, the Blueshirts banned. "We hate, I hate, anything that tastes of coercion," Dev remarked at the same time. "I hate it from the bottom of my heart."

The paradox of his using the coercive laws in the name of democracy could not escape him, but it was impossible to stand by and allow Irishmen to be offered up by O'Duffy and those he called the latter's *claque* on the altar of statism. In the Dail he read aloud from one Blueshirt leader's speech boasting that if a dictatorship was necessary in Ireland there would be one; that it would be better than their so-called democratic government run by foreigners and Jews. He put down the paper from which he was reading and lifted his eyes to the deputies across the house. "There is not, so far as I know, a single drop of Jewish blood in my veins." In disclaiming Jewish blood he did not want it to be interpreted as an attack upon the Jews, but as President he would not have his antecedents misrepresented. This sort of thing had happened to him before and with his words shaking on his lips he protested, "I say that I have been known to be Irish," his voice tightened, ". . . and that I have given everything in me to the Irish nation." The Dail's fears that the illegal movement was tainted with Hitlerism were strengthened by its racist innuendoes and the Government, kept aware by the Chief of the sinister movements he had observed on the Continent, introduced legislation to prevent the wearing of uniforms. With O'Duffy's downfall, Cosgrave assumed the active direction of the rightists' militant wing as well as of the United Ireland Party, and some degree of moderation was restored. The Blueshirts after 1934 declined but did not disappear.

De Valera waited, hopeful that there would be a commen-

surate falling off of I.R.A. activities and issued a public appeal,
". . . if the name 'I.R.A.' . . . has your respect, you should resent,
as we do, that it should be brought to disgrace by associating it
with either preparations for a factional war or with murder naked
and unashamed." I.R.A. leaders continued to abstain from all
contact with Dail Eireann though De Valera felt he had cleared
the way for them to enter. The necessary interval since the general
election had elapsed so that the oath had been constitutionally
abolished without the consent of the *Seanad*. Not only was this
imperial symbol gone but another token of inferiority, the right
of appeal from Ireland's Supreme Court to the Privy Council in
England, had been wiped off the books. The President had, in his
own language, worked to remove "these forms one by one so
that this state . . . may be a republic in fact and that when the time
comes the proclaiming of the republic may involve no more
ceremony than the formal confirmation of a status already
achieved." Listening for outright declaration of the republic,
the extremists heard the President say in 1934, "The time has not
yet come for a new proclamation restoring the Republic."

New resistance from the Republicans outside the Government
began, and Cosgrave was not slow to challenge the Government
for any suspected distinction in enforcing the public safety acts
between the Blueshirts and the I.R.A. It was charged that communism was infiltrating Republican ranks, that Dev himself was
communistic. Some decisive strategy against such a predicament
seemed on his part imperative and at the end of the year 1934
a messenger was sent to ask Sean Russell to come to Government
Buildings. Russell, delaying only to get the authorization of the
I.R.A.'s Executive Council, appeared the same afternoon at the
President's office. Of all the problems confronting the Government, Dev explained to him—the land annuities, the economic
war, the Blueshirts—only one appeared insoluble, the I.R.A.

"What do you suggest?" Russell parried.

"Firstly," Russell heard the President commence in didactic
tone, "the I.R.A. should hand up its arms to the Government."
But, Russell interrupted, had it not been on Dev's own order at
the close of the civil war that arms had been retained for the next
attempt to defend the Republic? "I admit," Russell heard the
President continue, "that I left you that legacy." He pleaded with
Russell to cease drilling and parading in the open with arms, but

when he got no response he sat back. "What have you to suggest?"

Russell scarcely hesitated. "Put the issue of the Republic before the people at the next general election and support it or declare the Republic within a reasonable time."

It was de Valera's turn to hesitate. "What do you consider a reasonable time?"

"Five years," Russell hazarded, "and in the meantime you need have no embarrassment so far as we are concerned. . . ." A republic for 26 out of the 32 counties was not Dev's intention, and he had no more way now than he had had before of making a republic effective in the six Northern counties. So Sean Russell was escorted out as secretly as he had come and Dev, concluding that the Republican Army would not co-operate, authorized his police to search out and arrest its leaders. "We have been disappointed," he had to confess in the Dail. "I frankly admit that we have not been met in the way we hoped to be met." No more would he tolerate a dictatorship of the left than a dictatorship of the right.

The arms-carrying Republicans, undeterred, took the occasion of Easter, 1935, to muster on the rain-swept hillside in the civil-war country where Liam Lynch had fallen to unveil a memorial to him as their special martyr. Other anniversaries were even more defiantly celebrated. When the I.R.A. announced that, contrary to Government policy, a Wolfe Tone demonstration would take place at Bodenstown in June 1936, President de Valera issued a proclamation declaring the I.R.A. an illegal organization, just as he had done in the case of the White Army. Maurice Twomey, Chief of Staff of the I.R.A., was summarily arrested. As had happened to the Blueshirts upon being banned, the I.R.A. seemed to drop from sight, but the roots of both organizations reached underground and the Government had to cast about for still more specific action.

The law to prohibit the wearing of uniforms introduced earlier had been approved by the Dail but rejected in the *Seanad*. The President, his temper shorter than on previous encounters with the senators, discounted them as "old fogies" flouting the will of the people which was represented by the majority in the lower house. The antagonisms of the young he could stand, he said, as having something generous about them, but the antagonisms of the old were burned into the bone. Already he had

tried to shorten the period of time the senate could delay legislation. "I discover now," he explained to the deputies, "that if
I were to . . . abolish the present *Seanad* we would have a larger
majority of support. . . ." He added, "I am beginning to discover
that I am more conservative than a large majority. . . ." He
confessed his own "hankering" for a consultative upper house
representing vocational groups perhaps or experts and public
administrators, and he asked for suggested schemes that would
not duplicate the Dail. When none was forthcoming, he decided
to recommend unicameralism temporarily. The vestigial chamber,
that last battalion of Ireland's old guard, those "spent forces,"
would have to go, and in 1936 the *Seanad* adjourned *sine die*,
observing proud punctilio to its reluctant end.

The President had other changes in mind too. That the Free
State had the power to abrogate the Treaty on the basis of the
Statute of Westminster, legal opinion in Britain as well as in
Ireland concurred. De Valera decided his country needed not
only to get rid of the Treaty but to adopt an entirely new constitution replete with ancient Irish liberties. In part, his view was
that of the political theorist; in part, that of the practising
politician. Late into the evenings at his home he laboured over
the draft, studying the constitution-writers of other countries:
Americans like Adams and Franklin; Frenchmen like Abbé
Sieyès and Condorcet; the British authorities like the third Earl
Grey. His wife attempted to keep in order all the papers upon his
desk in his Blackrock study. His eyes, suffering from the strain,
had to be protected by dark lenses and to read or write he wore
special glasses. In the mornings, he would carry with him on his
drive to Government Buildings his attaché-case full and he put
the manuscript in his top desk drawer where he could get
at it whenever there was a moment's opportunity. The new
Constitution was being written, he told the delegates at Fianna
Fail's *Ard Fheis* in the autumn of 1936, as if Britain were a million
miles away and it would contain no reference whatsoever to the
King. External association was still his formula.

While revision of the whole Constitution proceeded as rapidly
as possible, reforms that he felt could not wait were undertaken
as amendments to existing regulations. Irish nationality was one
of his most cherished concepts and he aimed to reduce it to
specific terms. When his proposals, cast in a form that would not

have to be changed if a Republic were declared, were eventually enacted by statute, Irish citizenship was established as distinct from British citizenship and from common citizenship. Though Britain interpreted the Dail's action as not depriving anyone of his status of British citizenship, de Valera announced that the term British subject no longer ran in Ireland. Irish citizenship became a fact. His own life-long dilemma was resolved.

His Party workers grasped at the news of the forthcoming Constitution as a means to re-inspire political confidence in the Government. The economic war had not been settled though the decline in Ireland's export trade was being partially offset by a drop in imports, and the country was beginning to manufacture its own boots, clothing, textiles, jams, stationery, shirts and other commodities. Due to a coal-cattle pact whereby Ireland exchanged tariff preferences on coal shipped from England for preferences given by Britain on Irish cattle shipped into England, conditions were easing slightly, but Irish farmers, the ones most acutely affected by the economic war, were being encouraged by Cosgrave in their determination not to pay the annuities at all, not even to the Irish Government. The President continued to preach self-sufficiency and by 1936 he claimed that the goal was in sight.

Fianna Fail did not achieve its results without continual partisan battles and political attrition. Verbal assaults from the deputies of the United Ireland Party raged round the President's ears. He was called a political centipede, a will-o'-the-wisp skipping from tussock to tussock in the bog. Remaining at the forefront of his Ministers on the Government bench, he would try to reply, his voice uneven with anger, sitting down at times to cover his face with one hand held at his forehead. Thomas O'Higgins, pointing a finger across the Dail, did not hesitate to impute to Dev the murder of his brother, Kevin. Other charges were levelled at him for the methods used to finance the *Irish Press* of which he was controlling director, a "kept" paper it was called. The fact that a number of Americans had transferred their interest in the Republican bonds to him for his journal was known, and when he insisted that the bondholders be repaid by the Government his motives were termed ulterior. "The Irish people know full well," he retorted, "that I personally never got one penny out of anything I did as far as Ireland was concerned." Nor did his son Vivion, who became a director, receive any money from the newspaper. There never had been any expectation, Cosgrave's supporters went on, that the money should be repaid to the bondholders. Not to be deflected, Dev held out that the original pledges must be repaid, that no one was going to prevent the *Irish Press* from getting what was legally due in the process, and in his complicated financial scheme he won. He now had a newspaper in daily circulation to serve as Fianna Fail's mouthpiece.

Since he had become President, the de Valeras had moved to the other side of Cross Avenue, into a large, ornate villa behind a high wall with its own oval-shaped drive around formal grounds. At the gate of "Bellevue," as the house was called, a sentinel stood guard. Mrs. de Valera kept up her interest in the Irish language by writing children's stories and plays. Though her husband was carrying on the language revival which his predecessor had launched, making Irish compulsory in all schools and requiring it for the civil service, still it did not gain ground as he and she had once hoped. At a gathering in Parnell Square, she welcomed home Dublin boys and girls from a summer they had spent learning Irish in Connemara. It was the voices of children, she told them in her own fluent Irish, that had brought St. Patrick back to Ireland, and the voices of children should spread the language throughout the country.

"Bellevue" was a family home where the father found a chance to be a family man among his sons and daughters, and it was for him tangible proof that an Irish-speaking, Irish-thinking way of life was possible. Vivion was studying law at the National University, keenly interested in debating and in politics from a childhood spent in the shadow of them. Mairin, no less a student in her steel-rimmed glasses than her brothers, was outstanding in botany at the National University where she was to win a travelling fellowship for the Continent. Eamon was taking honours in his medical training. Emer, Terry and Ruairi were still in their teens.

Brian, the third son, a dark, handsome young man of twenty-one, had finished his work like his older brothers at Blackrock College and was in his second year at the National University, where he was considered brilliant in mathematics. He rode sometimes with the North Kildare Hunt or with the Bray Harriers and on a February afternoon in 1936 he and his cousin, a young

dentist, Laurence Flanagan, were on horseback in Phoenix Park,
following the bridle paths between the bare gardens and round
the winter-stripped trees. Near the reviewing ground called the
Fifteen Acres, Brian's mount bolted under a low-branching tree,
sheering him out of the saddle. He lay on the ground, the left side
of his face bruised and a lump swelling on his temple until his
cousin found him. Taken first to Mater Misericordiae Hospital, he
was discovered to have a serious head injury and word was sent
to his father. The boy was moved to a private nursing home and
attended by two of Dublin's best surgeons, but died before
evening.

Vivion, in Birmingham, England, for a university debate,
hastened home and two days later the stricken parents knelt with
their other children for the Requiem Mass in the family church
in Booterstown. At Glasnevin, as snow fell into the newly
opened grave, the father stood hatless, the upturned collar of his
black coat protecting a face creased with agony. His umbrella
remained furled in his hand, the stick of it supporting him,
though Vivion stood on one side and Eamon on the other. The
mother, both sisters, all the brothers, the cousins, and dignitaries
of the Church and the State stood silent behind President de
Valera's dark figure, bent by emotion which he could not conceal
as the coffin was lowered.

It was only a few weeks later that de Valera left for Switzerland, this time not for the League of Nations but to enter the
clinic at Zurich as a patient. Dr. Alfred Vogt, professor of
ophthalmology at the University of Zurich, performed an operation the nature of which was not announced, but it was said in
Ireland that a cataract had to be removed from the left eye. Early
in the spring, Dev returned wearing dark glasses and in the Dail
a special light was fixed over his seat.

As he felt from his European contacts that international strife
was moving steadily closer, de Valera tried to concentrate upon
Ireland's best course. "Today, before the mangled bodies of the
youth of this Continent have been mercifully assimilated with the
clay," he entreated the League delegates in Geneva, in words
reminiscent of *The Hound of Heaven* by Francis Thompson whose
poetry had entered into another dark hour of his career, the
period spent in Belfast Jail, "before the anguished hearts of
countless mothers have even got a respite, we are awaiting the

result of an eleventh-hour attempt to postpone the opening of a conflict which may set the peoples of this world to mutilating and destroying each other again. . . ." With the idea of strengthening collective security, he voted to bring the Soviet Union into the League even though he represented, as he put it, a country where the religious beliefs were poles apart. Acting as his own Minister of External Affairs and adhering to his long-standing thesis of neutrality, he decided to adopt for Ireland the policy of non-intervention in regard to Spain and everywhere else, though he was under pressure from the right to recognize Franco's Government. That war was in the making on the Continent between fascism and communism, he became convinced. He detested communism but declared that fascism, if not equally bad, was bad, and whenever there was an opportunity at the meetings of the League of Nations, he raised his voice against both heretical ideologies. The delegates of other small nations were sought out by him because their problems were like his own—Belgium, the Netherlands, the small countries of Northern Europe. Only the big states would have the heavy armament to back up action, he surmised; the lesser powers would have no say.

The idea of peace which had dominated international counsels since the last war was, he began to fear, being subverted by a return to the old balance of power. By June 1936 he spoke of the possibility of Ireland's withdrawing from the League. The League had not prevented Japan from entering China; it had not brought Paraguay and Bolivia to a solution of their conflict; and Ethiopia, a country whose status had been solemnly guaranteed by some fifty other states, had lost its independence. The League's imposition of economic sanctions upon Italy for her actions against Ethiopia he had approved, but when nothing was done to enforce the sanctions, he concurred in removing them with a cynical dispassionateness, ". . . we must abandon the victim to his fate. . . ." During the session of the Dail that month, he was asked whether he believed in regional pacts as a substitute for the League of Nations. "Well, I do not know that there is any substitute in that direction. . . . I do not think anything is going to save us in the immediate future from another war of some kind or another." A commonwealth of Europe offered more hope in his eyes than the League.

So sure was he that hostilities lay ahead that he spelled out for

his own country the policy of neutrality. Ireland's position in the
Atlantic Ocean made her a logical springboard from which Great
Britain might be attacked by hostile forces. "The factor in the
whole situation that has to be borne in mind is that in their own
interest they [the British] would be prepared to put their forces
in the field so to speak, to prevent such an attack from being
successful." In the event of war, he indicated tentatively, Ireland
would communicate with Great Britain to see how British
assistance could be incorporated with Irish defence arrangements. British protection he took for granted, the one condition
to Ireland's war-time co-operation being the establishment of
friendly relations between the two countries. This, however, was
something which could never be so long as the British Navy was
in occupation of Irish harbours. "We want," he declared, "to
have our own country for ourselves."

Overt enmity between the two countries was actually diminishing. The President himself moved that sympathy be trans-
mitted to the royal family when King George V died in 1936, but
when plans for the coronation of King Edward VIII were undertaken, he eschewed any idea of attending. Apart from any other
reason for refusing, he was at that time—the autumn of 1936—
too.busy working on the new Constitution which he had promised at his Party's *Ard Fheis* to replace the document which he
considered had been forced down the country's throat at the time
of the Treaty election.

Events happened to prevent de Valera from choosing his own
time in regard to promulgating his Constitutional reforms, and
they happened in Britain, not at home. In December 1936 he
received from London, as did all dominion Governments, a
signed and witnessed instrument of abdication from King
Edward VIII. The matter of succession to the throne, according
to the Statute of Westminster, required the assent of the dominions. Many in Ireland saw an opportunity for the Government
to declare a Republic. De Valera summoned the deputies into
emergency session by telegram, for Edward would continue to be
King in Ireland until his abdication was accepted, and they arrived
at Leinster House breathless and confused. The Ministers had
worked throughout the preceding night to prepare for the
deputies' action two measures. The first was an amendment to
the old Constitution which would remove from it the King and

all the King's functions internal or external, and the King's representative, the Governor-General. This was exactly what Dev had told the *Ard Fheis* would be done in the new Constitution, though he had not yet finished drafting that document. By invoking the closure rule on debate, the Government secured the passage of the Constitutional amendment on the evening of the same day it was introduced, Labour lending its usual support. No nook or corner was left, the President gave his word, where Edward VIII or his disembodied spirit could hover.

The next day, December 12, 1936, de Valera pushed for equally expeditious action on his second measure, called the Executive Authority Bill. This was a statute, not a Constitutional amendment, recognizing George VI as successor to Edward VIII and authorizing him to act for Ireland in external affairs. The President and his aides were conscious that Republicans would not like this but they had framed it deliberately as the best hope of securing a united Ireland. The North was yet to be won over and the North had to be won, not dragooned. There was no intention on Dev's part of declaring a truncated republic for twenty-six counties only. The King was being retained as the symbol of co-operation with the other states of the British Commonwealth, the co-operation which might meet the sentiment of the North, but no power over Ireland's internal affairs was to be granted to the King, who would act on the advice of the Irish Government for the purpose of appointing the diplomatic and consular representatives and for concluding international agreements.

In the short, chaotic debate that ensued with humourless jests about a royal republic, the President was branded by the political opposition as a shifty politician and a slick opportunist. Why did he not come right out and declare a Republic rather than put over "zebra" legislation? He was clinging to the tow-rope with one hand and waving the Republican flag with the other. Ireland in the Commonwealth would be like a flea on the back of a dog. The Irish would be Republicans in the bog and imperialists in Piccadilly. To Dev, wearier than the rest with intensive preparation as well as with relentless effort on the floor, neither term—republic nor dominion—seemed wholly accurate though both were partially true. The ultimate objective of satisfying the aspirations of North and South could not be reached in "doctrinaire fashion." His way out was not by means of dogma but by means of compromise. "If we want, the day after this bill is passed, to repeal this bill or to declare a republic . . . we can. . . ." Late in the evening, Fianna Fail with the help of Labour secured the passage of the measure. After a decade and a half of patience compounded by defeat, the President at last saw external association come into full realization. Just as the Statute of Westminster had facilitated his unilateral action with regard to the oath, just so did the abdication suddenly permit Ireland to recognize the new King on Ireland's own terms. For all the adversity that had confronted him at home, the course of events in Britain had proved his greatest, if least expected, advantage.

Fair warning, the President felt, he had given to the Republicans in hiding in Kerry, Clare, Cork and Limerick at the time of the abdication that he was not going to decree a Republic in the Constitution he was completing. These young extremists would, he anticipated, write him off as an old "fogey" just the same. Suspicious as he was of their attitude, he was not entirely alien to them; he would not pretend to say whether they or he were wiser. "They, perhaps, have hopes beyond what our hopes are." *Bunreacht na hEireann* embodied most if not all of his early dreams and "this," he said as he picked up his finished draft of the Constitution, "is not the last."

For one year the drafting had been his preoccupation, a year broken by his son's death, by fear for his own eyesight, by threats against the peace at home and abroad. Not one but twenty years were in reality represented in the document, he let it be known, decades of personal participation in the fight for freedom. In these years he had grown from a young revolutionary priding himself upon his radicalness into the practical administrator insisting upon his conservatism. At the age of fifty-five, he had behind him a wealth of reading and study on which to draw. Experts and advisers from his own departments had been consulted—lawyers, economists and Churchmen. From the old Constitution, which he regarded as a product of contingency and the outgrowth of turmoil, little was carried over, but the charters of other nations, big and small, had been at his finger-tips. Much of it he had written himself, steering away from parliamentary draftsmen because he wanted the language to be simple like that of every day. For him, the document was the labour of a lifetime of love.

When he walked into Dail Eireann at the beginning of May

1937, he carried in his hand the full draft of *Bunreacht na hEireann.* The deputies perceived from the copies placed before them that the Irish Free State was to be no more; that a new name was to be given to their country—Eire, the Irish word for Ireland. Eire was to be used when speaking Irish and Ireland when speaking English. Eire the nation meant the whole island as distinguished from Eire the state, by which was meant the government.

The laws of the state would be applied only to the twenty-six Southern counties until such time as the six counties returned to the fold, a compromise in jurisdiction Dev made because he hoped it would bring the Northerners back into political partnership. He did not hesitate to admit in his presentation of the *Bunreacht* that except for the North, he would have put in a flat, downright proclamation of the Republic. No mention of the King appeared but association by statute with any group of nations was authorized for the purposes of external relations. This was the sequel to the External Relations Act of the preceding December which had already recognized the King for purposes of such association.

The deputies paid him half attention, drifting in and out of their seats while he pressed the case for the Constitution. He had tried to make it broad enough to transcend partisan opposition from Fine Gael, as Cosgrave's Party was now called, and sought from the deputies a vote of approval that would be unanimous. It would still have to be submitted to the people for final adoption. Dev did not let himself be pushed into saying whether Eire was in or out of the British Commonwealth.

Cosgrave's followers in the Fine Gael Party like Richard Mulcahy, Patrick McGilligan, John Costello and James M. Dillon, son of the old nationalist, attacked the clauses dealing with internal affairs as well as those concerning external relations. The working head of the State was no longer to be called the President but Prime Minister, or in Irish *An Taoiseach*, and Dev spoke about the necessity of having "a really strong Executive," touching off charges that he was seeking dictatorial powers, that he was carrying a copy of Machiavelli in his pocket, that he was putting the Dail through tricks-o'-the-loop. Dictatorship was a word calculated to strike alarm in the year 1937, and he called attention to provisions setting checks and limits upon the arbitrary exercise of power. "It is a terrible mistake to suggest that because the head of the Government selects the team . . . his colleagues are only 'yes-men'."

The titular executive under the new Constitution would not be the Governor-General but the President or *An Uachtaran* chosen for a seven-year term by the people themselves. As an experienced individual he could give the man "in the turmoil the view that the hurler on the ditch can get of the game looking at it from the point of view of the national interest." The President was to act for the most part upon the advice of the working executive, the Prime Minister. Suspicions that he was creating the new Presidential post with extraordinary powers for himself ran round the benches; when men sought to make a mighty fire, it was whispered, they began with small straws. The accused replied indignantly that it was not he but the people whom he had fought that were heading toward dictatorship. "We fought against that dictatorship," he said. This section of the Constitution did not pass until Dev made it clear that he had no desire to move up to any nominal headship himself; that there was still too much for him to do on the firing line.

In further disproof of any designs to build up arbitrary executive power, the *Bunreacht* restored two legislative houses. As before, the *Seanad* was to contain sixty members, but their powers were more limited and they were to be chosen on the basis of vocational representation to secure vertical lines rather than the horizontal division between capital and labour. This idea he traced back for the deputies to the functional groupings described in Pope Leo XIII's encyclical, *Rerum Novarum*, and Pope Pius XI's *Quadragesimo Anno*. The deputies felt as if they were in a classroom and the professor was conducting a class.

Into that part of the Constitution entitled Directive Principles of Social Policy, a phrase taken almost verbatim from *Quadragesimo Anno*, Dev had put his heart as well as his mind. The family was proclaimed as the fundamental unit of society and no law was to be enacted providing for the dissolution of marriage. In drawing upon his own concept of social policy, implicit not only in this section but throughout the Constitution, he stressed what his Government had already done in furthering health insurance, unemployment assistance, pensions, public housing. He held that the Government had an obligation to the weaker parts of the community, "just as good parents would naturally lean towards

members of the family...." For the resentment against
tutional references to women evoked from the women
...s, many of them prominent among Dev's own early
...rs, he was not prepared. They felt that any discrimination
result in their not getting jobs, but he argued that women
were not fitted for all kinds of work, not for the Army certainly
and not, he hazarded at random, for stoking a trans-Atlantic liner,
work which he knew something about. In his own home he had
seen the sacrifices his wife had made in a teaching career to give
their children first consideration, and he was determined to give
protection to mothers and to pay tribute where he felt tribute due.
"I do not mind," he declared with unsmiling humour, "being
a whole burnt-offering for that."

Fuel was added to the controversy over the Constitution by
its clauses setting up censorship of the Press, radio and films. The
campaign against "evil literature" had, however, been commenced under Cosgrave and a whole register of books was
banned including works by Huxley, Hemingway, Sinclair Lewis,
Faulkner, and by Ireland's own authors like Liam O'Flaherty,
Sean O'Faolain, Sean O'Casey. With the Abbey Theatre forbidden to take O'Casey's *Plough and the Stars* or Synge's *Playboy of
the Western World* on its tour to the United States, William B.
Yeats went to the President to demand that politics and aesthetics
be kept separate. The two men differed diametrically, but Yeats,
who had previously spoken his mind about his fellow-countryman
in the old days in New York, acknowledged that he was surprised
and disarmed by the other's personal simplicity and honesty.

The Roman Catholic Church itself was named in the Constitution as the faith of the great majority though religious freedom
was at the same time guaranteed. Dev had seen religious perse-
cution at first hand in the North and wanted to guard against it,
while at the same time according to religion a unique place: "As
Voltaire or some other Frenchman said, it would be necessary to
invent God if it was thought that He did not exist." The whole
purpose of government in de Valera's mind was the Thomistic
one of common good. Democracy had been brought to its
breaking point, he felt, in Britain and elsewhere by nineteenth-
century liberalism, and personal liberties now had to be balanced
by social regulation. Not only by such provisions as the censorship was personal liberty restricted. Legislation giving the

Government arbitrary powers in case of emergency received Constitutional authorization. The President, since assuming the responsibility for preserving order, had come to see the indispensability of public safety acts.

Impatience grew upon him as the Dail debated late into the spring of 1937. "The only thing that irritates me is the clock," he insisted. Conditions on the continent of Europe left Ireland little time to fortify herself. The restiveness of the dissident Republicans increased. In the Dail, Dev remained on guard, his features set in determined repose, his eyes cast down at his feet, no glee manifesting itself as each article was introduced, minor revisions accepted, and finally accorded endorsement by a majority of the deputies. At once he dissolved the legislature and called the general election and plebiscite for which he had been waiting. New hopes rose within him that his work would, in spite of the Dail, get overwhelming popular ratification.

Outside the Dail, the document was assailed not only by Cosgrave's Fine Gaelers but by the Republicans, who derided it as a new-fangled Free State charter and advocated that the election be boycotted. The mass of the people were unable to follow the technical minutiae and looked in vain for solution of the things that worried them most like partition, the quarrel over their ports, the high prices and the shortages. The farmers found in the draft no answer to the riddle of the land annuities and saw no end in sight for the trade war. The women remained sceptical. At the polls, there was no landslide for or against the new State of Eire. Only with the help of Labour did Dev himself manage to return to office. By a close margin of 686,042 to 528,196 votes, final approval was secured for the *Bunreacht* and Fianna Fail was returned with 69 seats, Fine Gael with 48, Labour with 13, and Independents with 8. Dev's majority fell slightly below what he had before this election and far short of what he had hoped to get, less for his own sake than for the Constitution. No one knew what attitude or action England might take at the supplanting of the old, Treaty-based Constitution.

CHAPTER XV

OUT OF THE TITANS' WAY (1938-1944)

OF his new title as *An Taoiseach* or Prime Minister, de Valera took scant notice when *Bunreacht na hEireann* went into effect at the start of 1938. What had been accomplished was of less interest than what remained, and his attention reverted to the hard core of unsolved disputes with Britain. If he could reunite the whole island under the flag of the new State of Eire, the Republicans might yet be reconciled.

So he began stopping in London on his trips to and from League of Nations' meetings in Geneva. Apart from his business of state, he liked to walk about the London streets, watching the people, pausing by the barrows of old books, picking up here and there treatises on Gaelic, on mathematics, or volumes written in French. At his London hotel room, he managed on occasion to get a glimpse of his daughter Mairin, now in her twenties, who was travelling in pursuit of her scientific studies. The Irish leader found in London unprecedented cordiality from the Secretary of State for Dominion Affairs, Malcolm MacDonald, and this sober-faced, unassuming young man seemed to welcome the opportunities for contact.

Mutual confidence was augmented when His Majesty's Government extended guarded recognition to Eire, announcing that the new Irish Constitution caused no fundamental alteration in the Irish position in the Commonwealth, although specifying that Eire had no rights over Northern Ireland. Small nations had only one hope, as Dev saw it, and that lay in neutrality. Russian might was an unknown quantity. Hitler had moved into the Rhineland and was turning greedy eyes on Austria. Now that Britain had recognized Eire's self-determined status in the *Bunreacht*, de Valera was ready to get on with a general settlement. A basis for co-operation was becoming, in fact, imperative to the security of both countries.

The quarrels outstanding with Britain centred around four things: partition, the ports, trade and finances. Harmony could be expected at home only if the Republicans saw partition ended, the ports restored, and the economic war stopped. Had he gone to London before external association was constitutionally authorized and recognized, his bargaining position would have been as vulnerable as Griffith's and Collins' in 1921 but now, for the first time, he could go as the represenattive of a "sovereign, independent, democratic state," as the Constitution expressed it. The chess-board looked to him ready for another move from the Dublin side.

Accordingly, Prime Minister de Valera sent a message to London. Formal negotiations were scheduled, and in January 1938 he crossed the Irish Sea with several of his Ministers. Restoration of Ireland's natural, sea-bound unity was his initial demand as he and Prime Minister Neville Chamberlain sat down together at Downing Street. Each met the other as a responsible executive having separate and distinct problems of his own, but each was thinking in terms of the common danger confronting them. A plebiscite would, de Valera told Chamberlain, show that only Belfast and its immediate environs favoured partition. Force, he gave his word, was not contemplated on his part, but the jagged frontier between North and South was several hundred miles long, and gerrymandering was an outrage upon his Motherland. His own formula for solving partition he then re-stated: one, All-Ireland Parliament with the jurisdiction over local matters devolving, if the people up there so desired, upon a separate Northern assembly.

Britain, Chamberlain replied, would be glad to see the border removed, provided only Ulster would consent. The earnest but harried British Prime Minister was conciliatory in manner but insistent that the disagreement lay between the Governments of Northern and of Southern Ireland. Lord Craigavon, as Sir James Craig had for some time been entitled, was in London keeping the British Cabinet members closely advised of the North's unwillingness to alter the *status quo*. De Valera continued to urge Chamberlain to use his influence with the North where oppression of the Catholic minority was of current concern to him. Irish Catholics had never oppressed others, he reiterated, citing from Lecky and other historians the sanctuary Ireland had given to Huguenots, Jews, Quakers and Wesleyans. Protestantism and Catholicism alone would not, in his view, keep North and South apart; religion was being made the cloak for shabby, political motives. The politicians of Northern Ireland, he was forced finally to conclude, would not let Britain withdraw, and in trying to describe London's own predicament when he returned temporarily to Dublin, he spoke of Humpty Dumpty: ". . . if you knock the egg off the wall, the fact that you yourself are the person that knocked it off is not going to make it any the easier to put it together again." What the British had done they might not now be able to undo. Over Radio Eireann on St. Patrick's Day, 1938, he acknowledged that he had been unable to get a settlement on the first of the four issues under negotiation—partition.

Back at the table in Downing Street, the next demand he presented was that the Royal Navy evacuate the ports of Berehaven, Cobh (formerly Queenstown) and Lough Swilly. The Government of Eire was prepared, in return, to deny any foreign power use of Irish domain as the base for an attack upon Britain if the ports were evacuated. But so long as they were occupied, Ireland might be drawn into any outbreak of international violence. She could neither assume responsibility for her own defence nor expect to be regarded as neutral by hostile powers. Chamberlain, even more conscious of Hitler's lengthening shadow, decided that the chances of having a friendly Ireland at his back would improve if he acceded to Ireland's demand for her ports. Lord Halifax as Secretary of State for Foreign Affairs consented and so did the British Chiefs of Staff. Circumstances alone, de Valera owned, won him this major point; England's danger was actually proving Ireland's opportunity.

Churchill, not a member of the Government and unheeded, did not agree with the return of the ports. "In a war against an enemy possessing a numerous and powerful fleet of submarines," he protested, "these are the essential bases." Threats to British security were accelerating—Hitler's imprecations in the Reichstag, pressures from Italy—and to many observers English appeasement seemed to be in full motion. De Valera himself might mean no harm to Britain, Churchill admitted, but de Valera would not be able to hold in check the dark forces of the Republican underground, "a whole organization of secret men bound together." By withholding future access to the Irish ports, de Valera might in case of hostilities bludgeon Britain into giving up partition. Chamberlain had, in Churchill's summation, put his head into a noose because if the British should violate Irish neutrality in time of war, it would put them out of court in the judgment of the world.

The Chamberlain Government, nevertheless, promised to evacuate the ports and other questions between England and Ireland were thereupon quickly resolved. The Irish negotiators agreed to pay Britain £10,000,000 to wipe out the sum of £98,000,000 for which Britain held them responsible. This meant that Britain gave up all demand for the land annuities. ". . . these land annuities," Churchill again objected, ". . . were the purchase price by which a peasant proprietor . . . was established on Irish soil." Dev claimed that the real indebtedness was the other way round, but concluded it was in the public interest to compromise and facilitate agreement in regard to trade, in order to stop the "economic blizzard," whereupon Britain agreed to drop the penal tariffs imposed on Irish imports, and in return Ireland lowered her import barriers.

The Agreements were ready for signing late in April 1938, and de Valera arrived for the ceremony at the Prime Minister's residence, his face composed, almost relaxed, his hands plunged into the pockets of his long coat. With the formalities around the Cabinet table completed, Chamberlain rose and handed to his guest a pair of battered, old-style field-glasses, explaining that he had received them from a former officer in His Majesty's forces named E. J. Hitzen, now a biscuit manufacturer in Leamington. At a glance, Dev saw that they were the binoculars he had carried through the Easter rising until he had had to surrender them to his captor that April Sunday twenty-two years before. Into his mind's eye flashed the picture of the quiet-spoken young captain who, in 1916, even in the hour of battle, had spoken to him in comradely terms. Before packing for the night mail-train, he sat down, took a sheet of hotel stationery, and in his meticulous and graceful script, wrote:

Dear Captain Hitzen,

I have just received from Mr. Chamberlain the field-glasses which I surrendered to you twenty-two years ago. I am very pleased indeed to have them back and I want to express to you my appreciation of your kind thought in sending them to your Prime Minister for presentation to me on this occasion.

I am glad to note that you have come safely through the
Great War and I wish you many years of health and happiness.

Sincerely yours,

(signed) Eamon de Valera.

The friendship between Englishman and Irishman that had been
his dream was, it seemed, coming true.

The Anglo-Irish Agreements impressed the Irish people in
a way that the Constitution had failed to do. Only from deep
down in the country were there Republican rumblings about
betrayal of the Northern nationalists. Freely Dev admitted that
the North still worried him and promised to work to pluck out
the single thorn remaining in Eire's side. Dail Eireann, like the
British Parliament, quickly tendered its approval of the Agreements. Basking in the afterglow, the Fianna Fail Party looked for
the chance to hold a general election to secure a clear majority for
the Government. "The hay is ripe," *An Taoiseach* put it. "Let us
save it while we have the opportunity." For a year he had had to
depend upon deputies outside his own Party with not a single
vote to spare in carrying the house. Sometime earlier he had
declined to stand for re-election to the Northern parliament
which had abolished proportional representation, the minority's
chief protection. Stormont was also requiring oaths of loyalty.
In the South, the popularity of Fianna Fail soared with the end
of the five years' economic war.

The Chief appeared unusually sanguine for all the signs that
he was neither carefree nor young. In face and figure there was
no longer the leanness that used to make him seem more spectre
than flesh and blood. No more was he regarded as a revolutionary
leader but as a respectable statesman, almost as the conservative
he claimed himself to be. He stood at the political centre, not on
the left and not on the right.

He himself was reminded that spring of his roots in the old,
peace-bound nationalist movement when he was called down to
Bruree by the death of his aged uncle, Patrick Coll. Through this
uncle he had acquired his earliest political leanings, his first
schooling, and at the low-beamed labourer's cottage he had
received the strict rearing of a farm boy. The cottage on the
country road was still the home of his uncle's grown family and
it looked to him as it had in his youth with its open hearth at one

end. The older *An Taoiseach* grew, the more conscious he was of Bruree's influence upon him, and the more he spoke about his intimate associations with the "ordinary, plain people of the country." It was while he was in County Limerick for his uncle's funeral that a minor political crisis was precipitated in Dublin when his marginal Government was defeated on a technical question by one vote.

As soon as he got back to the capital, he seized this opening to dissolve the Dail and set a general election for June 1938. His son, Vivion, lawyer and ardent Fianna Fail advocate, took part as an election speaker, stressing the need for increased support so that his father could get on with national reconstruction and defence. Fianna Fail got its clear majority over the combined strength of the opposition parties: Fianna Fail, 77; Fine Gael, 45; Labour, 9; and Independents, 7. Bonfires were lighted upon the mountain-sides of County Fermanagh as near the border as possible, and the flames cast a glow of victory into Northern skies. This far and no farther could the celebration go but lettered in gold on the Parnell column in Dublin were the words, "No man has a right to say to his country this far shalt thou go and no further."

"Now," Prime Minister de Valera declared, "it is possible to pursue a steady path." On the heels of his electoral victory, he prepared for the gala installation of Ireland's first President under the *Bunreacht*. By common consent, the parties had joined in naming *An Craobhin* to the post. At the age of seventy-eight, Douglas Hyde still retained his political detachment, was still the enthusiastic Gaelicist, the embodiment of Ireland's spiritual emancipation. For Eamon and Sinead de Valera alike, he was a link with their past. On the morning of the inauguration, Dr. Hyde, a Protestant, attended religious service in St. Patrick's Cathedral, once Swift's own, while the Prime Minister with Sean T. O'Kelly, *An Tanaiste* or vice-Prime Minister, and the Cabinet Ministers took part in a votive Mass in the Pro-Cathedral. Religious tolerance was being made manifest for all the world to see. A distinguished company—Ireland's own—assembled at noon in Dublin Castle: diplomats, prelates in their robes, Lord Mayors wearing their chains of office and other regalia, judges in wigs and robes, University dignitaries in academic costume of scarlet, blue and green on lustrous black. With a military escort in full-dress uniform, the bent little old man, his eyes alight, his wide moustache twitching, arrived in tail-coat, striped trousers and a top hat. De Valera came wearing his black homburg and black sack suit with his Cabinet members in the same unvaried style of dress. As Dr. Hyde was led into the pillared St. Patrick's Hall amidst a flourish of trumpets, *An Taoiseach* rose from his chair on the dais to deliver the official salutation in Gaelic. Not a word was spoken in English throughout the inaugural ceremony.

This year of 1938 brought for Prime Minister de Valera a lifting of the clouds. The new Constitution was in effect. President Hyde was in the Viceregal lodge. External association was at last in operation, and in Neville Chamberlain he had an English statesman whom he deemed congenial. He himself possessed a clear majority in the Dail and could govern independently. "We have got here," he proclaimed, "a situation . . . beyond the hopes of many of us . . . the rest of the road can be travelled and . . . in our generation we will be able to see the completion of that work." As soon as he could get international opinion on his side, he gave his word, a Republic would be possible. "We have only to wait our time." The Republicans in jail—six in all—were set free. He could pursue peacefully the reunification of the nation if the extremists would give him the chance and if European troubles stayed below Ireland's horizon.

Europe, already an armed camp, was quaking beneath the weight of marching feet, and in Ireland Dev could not tolerate any disregard of his authority. Violence was not the way to internal unity, he stressed, because the territory of the North was not all that had to be won: the hearts of the Northerners were needed as well. External association, unpopular though it had proved with the Republicans, was not, he repeated, the last word. ". . . nobody is denying the right of anybody in this country to go out politically and say, 'We want the repeal of the External Relations Act.'" The reformist line was what he was resolved to pursue, not the revolutionary line, preferring as he grew older to balance what he described as the progressive force, always putting out its tentacles, and the conservative force, always trying to maintain what had been achieved. The only action he would initiate was pacific action, and during the months after his negotiations with Prime Minister Chamberlain he undertook extensive plans for an anti-partition crusade to America, including the acceptance of a White House invitation. At no other juncture in his life, he said, had he felt happier.

Then, at the end of April 1939, he walked through the swinging doors into Dail Eireann, took the few steps across the deep blue carpeting to his place and got the attention of the Ceann Comhairle. "Until yesterday," he said standing, his long fingers spreadeagled on the desk in front of him, "it was my intention to leave this week-end for the United States." His voice was low and level. "Certain grave events which . . . occurred yesterday have, however, changed the situation." Prime Minister Chamberlain, he had been informed, had a new military training plan which contemplated including conscripts from Northern Ireland. Churchill, though not in charge of British affairs, was insisting that England would before long need help whether from the North or from the South.

To the conscription proposal Belfast responded by offering to place all her resources at the disposition of Prime Minister Chamberlain. Sculptured into the high pediment of Stormont's great, granite parliament building was the figure of Ulster carrying the golden flame of loyalty to the Empire and Craigavon, making his last stand under the royal coat of arms emblazoned on the walls, took the occasion to rebuke de Valera for cowardice in the face of oncoming war.

The restraint which Dev had exercised during recent months toward Belfast was not producing the North-South *rapprochement* which he hoped thereby to induce. The tactics he had of late employed toward the Orangemen he described as the tactics of indifference like those in the old ballad which he and all the Volunteers had sung on their road marches about McGrath, the cattle-jobber, courting the coy Eileen:

> *He never seemed to see the girl at all,*
> *Though she looked at him from underneath her shawl.*

". . . the best way," he had thought, "to get them to go after you was to walk the other way," but he could not now allow Northern nationalists to be conscripted into a cause not of their choosing. Conscription if applied anywhere in Ireland would instantly undermine the neutrality policy which was Southern

Ireland's only hope for keeping out of world conflict. His mind flashed back to 1914 when he had led his company of Volunteers out of the hall in Donnybrook rather than take Irishmen into the British Army, and to the tense time in 1918 when once before he had helped fend off conscription. His Government notified the British Government, "We claim the whole of Ireland as national territory and conscription of Irishmen . . . we will regard as an act of aggression."

Prime Minister Chamberlain, hard pressed as he was to reinforce British defences, wanted above all to preserve the general policy of peace he thought he had implemented at Munich the preceding autumn. Solicitous of Irish sensibilities and protective of the accord he had established at the time of the Agreements, he dropped the conscription proposal for Northern Ireland regardless of Churchill's prognostications.

That crisis, though surmounted, roused in the Irish people a sense of dread. Previous signs of global war they had ignored but now they faced the fact that they, for the first time, might have to defend their own shores and skies. An Taoiseach and his Minister of Defence, Frank Aiken, going to inspect the ports which the British had evacuated, saw that the installations dated back to the Napoleonic era. Any belligerent could take them in the event of hostilities and Ireland had no navy and only a handful of soldiers. As Dev turned to the task of recruiting and arming Ireland, necessary though it was, some spark went out within him. He had to divert his eyes from his first and his final objective: a united, Irish-speaking, Christian island, St. Patrick's island, Parnell's island, the island nation he had seen first in incandescent phantasy from a Limerick farmyard, then through the white dust of Boland's Mills, and after that from many a fog-steeped prison cell. Whether the unity of the country would be achieved in his generation as he had predicted he began to wonder. His campaign against partition would have to wait, and he prayed God to give strength to their arms as He had given it to David's.

Sitting in his office in Government Buildings, resting his elbows on the arms of his swivel chair, his plain face reflective, he called his team of Ministers into conference about Ireland's defence needs. The opposition termed them a moth-eaten list. Most of them had, it was true, been together since 1916 or before; had been imprisoned either by the British or the Irish or by both;

had voted against the Treaty; and had taken up arms again only
to follow Dev finally into the Dail. "The members of this
Government," the Chief liked to point out, "are relatively young
men. I am the oldest." The insinuations made by the opposition
that they would go with him like sheep through a gap he vehem-
ently denied, insisting rather that they constituted a political
family bound by seven years in power together. Among them was
O'Kelly, short but imposing, particular about official amenities;
Ruttledge, the bluff Westerner who had served as Acting President; Lemass, a younger man, shrewd for all his hanging head
and pendulant features; Ryan, matter of fact and inconspicuous;
Aiken the Northerner, big and bulky of build, his black moustache
bristling on an expansive face, fierce to look at but soft to listen
to; Gerald Boland, sensitive, his impulses constrained by experience, his mouth a quizzical line; Derrig, square-faced, hair stiff
as a brush, the sight in his one good eye supplemented by dark-
rimmed glasses; Traynor, his face thickly fleshed, his features
heavy; MacEntee, piercing of eye, his hair a wavy pompadour,
his chin a wedge of determination.

The Chief, securing first their assent to a programme protecting Irish neutrality, crossed the country to his familiar stamping
ground in County Clare to issue a call to the Irish colours. When
he stepped on to the small, garish stage in the Gaiety Cinema in
Ennis, he saw a frozen-faced audience, the rows of seats in front
of him half filled, and looked in vain for his old Irish Republican
Army comrades. He commenced by saying that they must all
become stark realists, for the world was nearing the precipice.
"We must have unity." Behind an inarticulate reserve, the
audience shielded its doubts. The women were thinking, while
the Chief pleaded for all able-bodied men to join the national
army, of rebel sons or husbands or brothers on the run again, up
in hide-outs in the North or across in England biding their time.
The outlawed Republicans, instead of heeding his appeals, were
seizing upon England's difficulties as their next opportunity.

From undisclosed headquarters, the I.R.A. issued to Lord
Halifax, as Chamberlain's Secretary of State for Foreign Affairs,
an ultimatum of war against England, signed by Sean Russell and
others, unless, the statement read, the Crown agencies withdrew
from the North. De Valera was informed indirectly by Sean
McCaughey, Adjutant-General of the reconstituted I.R.A., that

the Republicans would, if the Dublin Government refrained from interfering with them, respect *An Taoiseach's* jurisdiction and commit no depredations against the South. The South, in other words, would be used merely as a base for the I.R.A.'s projected attack upon the North and upon England. To this de Valera deigned no reply and instead put through the *Oireachtas* two pieces of legislation so that the Government would have emergency powers in the event it needed them: a Treason Bill providing the death penalty, and an Offences Against the State Bill providing for internment.

The ricochet of bullets made itself heard again and outbursts of rabid oratory arose from street-corner rallies. Dubliners, meagre and hungry-looking in their coarse jackets shrunk by rain, were quick to congregate in O'Connell Street or in College Green, their eyes wide, brows arching up into their foreheads with the look of perpetual apprehension. There would be bars of shrill music in the distance, banners stamped with the red hand of Ulster as the anti-partition sign. In a cluster of speakers stood the tall bending figure of an old lady in black crêpe, her eyes deep and filled with a vision the crowd longed to share. This was Madame Maud Gonne MacBride, once the Abbey Theatre's Kathleen ni Houlihan, the woman whose beauty Yeats had apostrophized. Her life, as once her husband's and now her son's, belonged to the Republic. Secret responsibility for the *de facto* Republic which had been exercised by Mary MacSwiney was turned over by her to the executive of the I.R.A., and this body re-proclaimed itself as the only legitimate government of Ireland.

Soon after the I.R.A. ultimatum reached Lord Halifax, sporadic explosions broke out in England in hotels, in cathedrals, in railway terminals. One blast in the city of Coventry during the summer of 1939 ripped open the main street, killing and injuring afternoon shoppers. Disconcerting reports came from across the Atlantic as well. On the day the Canadian tour of the King and Queen took them to Windsor, Ontario, Sean Russell was apprehended by American authorities in Detroit, Michigan, just across the river, and travelling with him was the ageing Joseph McGarrity. Russell identified himself as the "head man" of the I.R.A. While denying that he had any designs on the life of the royal couple, he stated that England was the I.R.A.'s enemy. Dev he spoke as of too temperate and tolerant. After he was released on bond raised by the Clan-na-Gael pending his departure from the country, trace of Russell's whereabouts was lost.

The Irish deputies converged upon Dublin for an emergency session when hostilities actually commenced in Europe. All the dominions but not Eire at once joined the United Kingdom in declaring war against Germany. *An Taoiseach*, with the air of one who had foreseen and foretold all that was happening, took his place on the Government bench. One of the most terrible catastrophes in history lay ahead, he announced: ". . . it will ruin victor and vanquished both, and the settlements it will secure will be short-lived. The defeated will have to submit to the dictation of the conquerors, but sullenly and with the grim resolve to bide their time until they in turn can impose terms. . . . Hardly will the 'cease fire' have sounded when the conquering group will begin their own rivalries and in the new war that is set in train they may well be found on opposite sides." The deputies, uniting in a determination to stay out of war, as alarmed at their defencelessness as they had been indifferent over their isolation, promised to pool their thoughts and emotions. The faintest hint of taking England's part would, they knew, provoke an uprising from the Republican extremists. The Dail formally declared Eire's neutrality and proclaimed a state of national emergency to be in existence.

Dozens of Irish Republicans were soon being deported from England as that country took measures for her internal security, and the impact of their activities shifted home. Dublin authorities intercepted a letter addressed presumably to Sean Russell in America, signed merely "Busher." "Dear Sean . . . The war has changed the whole position here. . . . The lads are anxious to have you back as soon as possible; you will be needed here at once. Ask Clann to try and rush supplies." Regretfully Dev concluded that the war threw some back into the psychology of twenty-five years earlier, but that these were overlooking the changes that had since taken place, changes that had given Ireland a legitimate Government of her own, a Government whose prerogative was not to be usurped. The Fianna Fail Ministers found themselves in the grim position of having to outlaw the same resistance methods which they themselves had used, and of having to adopt the repressive methods which they themselves had abhorred. By bringing into operation at once the emergency measures on the books, the Government interned the deportees from England at Mountjoy and at Arbour Hill. One of them, after going without food for thirty days, was released under pressure from other politicial groups.

"What happened?" Dev postulated ruefully. "Next day a half-dozen more went on hunger strike," and by November 1939 four more were on the point of death from starvation. General sympathy stirred in their behalf and the Labour Party asked for clemency for them. Down in County Kerry the walls were lettered in whitewash, "Has Dev sold us out?" Two of the four he finally sent to a hospital, the other two home. At the same moment, efforts to get all the Republicans released on *habeas corpus* were being made by their attorney, Sean MacBride, on the grounds that the emergency legislation did not make it constitutional to intern without charge or trial. Justice Gavan Duffy, having listened to MacBride's argument that the Offences Against the State Act was repugnant to the Constitution, ordered that the prisoner whose case was before him be set free, and de Valera, in view of the High Court's ruling, released all the Republicans rather than risk holding them illegally. Not long after, a number of the released men, by commandeering motor lorries, seized a million rounds of ammunition from the Government's arsenal in Phoenix Park. Lest there be any doubt in the resulting uproar as to where Fianna Fail stood on the matter, de Valera delivered a denunciation of the I.R.A., "We all know that in the last year its activities have taken a new turn." Non-partisan support for whatever he might have to do to quell anarchy was what he wanted, and the Dail sat through the night to make the necessary changes in the emergency legislation so that the Government could exercise the power of internment without danger of reversal.

As the winter of the cold war ended, the Continent was crumbling piece by piece under the onrush of Hitler's divisions, and doubts that Prime Minister de Valera could keep Ireland neutral multiplied inside and outside the country. The Irish would have to fish or cut bait, President Roosevelt was writing confidentially to the American Minister in Dublin, David Gray. Not only was pressure being brought to bear upon Ireland from the American side but from another side as well. Edward Hempel, the German Minister in Dublin, called in person on *An Taoiseach* to find out whether he would welcome German help. Hitler was urging upon his naval leaders the suggestion that the war might be brought to an end if they made a landing in Ireland. Hempel got no response. De Valera, adding up the list of other small nations, realized that Norway had been overrun by Hitler, then Holland, then Belgium. The leaders of the countries now under occupation had been the very men he had sought out at Geneva, their problems being most similar to his own. "I should be unworthy of this small nation," he said in the Dail in June 1940, "if I did not utter our protest against the cruel wrong which has been done them." That same month France fell, leaving only the thin wedge that was England between Ireland and the Nazis.

In the quick turn events were taking, de Valera appealed to the members of the younger generation to enrol in the Irish Army as had their fathers a quarter of a century earlier. "Let it not be said of you that you have grown soft on the freedom that your fathers won." At a mammoth recruiting rally in College Green, he took the platform in company with Cosgrave and though the two, so long opposed to each other, neither exchanged greetings nor smiled, the fact that they appeared together at all struck Dublin with the extremity of the international situation. Dev realized that for every uniformed youth who passed before him on review, there were many others hanging back on the pavement.

Intent as an old soldier upon making the Army the nation's backbone and trying to rouse the people to their danger, he crossed the country on a recruiting mission, but reproach crept into his voice. "When your neighbour's house is on fire and the sparks are coming on to your roof, it is not time to talk of business as usual." Minister of Defence Aiken reported that the armed forces, as a result of new enlistments, neared 170,000 men. Vivion de Valera interrupted his law career to join, advancing soon to a captaincy, and his younger brother, Ruairi, having graduated from the University, marched off to camp as a private, swinging his long arms stiffly like his father.

People in general, Dev feared, were working only by fits and starts. His face, the face of someone waiting without knowing how long he would have to wait, grew drawn and he fell back into the role of teacher and docent, lecturing them on the steps that had to be taken for their safety. Before the end of the summer of 1940, the first bombs fell on Ireland, hitting a dairy in County Wexford

and killing several girls at work there. In the official announcement issued from Government Buildings the aircraft was not
identified as either British or German, but the raid came at a time
when one question was forcing de Valera's attention. Was there
collaboration between the I.R.A. and German agents? Gerald
Boland as Minister of Justice believed there was, and from the
other side of the house Dillon was openly declaring that Nazi
help was contaminating the I.R.A. Frank Aiken commented
afterward, ". . . when Germany became public enemy No. 1 to
Britain . . . the I.R.A. changed its whole outlook from being
Reddish to being of another type."

Guardedly, Dev stated only that "an organization," by which
he meant the I.R.A., was toying with the idea of bringing "other
people," by whom he meant the Nazis, into Ireland; that the
"organization" had declared "war" on one of the countries
engaged in the European conflict. It was clear he referred to the
I.R.A.'s earlier ultimatum against England. "Is it not obvious that
that particular organization is likely to be trying to work with the
others?" Whosoever brought in any foreign power, he warned,
would have their names for ever execrated. "The Irish people
want neither an old master nor a new one." The German Legation's wireless equipment was impounded and de Valera gave
his word that German diplomatic personnel, rumoured to
number a hundred, was actually limited to six under Minister
Hempel.

Shortly before the bombs had fallen on County Wexford,
a German parachutist, it was known, had landed somewhere in
Ireland, and when the police raided a house at Templeogue
named "Konstanz," they nearly caught up with him. In a locked
room they discovered the cap of a German air force officer, an
iron cross, a parachute and travelling bag; also $20,000 in
American currency, a radio transmitting set, and papers containing notes which gave some evidence of plans for a German
invasion of Ireland. Not until some months elapsed was the
owner of these belongings captured, Hermann Goertz, and it
became clear that he had in the interval been in touch with the
I.R.A.; that he had seen Hempel; that the German High Command regarded the I.R.A. as its ally.

"Danger," de Valera tried to tell his people, "threatens now
from within as well as from without." In a house in Killiney,

south of the city, the police discovered a laboratory stocked with materials used in the manufacture of bombs—sulphuric acid, phosphorus, red oxide iron—and the two men found on the spot with thousands of American dollars in their possession were arrested. Early one morning, a mysterious blast damaged Dublin Castle, fragmenting its stained-glass windows. When postal officers taking mail to the British representative in Dublin, Sir John Maffey, were fired upon from a hidden machine-gun, the Irish Prime Minister burst out against the dastardly act. On the day that England executed two Irishmen for their part in the Coventry deaths, the new Belfast steamer, s.s. *Munster*, sank after an explosion on board as she came into her Liverpool berth. His self-restraint almost swept away, *An Taoiseach* declared in savage indignation that a deadly conspiracy existed.

Realization of the existence of Irish-German intrigue underlined the instructions he issued to the people to give no countenance to "this organization." Two new hunger strikers, Darcy and McNeela, were allowed to die, and the number of I.R.A. members in jail rose to over 600. Special tribunals carried out the sentence of death on individuals who killed policemen, and in the stern measures being adopted Mulcahy gave de Valera his support. Sean MacBride, on his part, begged Republicans who were still using force to desist. Mary MacSwiney, eking out her last year or two, had gone back to teaching school in her native Cork. The I.R.A.'s adjutant-general, McCaughey, in whose possession were found notes regarding interviews with a parachutist and maps showing the disposition of Irish army units in the South and of British army units in the North, was put in prison.

By dint of continual vigilance, the Government eventually brought to a standstill the internal violence. Authorities arrested one German as he waded ashore at Waterford bearing no papers but supplied with American money. In an effort to prevent strangers from identifying locations, signposts were removed from all the roads. The Government put trawlers on patrol to prevent the landing of men from submarines. In the secrecy of the times it did not become generally known that, 200 miles off the Irish coast on board a German submarine, Sean Russell died and was buried at sea. That Eire would not be used as a base of attack against England Dev had given his word at the time of the Anglo-

Irish negotiations in London, and it was a word he laboured to make good. His struggle to keep Irish neutrality unimpaired required a protracted vigil against both warring sides.

Though the Irish people had been accustomed since the beginning of hostilities to the fear that they might be overrun by the Germans, new fears arose lest the British reoccupy Irish territory. Churchill, after succeeding Chamberlain as Britain's Prime Minister in 1940, made it known that British defences would have to cover Ireland and advised his own colleagues that if England's security should come to depend upon access to the Irish ports, England would have to act in accordance with self-preservation. Privately Churchill instructed his military heads to prepare a plan for getting a division into Ireland in the shortest possible amount of time. "The fact that we cannot," he told the House of Commons, "use the south and west coasts of Ireland to refuel our flotillas and aircraft . . . is a most heavy and grievous burden. . . ."

De Valera chose to interpret Churchill's remarks not as a demand for the ports, but as an expression of regret over the lack of them. Refusing to modify his neutrality, he said he would not make his island a cockpit of war with its homes levelled, its people slaughtered. But Dillon felt so strongly that the ports should be made available to the Royal Navy that he broke with his own Party, Fine Gael, to become the Dail's lone dissenter. The Irish people as a whole took refuge in the conviction that, so long as Eire stood upon her rights, British seizure of the harbours would lend justification to any counter-move Germany might make and that if Hitler did invade Eire, British forces would have to be diverted to protect her. After the French coast fell into German hands, necessitating the re-routing of British convoys around the North of Ireland, the strategic importance of Cobh and Berehaven declined. "So far," de Valera cautiously allowed in 1941, "our rights have been in the main respected," and when Churchill did not move to reoccupy the Irish ports, de Valera went on to say, "I think it is only fair in this connection to acknowledge that the belligerent nearest us, Great Britain, despite the temptations and urgings of certain propagandists, has not succumbed to them and not behaved unworthily."

Southern Ireland underwent a second and then a third air attack worse than either of the previous bombings, by 'planes this time unmistakably German. Dublin was hit so directly that the windows in President Hyde's residence were broken. The Chief, standing in Glasnevin Cemetery at the mass funeral for the victims, felt events pushing him closer to Britain and America. England was their nearest neighbour, he said, and natural instincts could not be denied; theirs was a neutrality friendly to Britain. He could not, he closed, speak of all he was feeling, and facts that could not be made known bore out his own personal leanings. He could not say that British 'planes making forced landings on his territory were not being interned but repaired and permitted to depart; that a British rescue ship had access to Killybegs Harbour. It was not a secret, however, that the Government put no obstacles in the way of thousands of young Irishmen who were going to Belfast or England to join the British Army. English women and children, driven out of their homes by the Luftwaffe, were finding open-armed welcome in Ireland. The middle of one night, Dev answered his 'phone to learn that Belfast, ablaze from a German air-raid, wanted help. Sending fire-fighters might, he speculated, be interpreted as a violation of neutrality, but there in the solitude of his own house he thought of the people in Belfast and called back to instruct the Dublin fire department to dispatch all aid possible. "They were our people," he explained after this crisis passed.

In December 1941, when America was driven by enemy action to abandon her neutrality and joined Britain as an ally, Dev owned that his heart would have to be made of stone to feel nothing after all America had done for Ireland. From President Roosevelt he received the message, "Your freedom too is at stake." To Churchill's mind, this occasion presented a last opportunity to win Irish co-operation and, banking on Irish-American ties, he wired de Valera: "Now is your chance. Now or never! A nation once again! I will meet you wherever you wish!"

The Irishman sent no reply, and within a few weeks after the United States entered the war, a vanguard of American troops landed in Belfast. But for the fact that what the South had withheld in the way of facilities the North of Ireland was extending, Churchill would, as he expressed it, have had to "come to close quarters" with de Valera. At once *An Taoiseach* protested to Washington that he had not been consulted about this use of territory he claimed as part of his. The presence of American troops in the North precipitated new alarm in the South lest it expose the whole island to German invasion. Farmers in the depths of Kerry and over in the stony reaches of Connemara looked up from their potato patches and cocked their ears for bombers. Roads leading down from the North were watched lest the British or Americans themselves swarm down upon them. President Roosevelt sought to give reassurance to the Irish, speaking of de Valera to the Press as an old friend, one who had a standing invitation to the White House. "If he would only come out of the clouds," the American President was at the same time saying in confidence to his own colleagues in the State Department, ". . . we would all have higher regard for him." If any belligerent should attack, de Valera warned, "we ourselves will take a hand in it, too," and he redoubled his troop inspections. Standing outside the General Post Office to take the salute, bareheaded, his hat held across his buttoned overcoat, he watched as his son, Captain Vivion de Valera, led one of the companies past him.

There were fewer afternoons now when he could pull his dark beret over his greying hair and walk up into the Dublin mountains. His bony frame, as he strode ahead of younger members of his family, was not as spare or straight as once, but he set his feet down firmly and precisely and walked with a steady rhythm. The fixity of his gaze gave him the aspect of one straining to see something that lay on the other side of the troubled times.

Every morning early he drove from Blackrock to Government Buildings, returning home for his mid-day and evening meals whenever the day's events permitted. Out of doors, he wore dark glasses, and people knew that on his last trip to Switzerland before the war he had visited his eye specialist and had since then been under treatment in a Dublin clinic for his eye trouble.

Emer, though one of the younger members of the big family, left to set up her own home after her marriage to the son of a Gaelic linguistic authority and close associate of her father's, Sean O'Cuiv. Her wedding was celebrated quietly with relatives and a few friends in the church at Booterstown and afterward at "Teach Cuilinn"—holly house—on Cross Avenue, the large home hidden in its own spacious grounds behind a high wall to which the de Valeras had moved from "Bellevue". Not long after Emer's marriage came that of her doctor brother, Eamon Junior, who was completing his medical training at the National University and already assisting in the National Maternity Hospital. Mairin was teaching in Galway and continuing her scientific research. Ruairi, upon completing his military preparation, returned to the study of archaeology at the University. Terry, the youngest, was interested in the law like his oldest brother but his Army duty lay ahead of him. As the children left home Mrs. de Valera, now white-haired, turned to her old interests in the language revival, and she re-wrote the legends of Cormac and Queen Gormlai which her own children had loved. Some of her playlets and stories she set to the music of old, native airs and lullabies like *Up in the Airy Mountain* and *Come to the Hedgerows*.

Because of the times, everyone had to live simply, which was how the de Valeras had always believed in living. The outward flow of emigration was cut off by the war and Irishmen were flocking back from England, making more mouths to feed at a time when there was less to feed them with and fewer jobs by which the wherewithal could be earned. Raw materials became so scarce that factories turned off their workers. Labour blamed the Government. Early in the course of the war the United States had placed Ireland in the combat zone, and with few vessels of their own, the Irish could get few more from America. The belligerents, in blockading each other, were blockading Ireland and the original Sinn Fein self-sufficiency programme was being put to a new test. "Ours is an island country," Dev reminded the grumblers. "Everything which we use and do not produce ourselves comes to us in ships across the seas." Eire, after the fall of Denmark, helped supply England with butter, eggs and poultry, and got good prices for what was sold abroad. Because of the lack of coal, *An Taoiseach* suggested that every possible sod of turf be cut in springtime and stacked for the winter's use. There was not enough grain to feed the cattle and the Minister of Agriculture, Ryan, ordered an increase in the amount of land to be tilled. Aiken, going to Washington to enlist President Roosevelt's aid, had been considered anti-British and the help he brought home was only a fraction of what was needed. But prices and wages had to be frozen and after 1943 the cost of living was stabilized. With the introduction of rationing, profits were brought under government controls and food subsidies granted.

Economic conditions were making the Government's task

increasingly unpopular and the Labour Party became an out-spoken critic of de Valera. Its following expanded as did that of the Independents and of a new Farmers Party. At a general election in 1943, Fianna Fail did not win a majority. At the same time, Fine Gael's seats decreased and Cosgrave, no longer robust in health, resigned as its leader leaving Mulcahy to take over the Party's direction with the aid of O'Higgins, Costello and one or two others. Only because the smaller parties could not unite under any other leader did de Valera, lacking a majority, retain the premiership. No longer was he a young man leading a forward march, nor was he even the optimist of his foreshortened middle age. Being over sixty years old with his children grown and leaving home, with his eyesight a recurrent worry, with partition an unsolved problem, the long history of crises was beginning to tell upon him but, refusing to compromise his programme, he managed to hold on with an uncertain margin until he could call another election. The people were instinctively drawn back to him as their fate and fortune both, regarding him as their bulwark against the pressure from David Gray or from any quarter.

In 1944 he managed to restore Fianna Fail's lead to seventy-six seats, while Fine Gael declined still farther. As the war lengthened, he was demonstrating his ability to preserve neutrality in the face of doubt, suasion and coercion. Since the interlude after the Anglo-Irish Agreements when he had felt in a stronger position than ever before to end partition, the outlook had altered radically. Then, he seemed to have brought to fulfilment his long belief in external association between England and Ireland, dating back as far as the Cuban analogue first suggested to his mind in the United States. The economic war had been settled, the ports restored, financial disputes overcome, and as the Chief he had confidently anticipated a full-scale mission to America, the second of his lifetime, to be directed this time against partition. The only old wound external association had not closed was the border dividing North and South, the existence of which, so long as it lay upon the country, would deter him from re-declaring the Republic of his earliest comrades. Then came the onset of another world war, changing all prospects at home and abroad. He was no more willing to become England's ally than to declare the Republic on account of that border, and the tightrope of neutrality became the only path he and most Irishmen could walk.

He had to cudgel the people at home to prepare for their own defence and had to shift course in regard to the outlawed Republicans. Because of the tough policy adopted against this handful of his own countrymen, and because of his refusal to grant England use of the ports, Ireland lost sympathy among diverse groups in America as had happened in World War I. With his brief optimism replaced by a stubborn, impenetrable determination, de Valera could only wait for hostilities abroad to come to an end.

CHAPTER XVI

THE ONWARD MARCH (1944-1953)

BY the time the final test came of Ireland's ability to maintain neutrality, de Valera's resiliency, both personal and political, was put to serious strain. From behind a desk equipped with several 'phones and a small switchboard operated by hand, he was co-ordinating the activities of his Government, serving as his own Minister of External Affairs. Neutrality had been his prescription for Ireland's policy since his 1920 proposition that England treat Ireland as the United States had treated Cuba, accompanied by the pledge that Ireland would not take sides with any enemy of England's. This he had repeated at the time of the Anglo-Irish Agreements, and the policy had been carried out to the letter from the onset of the war. The Irish people could not understand why it was resented abroad when Swiss or Swedish neutrality was, by contrast, accepted. That Ireland owed England a debt of gratitude was a notion incomprehensible to people who felt no thanks for any protection that had in the past been extended to them in the place of their freedom.

In Dev's office in February 1944, the American Minister waited upon him with a note from President Roosevelt requesting that the German and Japanese representatives in Dublin be sent home. "Axis agents," de Valera read, "enjoy almost unrestricted opportunity of bringing military information of vital importance from Great Britain and Northern Ireland and . . . transmitting it by various routes and methods to Germany." What President Roosevelt was asking was that Ireland break diplomatic relations with the two enemy powers.

Dev's first reaction upon lifting his eyes from the paper in front of him was one of pained surprise and instant refusal. To dismiss the Germans and the Japanese from Dublin would be to endanger the neutrality of four and a half precarious years, a prelude to possible declaration of war between Eire and the Axis. Before replying to the American President, however, he called into conference his Ministers and the leaders of the other political parties as well. With his opinion that the request was impossible, the others agreed. Neutrality was the rock and fortress of their security, all concurred. Even Mulcahy of Fine Gael commented that "the position is as the *Taoiseach* definitely put it." In the refusal sent to President Roosevelt, *An Taoiseach* stated that his Government would safeguard American interests within the limits of its power, but that its first duty was to protect Irish neutrality. He felt keen reluctance to do anything that would offend Ireland's friends in the United States and sympathized inwardly with the fight being waged against totalitarianism.

For reasons of security, the British then undertook at this crucial juncture to isolate Southern Ireland. The criticism of Americans and of British alike intensified. Travel into Ireland from Britain was banned and there was talk about cutting Irish telephonic facilities and other communication lines. Barriered by their isolationism from what was going on, the Irish conceived a fear of American invasion of their island as a result of the refusal to co-operate in President Roosevelt's request.

While nothing happened in Ireland in the summer of 1944, World War II moved into its final phase with the invasion of the Continent. For another year and more after the Normandy landing, de Valera maintained his guard against betraying openly favour or disfavour to either warring side, meticulous in demonstrating impartiality toward the united nations and the axis nations alike. In April 1945 he adjourned the Dail over the death of President Roosevelt, mourning him as one who could have been counted on when the fighting stopped to strengthen international organization. But the following month, when Hitler was reported dead, de Valera was careful to offer condolences by calling upon Hempel. "I did what I did as my duty," he defended himself in the Dail against an onslaught from Dillon, "and I was quite well aware . . . that it was capable of being misrepresented."

On V-E Day in May 1945, soldiers in American uniforms trooped down from across the border, given leave for the first time to do so, and found in the South a quick welcome and relaxation of tension. De Valera, listening to the jubilant broadcast made by Churchill from London, hearing the *bravura* of that voice rolling around the airwaves of the world, steeled himself to the recriminations cast upon him for refusing to grant use of his ports or to get rid of the axis representatives. "That," Dev replied to the indictment when he went on the air himself a few days later, "is precisely why we have had a disastrous succession of wars—World War I and II and shall it be World War III?" *An Taoiseach* sought to roll back the years to where Ireland and England had stood before the war, on the eve—as he had thought—of his international, anti-partition campaign. "I could not have hoped," he confessed, "that we would pass through five years of war with the social fabric as intact as it is at the moment."

The war had not left Ireland's position altogether unaffected. She was not a member of the United Nations organizations that had been created in the place of the League of Nations. Within the United Kingdom, the North occupied a surer spot than ever, for the United Kingdom owed the North a special debt of gratitude for the use of bases there. Chamberlain was dead, appeasement discredited, and the world weary of causes. The sympathies of some in the United States had been alienated by de Valera's unyielding neutrality. Others, prominent Irish-Americans, had turned against him for his strong-arm attitude toward the extremists, his old friend McGarrity among them. At home, the Republicans who remained active did not forget those allowed to die on hunger strike.

Those Republicans who were still interned Prime Minister de Valera set free in his immediate relief at the ending of the war. Priding himself upon his own kind of Republicanism, he did not relinquish the hope he could exact fealty from other Republicans. No less than they did he stress the coming of the day when the whole nation could be a Republic, the difference being that he would not grasp at half a loaf or any fraction thereof. His plan was, as it had been before World War II, to obtain a Republic for the whole of Ireland including the six Northern counties by reactivating his campaign for peaceful reunification. He was aware that danger had existed from a conspiracy between the I.R.A. and the Germans, a situation with which he had been familiar in the first world war as well as the second. He personally had never been known to have had any such entanglements and had, this time, owned his sympathy for those fighting Hitler. With the termination of hostilities, the Nazi prisoners who had parachuted into Ireland were ordered to be deported, among them Hermann Goertz who had been in an Irish jail for several years, a disillusioned man. While Goertz waited on his last day at Dublin

Castle, he unscrewed the stem of his pipe and removed a vial of poison which he crushed between his teeth. The would-be ally of the Irish Republican Army died in a Dublin hospital. That organization itself acknowledged no defeat in 1945.

As soon as its leaders got their freedom, violence recommenced and when a former I.R.A. chief of staff, Sean McAteer, was caught recruiting in defiance of the ban upon the Army, de Valera asked for an extension of the power of internment, and McAteer with dozens more was lodged back inside prison walls. The Republic by force and violence was still the demand of the militants, but Dev was no longer their leader and, since their Nazi collaboration, not even their friend. Not since the North had been partitioned off by its own wish and by British act had he advocated other than civil means to bring it back into the fold. But blame for the renewed turbulence in the South was laid upon his doorstep, not only by Fine Gael members but also by certain deputies among the Independents like the young, hammer-tongued Oliver Flanagan. When one of the prisoners, former I.R.A. Adjutant-General Sean McCaughey, neared death on hunger strike in Maryborough Prison, Flanagan demanded that the Government intervene. *An Taoiseach's* reply was that he would leave the Government benches before giving in again to hunger strikers, to men who had done everything they could to involve the country in war. There would have been no such thing as neutrality had they had their way. McCaughey died and Flanagan shouted across the house that the *Taoiseach* had blood on his hands; that he was the greatest traitor the country had ever had; that there was sufficient information to hang him. The old charge, Ireland's most damning, that of being pro-British, fell upon de Valera. Ageing almost before the deputies' eyes, his face pinched and white, he had to listen. ". . . however I dislike it, I have got to lump it." The recourse to politics instead of other methods of attack, what he himself had recommended, was being pursued with a vengeance by those opposed to him.

To refute the charges that he had not gone far enough in his own Republicanism, Dev undertook to show that Eire was already a Republic in fact if not in name; that Eire had had Republican status since the *Bunreacht* of 1937. Whether it was called a Republic or not did not matter; the American Constitution had not used the term, but nobody doubted that the United

States was a Republic. "We are," he asserted in answer to a question raised by Deputy Dillon as to what Ireland actually was, "an independent Republic associated as a matter of external policy with the States of the British Commonwealth." To the deputies he read aloud definitions of that word from the *Encyclopaedia Britannica*, from the *Encyclopedia Americana*, from the *Shorter Oxford English Dictionary*, from Webster's *Dictionary*. This, remarked one deputy, made the situation as clear as a pikestaff. So insistently were his contentions challenged that he himself began to doubt how much longer external association could be made to last. He had never regarded it as a final solution, only as a means of bringing North and South together, what he described as a bridge across which their hands could touch. But after eight years of external association with Britain, he could not discern any alteration in the Northerners' attitude towards the Southerners, something he called heartbreaking for himself and for every Irishman who loved the homeland.

To keep his mind and his heart too on the strict course he had, upon entering the Dail, marked out was the more difficult because of his own past. The emotions of the extremists he could understand, having been in 1916 himself up in arms against England. The feelings behind their persistence against Ireland's own Government, deemed by them tainted with compromise, he could also fathom in terms of his own action in the civil war. But by asserting his mind over his emotions, year by year and step by step, he had moved away from rebellion and insurrection himself, the difference being made possible for him by the great changes that had actually been wrought in the status of the country. So gradually had they been effected that they lacked the appeal and the glory of the old revolutionary programme. De Valera, having eschewed his own early methods, had committed himself long since to tactics suited to political combat and in so doing had found himself coping more and more with internal needs. So adjusted was he to all of Ireland's problems that he took each in stride and governed by doing less while waiting for more.

The longer Fianna Fail remained in office, the more complaints there were against its lack of progress, the more outcries against hard times, and the more charges of corruption. With the discarding of other weapons, politics became increasingly bitter. No form of political attack was left untried. Deputy Flanagan in the Dail insinuated that a gift had been given through a patient to Dr. Eamon de Valera, practising as a gynaecologist with an office in Fitzwilliam Square, to "soften up" his father. Dev denied that his son had even heard of such a gift. When Emer's husband entered government employment, it was hinted he owed his post to favouritism. Ruairi de Valera's work as an archaeologist and civil servant in ordnance survey was called political jobbery and his father wrote this off as blatant falsehood. His family was becoming, he objected, a target for the mud thrown by every Jackeen. His children seemed to him in the position of "dogs tied, stones loose."

Only within the protecting walls of "Teach Cuilinn" did the Prime Minister and his wife find peace and quiet. The family at home became smaller when Vivion, in the Dail as a "Fianna Fail Republican," was married. Terry, the youngest, was at "Teach Cuilinn" after completing his military service, and though qualifying as a solicitor, his musical talent gave him a reputation among family friends as an "artist." As the official black car of the Prime Minister turned in through his bright green gates on Cross Avenue, it angled past the stone lodge of the gate-keeper and out of the public gaze. "I believe that I live as simply as most people," Dev commented. "A number of expenses that the average person has, I have not got. I do not smoke or drink; I do not entertain to any extent." He enjoyed additional freedom after Sean T. O'Kelly in 1945 succeeded to the Presidency and assumed all the ceremonial functions that had become impossible for one of Dr. Hyde's age. It was privacy that de Valera cherished. "The newspapers, the opening up of areas by buses, the radio, and the cinema, all these things," he complained, "are breakng in." The frugality of his Limerick boyhood was the preference if not the necessity of his old age. Anyone brought up in the country might, he supposed, say, "You are in the country all your life because you understand fully what country life means."

Half-humorously, half-despairingly, his wife confided to friends that she could write a play about her husband's career, but that she did not "know yet whether it would be a comedy or a tragedy." On the few occasions when she appeared publicly, she dressed plainly and the trace of a stoop in her shoulders made her look smaller than ever as she stood beside her husband. Another generation was added to the family when a baby was born to Emer, a baby that was to be one of a large number of grandchildren. The Prime Minister welcomed to "Teach Cuilinn" the winter after the war his half-brother, a man of fifty-five, tall like Eamon but heavier and of sandy colouring. Though his life as Superior of the St. Alphonsus Retreat House in Pennsylvania had been far removed from his older brother's public career, he was among the very few permitted by de Valera to enter closely into his personal orbit. Not long after Father Wheelwright's return to America came the news of his death due to an automobile accident. Just a few months before, de Valera had spoken of the loneliness he felt over the death of his eighty-six-year-old uncle, Edward Coll, in Connecticut. He called it the severing of links with his youth. His brother's death was another. "These events," he wrote his American cousins, "only help us to realize that 'not here have we a lasting city.'" By means of his religion and philosophy he tried to reconcile himself to all that happened, privately or publicly.

"I am getting older, my time is getting short," he said in the Dail during a burst of impatience over his unfulfilled objectives. Only when North and South were no longer divided by trumped-up excuses could his friendship with England be complete, and only then would the people of his island and the people of the other island live side by side as good neighbours. "I still hope to see the day." The idea of natural neighbourliness he had cherished for thirty years. "I have dreamed dreams," he mused, then pulled himself up short. "But I have had the task . . . to make our dreams come true." For good or for ill, he reminisced, he had been representing the country for longer than anybody living, a fact attested by the second generation rising round him, by the sons succeeding in the footsteps of their fathers, of whom Vivion was only one. For a long time, brothers and sisters had carried on for the dead of their own generation and names like Mac-Swiney, Pearse, Plunkett, Lemass, O'Higgins and Boland had become family names in Irish politics. The next generation would play its part differently. Redmond's son had finished his role early but Dillon's son was still in the ascendancy. Cosgrave's son entered the Dail and Larkin's. Tom Clarke's son was politically active. Erskine Childers, Junior, came into the Dail for Fianna Fail and rose rapidly. Cathal Brugha's son Richard, married to Terence MacSwiney's daughter, was a member of the militant Republicans.

Sean MacBride, son of two distinguished patriots, was gaining a unique prominence of his own. Having renounced violence during the war, he was now considered half in and half out of the I.R.A., and for the purpose of getting a Republic declared he undertook to organize a special political party. Dev remembered that, having decided to dissociate himself from militant action, he had organized Fianna Fail and come into the Dail to fight the established regime by political means. He himself now represented the established order. Clann na Poblachta, as MacBride named his Party, made political capital out of Dev's inability to gratify Republican ambitions and the economic difficulties that were plaguing the Fianna Fail administration in the post-war period. Taxes were rising and the national budget went higher than ever.

By 1947, after a series of by-elections, MacBride captured the seat he coveted in the Dail, the springboard he wanted, and Fianna Fail backing weakened to the point where Dev called a general election for February 1948. People forgot, he observed, campaigning from crossroad to crossroad, that there had been a world war raging round them out of which they had emerged safe and sound. His jaws were clenched as he hurled back the blame his Ministers were getting for everything. "Some people suggest . . . that I should pass off the stage, but when that happens I shall have the great satisfaction of knowing that there are many magnificent Irishmen in the ranks of Fianna Fail from the *Tanaiste* [Sean Lemass] down—who will take my place."

"What about the Republic?" someone heckled him in Ballina. MacBride's Clann na Poblachta was pledging itself to declare a Republic and Fianna Fail had to show its colours. Dev's Republicanism was, by his own definition of that term, consistent from the beginning. Though not among the signatories of the 1916 declaration of the Irish Republic, he had fought for it, often gone to prison for it, become its chief executive, raised millions for it, taken an oath in the legislature to uphold it, and fought again for it in 1922. But it was really for a sovereign, united nation he had done all this, not for a particular system of government, not as a doctrinaire Republican by his own protestation, and not since partition went into effect for anything but sovereignty and unity. Although his scheme of external association had not brought the hoped-for results, mere nomenclature such as formal use of the word Republic would never, in his estimation, reunite North and South, would in fact only further antagonize the North. As things stood, the Southerners already were in possession of the substance of republicanism.

"Do not try to fool yourselves that you have not an independent Republic established," Dev retorted to his heckler. With terminology and gesture he had no patience, and Clann na Poblachta's electioneering platform was for him purely artificial. He recommended that if any wanted guidance for the future, they turn to the past. "Is there any party or combination of parties that can produce a government that is as Republican as our Government?"

The answer was given by Deputy McGilligan for Fine Gael, "If we have to make a choice between living a lie (by which he meant pretending to have a Republic) and some trouble arising in our international relations (by which he meant British reaction to repeal of external association) I would rather have the trouble in our international relations." Fine Gael, not powerful enough to win the election alone, thus aligned itself on the side of MacBride. After the election, Fianna Fail was returned with two fewer seats than it had before, 67 in all, not enough to out-vote Fine Gael in combination with the other parties. Fine Gael secured 30 seats, Labour 19, the Farmers 5, the Independents 17, and the new Clann na Poblachta in its debut scored with 7.

The Fianna Fail Chief arrived at Leinster House in his car to hear the crowds greeting him as "Good old Dev". Unsmiling, he waved his black hat as he circled the driveway where a granite walk bordered with ornamental urns and lamp stanchions now replaced the unloved statue of Victoria. As soon as the *Ceann Comhairle* called the new Dail to order, some of the deputies appealed to Dev to throw in his lot with the other political factions in order to head a coalition. To hawk "the dead cat of coalition" around again he called absurd. Democratic government had to be responsible, and only governments of known and positive leadership could be held responsible. Everybody's business would be nobody's business and real power or no power was his final reply, meaning he would go out of office.

"Thanks be to God," ejaculated Deputy Flanagan, "that I have lived to see this day." Then, upon Mulcahy's motion, Deputy John Costello of Fine Gael was named to preside as Prime

Minister over an inter-party Government. The Chief took his defeat with an air of manifest indifference, moving back for the first time in sixteen years to the other side of the house as leader of the opposition. His salary fell from £3,000 to £1,040. Lately, he had found it easier to sit back and wait, to refrain from hasty action, to yield himself more readily to circumstances. The mere bandying about of the word Republic he was sure would not end partition, for all the hopes of Sean MacBride, the new Minister of External Affairs.

While Costello and his new Ministry had to reckon with the consequences of their election pledges, the ex-*Taoiseach* took advantage of his comparative freedom in the spring of 1948 to set out on his long-postponed, anti-partition campaign. His mission had more to accomplish than when originally planned because the unpopularity of Irish neutrality during the war had to be counteracted. Flying with Frank Aiken to the United States, he was hailed from New York to San Francisco with showers of green confetti and pipers' bands playing *When Irish Eyes Are Smiling*. It was, he told welcoming parties, almost like coming home though he missed faces remembered from his other visits. His old suitcase some recognized as that given him almost thirty years before by one of those now dead, Joe McGarrity. During the war, when Dev had not released the hunger strikers or spared other Republicans, it was no secret that McGarrity had taken up Sean Russell's cudgels. "Tell me," the Chief asked a mutual friend in Philadelphia, "was Joe's break from me personal or political?" At the assurance that it had been politics and nothing else, the tone of his voice changed to grateful relief. In Washington, where President Truman received him, he laid the ground-work for resolutions subsequently passed in the United States Congress endorsing the unification of Ireland. As "Good old Dev" he found a respectfully affectionate welcome and an avid audience on this and on later journeys wherever he travelled—to Australia and New Zealand and then back to England and as far North as the Hebrides, one or two of his sons or colleagues accompanying him.

Back again in Dublin in his place on the Dail's opposition bench, he found the administration moving rapidly to carry out Minister MacBride's pre-election promise of a Republic by abolishing external association. A sardonic smile spread across

Dev's face at Prime Minister Costello's insistence that this would take the gun out of Irish politics, and when Dillon asserted that in future the Republic would not owe its existence either to the dictionary or the encyclopedia, he smiled again. He had done his best, he was thinking, and all he had got for his pains was a jibe. If what the people wanted was a united country, it would take more than a word to do it, but he could understand the prevalent impatience. In open session he tendered Costello his co-operation "because we have been in public life not to retard, not to put barriers to the onward march of the nation." It would be more than it was worth to Fianna Fail to appear to hold out against the declaration of the Republic. He took his cohorts aside; time would tell; those who supped with the devil, he quoted, would need a long spoon. Playing politics with the outlawed faction would not produce lasting results. The inter-party Government's legislation repealing the External Relations Act and setting up the Republic passed unanimously at the end of 1948. Dev had to reckon with his realization that this was no more than he himself had said, when he introduced the new Constitution, could be done.

The declaration of the Republic quickly turned into a hollow victory when the law passed by the British Parliament granting recognition to the new Irish Republic also stated that there was to be no change in the relation of the six counties to the United Kingdom. Although Prime Minister Attlee's Labour Government declared that factual ties with the South of Ireland would not be severed, and although the two Governments agreed on reciprocal citizenship and trade preferences, the British Parliament's move perpetuating partition in a specific statute brought resounding protests from the Dail, and it was Dev's prediction that new seeds of enmity had been sown. Ireland could not be expected to be grateful, he observed, just because Britain tolerated the declaration of a Republic in the South. "If a man takes your watch and chain and then gives your watch back you still want the chain too." But Churchill pointed out that the unilateral declaration of the Republic by Dublin made the North more important than ever to Britain. In view of the possibility of future warfare, Britain would not soon give up her foothold there.

The state of the world had been of as much concern to Dev since his travels abroad as Ireland's internal changes. The globe was being dangerously divided by the threat of Russian aggression, yet both he and Costello knew as practical politicians that, until the Republic included the North, no Government could survive in Dublin if it walked into a military alliance where Britain was co-partner. In 1938, at the peak point of Anglo-Irish co-operation when Chamberlain had been Prime Minister, de Valera had gone so far as to indicate that his country would, in time of war, co-operate with England on one condition, but that condition—the ending of partition—was not yet met and new danger confronted both countries. Two antagonistic international groups were unmistakably forming, in Dev's opinion, and whenever both were ready he was sure conflict would commence. Any hint of contamination with the Russian communists became damaging in Ireland. After Russia temporarily blocked Ireland's membership in the United Nations, it became more so and Dev's opponents in the Dail revealed for the first time the story of the old loan that had been made in 1920 by him and Gerald Boland's brother Harry to the Soviet representatives in Washington. Gerald Boland explained that the Russian jewels taken as collateral had now been turned over to *An Taoiseach's* department. The Costello Government called upon Russia to repay the money and when it was forthcoming from Moscow, the jewels were duly returned. The Irish people showed little political reaction to this evocation of the past, being more engrossed with the present.

Although no one realized better the need for collective security, Dev did not favour lining up to fight side by side with the British so long as part of his own nation remained subjugated. Two alternatives became clear to him for Ireland: joining the North Atlantic Treaty Organization sponsored by the United States, or going a lone way. The specific proposition of entering N.A.T.O. came before the Dail in due course, and all parties united against it. Until England withdrew from the North, Ireland would not co-operate save at the risk of a revolution at home. The I.R.A. had not disappeared nor had the gun gone out of Irish politics after all. Posters mocking the repeal of the external relations law appeared on Dublin walls; the border was seen to be as much a dividing line as ever. The people tired of the partition talk after the latest disappointment and turned their attention to their struggle to make a living.

The inter-party Government now got the blame for their daily privations. In an effort to relieve Ireland's economic shortages, Prime Minister Costello decided to accept an American loan through the Economic Co-operation Administration. Dev gave only cautious assent because of strings that might be attached. ". . . drinking is very pleasant," he recited from an Irish proverb, "but paying for it is bitter. . . ." It was not to be denied that economic issues were taking precedence over the old, ideological ones and practical realities dominated the politics of the day. By 1951, de Valera's standing question about the cohesion and responsibility of coalitions got an answer when a breach occurred within the inter-party Ministry. The Minister of Public Health, Noel C. Browne, disowned by Minister MacBride for the Clann and denounced by Prime Minister Costello for the free health services he advocated for mothers and children against the wishes of the Church, resigned, and in the pursuant split Costello was forced to call a general election for the spring. Fianna Fail built its platform for a return to power on the idea of one-party rule, and the electorate's penchant for infallible guidance was ready to respond. "Is each Minister," de Valera asked, "in each particular department to be allowed to run that department without consideration of general policy?" His Fianna Fail Cabinet had functioned, he stressed, "as a group, as a team, as a body bearing collective responsibility. . . ."

On election day he voted early in Blackrock, then went by car in the warm spring sunshine across the midlands to his old constituency in the west—to Ennis in the Banner County—where he was driven slowly down the dipping defile of the old street, darkened by the chimney-potted roof-tops. On all sides the people turned out to greet him as their own, enjoying with him the sensation that history was repeating itself. A third of a century earlier a young man, somewhat leaner and blacker-haired, had come to town with the same tricolor, but a man no more serious of countenance or intent of voice than Dev on this day in 1951. He had been forbearing with the Claremen when they had stepped from the straight course, and he smiled upon them now as he called for their votes.

Enthusiasm for the new Party had vanished with the indissolubility of partition. Sean MacBride was able to hang on to his own constituency but Clann na Poblachta retained only one other seat. In the new chamber sat six deputies from the Farmers Party, 14 Independents, 16 Labour, 40 Fine Gael and 69 (instead of 67) Fianna Fail. Costello, because of his alienation from his former Minister, Browne, and several others who had come back this time as Independents, was not able to win re-election as Prime Minister. The 69 Fianna Fail members were not enough to give de Valera a clear majority either, but when Browne and fellow Independents cast their ballots in his favour, he became *An Taoiseach* again. Without a sign of surprise, calmly and serenely, he thanked the house and moved back to the Prime Minister's suite in Government Buildings, putting up his photo of Pearse and his few office effects. The same thick, green tweed hung at the big windows and covered the chairs of the reception-room, and in the corner on its own pedestal was the bronze statue of Abraham Lincoln, who in his time and country had fought against a national partition.

Dev's old preachment of austerity became the order of the day, but it was austerity on top of austerity, hardship compounded. Within a few months after Fianna Fail's return to office, participation in collective defence was made obligatory by the United States for recipients of American aid, and Prime Minister de Valera regarded this as impossible so long as partition lasted. Neutrality was as much his post-war policy for Ireland as it had been his war-time policy. The E.C.A. mission departed from Dublin at the beginning of 1952, and the Irish people were warned by their Government that their level of industry and agriculture must be raised to meet the rate of consumption. Ireland was going it alone in a changing universe, paradoxical as this was under a leader once at the head of a world organization. ". . . everybody knows that the United Nations Organization is a failure," he said in the Dail. "The whole situation gives rise to despondency." As far as he could see, only an international confederation held any hope—"states confederated in such a way that there is . . . a law-making authority, an executive . . . and a court"—and that he considered to be a long way off. To the Council of Europe at Strasbourg he gave wholehearted support, sending Irish delegates to work in the direction of a United States of Europe.

As a pragmatist, de Valera took each turn of events as a fore-runner to the next and his sense of humour got freer play. The new census showed that the population had ceased its fall. People went about their jobs and their leisurely way of life as they had not done for decades, singing to themselves in the streets, following the races, setting their store by their books and plays, loving their own landscape, and enjoying witty sallies at the outside world. New schools, new hospitals, new churches were under construction. A scheme for utilizing peat to generate electricity brought dinosaur-like machines on to the Bog of Allen. One undertaking related to his own early proclivity for Irish culture gave de Valera prime satisfaction. With governmental backing, he had created an Institute for Advanced Studies. "I do not pretend," he said in arguing for funds for the project, "to be a Celtic scholar any more than I pretend to be a mathematician," but the Institute was the expression of something the course of events had denied him in his own career. He saw coming true some, at least, of his early dreams of an Ireland living her own life at peace with her nearest neighbour.

During a visit to London he accepted an invitation to lunch with Churchill, who was also back in power after a post-war lapse from it, and on the doorstep of 10 Downing Street the two contemporaries shook hands genially; Churchill, who had been speaking out for home rule four decades earlier; de Valera, who had at that same time been possessed of the hope that home rule might bring Ireland's salvation. When, early in 1952, England lost her King, Prime Minister de Valera tendered to the royal family and the British people "a neighbourly understanding and a neighbourly sympathy." It had been in the reign of George VI's father that the young Commandant de Valera had been condemned to death. Not only had the condemned man survived, but at the age of seventy he was again in command. He showed himself as ready as Costello had been to put the past behind the present, even to do business with the North when it was necessary. The Dublin and the Belfast Governments entered into conferences over the joint operation of the connecting rail line, over drainage operations, and over the hydro-electric development on the River Erne. Nothing was left in the issue of Republicanism but partition, and when anyone asked Dev if he had the solution to that problem his laconic reply was, "I have not and neither has anybody else."

Infirmities were something he put from him with silence, though his people worried for him when he made a trip to the

Zurich clinic for treatment of his eyes. Dr. Vogt, his surgeon, had died during the war. People saw Dev at the Hill of Tara early in the summer of 1952, lifting his broad-brimmed hat with sober, old-style courtesy, but bending his head to watch his step across the wide, grassy, windblown plateau as he went to turn the first sod in excavations at the site of the palace of the ancient kings of Ireland. Before the end of August, he left Dublin accompanied by his physician son. He was threatened with total blindness from a detached retina. In Utrecht, Holland, the Dutch eye specialist, Dr. Weve, operated on him and in the weeks that followed, and then the months during which his return was postponed, he underwent two additional operations. Word came that the patient was working in the hospital with his son to read at his bedside and late in the autumn, his secretary of many years, Kathleen O'Connell, was flown to the Netherlands.

At the end of December 1952, as he was escorted aboard a 'plane for his flight back to Ireland, he gave to Dutch newsmen the first specific information about himself: "As is well known, my eyesight for a number of years has been far from satisfactory. Last August a new condition was discovered. The retina had become partly detached, threatening total blindness. . . . The retina has now completely reattached, and my sight is at the stage where it was before the detachment occurred." At Dublin's airport he appeared to President O'Kelly, to the Papal Nuncio, to the foreign diplomats, and his own Ministers who awaited him, rested, younger and heavier than when he had gone away, but those nearest took his arm to guide his footsteps. *An Taoiseach* held his head up and walked fearlessly, able still to distinguish light and shadow, quick to turn his head in the direction of voices and to extend his own hand first in salutation.

Though he summoned his Cabinet the following day, he agreed that it would be a little time before he could resume the full round of his public duties, and in by-elections that occurred early in 1953 Fianna Fail suffered. This time he did not call for a general election but asked the deputies themselves for a vote of confidence. A "ragged cloak to hide the Government's shame" was what Costello called this move. In preparation for the critical motion, neither Fianna Fail, Fine Gael nor the smaller parties set out to make it turn on the matter of national reunification. The Republic was disillusioned with its own politics and less concerned over the North, over England, over old grievances, than with bread and butter and jobs for the idle who were parading up and down the streets of Dublin. The partition issue had been worn thin by the diminishing minority of militants, although they were at the very moment demonstrating against Queen Elizabeth II's coronation visit to the North. In Leinster House, the younger deputies were weary of the old fight and impatient when the elder statesmen cast their eyes backward. Fianna Fail's chances of remaining in office did not rest upon reiteration of the past, but upon what its veteran leader could offer for the future. Upon him personally much of the outcome depended for he far outranked, in public opinion, any of his team of Ministers.

In the first few days of July 1953, the Dail opened its debate on the confidence motion at a desultory tempo, so few in attendance that the bells rang repeatedly throughout Leinster House to summon a quorum. The Government was represented by one or two of the Ministers relieving each other on their bench. On the other side, Mulcahy sat continuously, hunched and grizzled but possessed of pent-up opposition. The hour set for de Valera's summation approached on a hot afternoon. Dubliners were going drowsily about their business, many unmindful of the crisis inside Leinster House. Costello arrived to take his seat and Dillon, with his under-lip protuberant, lowering and alone; then McGilligan, small and pointed of face. MacBride, but recently bereaved of his mother and Ireland of a legend, was hovering alone in the anterooms, but finally sat himself down to the immediate right of the speaker, close to Fine Gael. Labour members were assembling in their places in the curve of the horseshoe, and next to them by the rear gangway of the house came the handful of Independents on whom the vote would turn. Whether the Government was cut down or not, it would be by a razor's edge with Fine Gael leading the No votes and Labour and the Farmers following in full cry.

The Chief entered almost unobserved through the swinging door behind the *Ceann Comhairle's* dais, moving acro ssthe few steps he knew so well to the first seat in the Government's row. Dressed in a blue-black suit with the *fainne* threaded in red in his lapel, he sat erect, his shoulders forced square, his eyes behind thick lenses fixed straight ahead. His hair was still less grey than black.

He rubbed his smooth, young-looking hands together. His

entry was the signal for attack. The seats filled up behind him
with Fianna Fail men emerging from the smoking-rooms, the
restaurant below, and lobbies. Paying no attention, he put his
elbows on the bench in front of him, pressed the tips of his long
fingers to his temples, and bowed his head as if in prayer. Insults
were fired from side to side, some with a wink and a smile, but
with a rabidness reciprocated. Among the Independents, one or
two spoke against *An Taoiseach*, one or two for him as a man of
moral courage, a man of vigilance, a man who had kept the nation
out of world war. It was Churchill, came the retort, not de Valera,
that had saved Ireland. Begrudgingly, Dev's personal magnetism
got acknowledgment, but simultaneously he was excoriated for
arrogance and egotism. Sean McKeon, grown bulky and bent
who, as the Blacksmith of Ballinalee, had nominated him three
decades before to the highest office, delivered the final charge
against him.

Promptly at four o'clock, *An Taoiseach* rose, pushed up his
seat, leaned back with his elbows on the ledge of the row behind
him, locked his hands across his chest, and began as every place in
the chamber, in the Press section, in the public gallery and in the
distinguished visitors' balcony filled to hear him speak. Without
seeming to hurry, without initial indignation, he commenced
a defence of his historic economic programme, of partial self-
sufficiency, of the full life for the farmer in Ireland. He wondered,
aside, why he had ever left it for politics, but there was the
Constitution to show for his record, there were the land annuities,
and there was neutrality. It had been said in the nineteen-forties,
he reminded the house, that the Brownshirts would win in
Germany, the Blackshirts in Italy, the Blueshirts in Ireland. "It
would have been better," came a voice, "than your hair-shirt."
The *Ceann Comhairle's* bell was struck for order and *An Taoiseach*
dipped his head, hesitating only for the second. No notes were
possible for him. His tone rose from its soft sibilance to a harsh
insistence, as he persisted over interruptions from across the
floor. With the flat of his hand he flagged down MacBride whose
smile was at times like a sneer. Dev, suddenly straightening up,
turned his head as if he could see the clock high on the wall over
the reporters. Assured he had plenty of time, he stopped only long
enough to say, "Thanks be to God." He had been talking, he said,
for thirty-seven years and he only wanted to know where he

stood; he and his Ministers would be glad to remain if they were wanted, but if not they would go happily into opposition.

The people must know that there were hard times ahead, splendid and easy as it might be to have it both ways. No socialist he, and he slapped the desk, but he did not believe either in the law of the jungle, nor that the Almighty created everyone equally capable of caring for himself. The Government would have to help the weaker ones, and he would rather be pitched out of his seat than mislead anyone. He would break stones, but if he ever had to have assistance he would not regard it as charity. His voice dropped and solicitude roared up behind him. Abruptly, he sat. The Republic had scarcely been mentioned, nor the civil war, nor partition. The division bells began their ringing throughout Leinster House, and when the chamber doors were fastened the deputies moved up the short flight of stairs at the rear, dividing to the right and the left through the Yes and No lobbies, and back down the forward steps to their places. Dev, with Aiken towering at his elbow, made his way back to his seat to await the tally. MacEntee slid toward him on the bench, Lemass came to perch on the stairs at his right, Childers whispered to him from a seat in front. The *Ceann Comhairle* rose, wrapped his black gown about him and announced the vote: 73 to 71 for Fianna Fail. In the din, Fine Gael tried to enter a protest but Fianna Fail raised the old cry, "Up Dev," drowning out everything else. Dev's face, mobile and relaxed, showed no change of expression but he ran his hand up and down his thigh. The march forward was after all to continue, and whether he was in or out of power, no halt in it would be called by him.

ACKNOWLEDGMENTS

What I have here to acknowledge, as one who has wished to serve honestly events of import for the people of one country—of import for the people of two, three and many countries in the outcome of the events—is not indebtedness.

So much help and courtesy were afforded me, without the idea of placing me under obligation of any kind, that I want to express gratitude beyond repayment to these and to others who shared with me professional skills, records, recollections, convictions—of the University of Michigan, Ann Arbor, Michigan: Roy W. Cowden, Lionel H. Laing, Eugene B. Power, Lawrence Preuss and Frederick D. Wieck. In Ireland: Robert Brennan, David T. Dwane, Felix E. Hackett, R. James Hayes, Florence O'Donoghue, Michael Tierney, and Joseph P. Walshe. Others in my manifold acknowledgment include: Cornelius Neenan of New York City; Mrs. William O'Brien of Neuilly-St.-Front, France; Mrs. Charlotte Whitney Allen of Rochester, New York; and the Rev. D. P. Falvey of the Villanova College Library in Villanova, Pennsylvania. Responsibility for what has been written down in this book as a result of the help extended to me is mine alone.

Just as the dimension of the word and the margin of the page are exceeded far by the extent of my thanks, so are they outstripped by the nature of my acknowledgment to a co-worker from beginning to end, Arthur W. Bromage.

MARY C. BROMAGE

BIBLIOGRAPHY

The following general publications, documents, newspapers and periodicals are those principally used in the preparation of this work.

GENERAL PUBLICATIONS

Arensberg, C. M., and Kimball, S. T., *The Family and Community in Ireland* (Cambridge, 1940).

Arthur, George, *General Sir John Maxwell* (London, 1932).

Asquith, H. H., *Moments of Memory* (New York, 1938).

Barry, Tom, *Guerrilla Days in Ireland* (Dublin, 1949).

Beaslai, Piaras, *Michael Collins and the Making of a New Ireland* (Dublin, 1926), 2 vols.

Beaverbrook, W. M. A., *Politicians and the Press* (London, 1925).

Beaverbrook, W. M. A., *Politicians and the War* (New York, 1928).

Becker, B. H., *Disturbed Ireland, being the Letters Written during the Winter of 1880–1881* (London, 1881).

Birkenhead, F. E. (1st Earl of), *America Revisited* (London, 1924).

Birkenhead, F. E. (1st Earl of), *Contemporary Personalities* (London, 1924).

Birkenhead, F. E. (1st Earl of), *Points of View* (London, 1922).

Birkenhead, F. E. (2nd Earl of), *Frederick Edwin, Earl of Birkenhead* (London, 1933).

Bonsal, Stephen, *Unfinished Business* (New York, 1944).

Boyle, J. F., *The Irish Rebellion of 1916* (London, 1916).

Breen, Dan, *My Fight for Irish Freedom* (Dublin, 1926).

Brennan, Robert, *Allegiance* (Dublin, 1950).

Bretherton, D. H., *The Real Ireland* (London, 1925).

Briollay, Sylvain, *Ireland in Rebellion* (Dublin, 1922).

Butler, Matthew, *Eamon de Valera—A Biographical Sketch* (Waterford, Ireland, 1932).

Callwell, C. E., *Field-Marshal Sir Henry Wilson—His Life and Diaries* (London, 1927), 2 vols.

Carty, Frances, *Legion of the Rearguard* (London, 1934).

Casement, Roger, *The Crime Against Europe* (Philadelphia, 1915).

Casement, Roger, *The Crime Against Ireland and How They May Right It* (New York, 1914).

Chamberlain, Austen, *Down the Years* (London, 1935).

Chamberlain, Neville, *In Search of Peace* (New York, 1938).

Childs, Wyndham, *Episodes and Reflections* (London, 1930).

Churchill, W. S., *A Roving Commission—My Early Life* (New York, 1930).

Churchill, W. S., *Mr. Winston Churchill's Message to Ulster* (London, 1912).

Churchill, W. S., *The Second World War* (London, 1948–1954), 6 vols.

Churchill, W. S., *The Aftermath* (New York, 1929).

Clarke, T. J., *Glimpses of an Irish Felon's Life* (Dublin, 1939).

Coffey, Diarmuid, *Douglas Hyde, President of Ireland* (Dublin, 1938).

Collins, Michael, *Arguments for the Treaty* (Dublin, undated).

Colum, Mary, *Life and the Dream* (New York, 1947).

Connolly, James, *Labour and Easter Week* (Dublin, 1949). Edited by Desmond Ryan.

Crain, Maurice, *Rulers of the World* (New York, 1940).

Creel, George, *Ireland's Fight for Freedom* (New York, 1919).

Curtis, Edmund, *History of Ireland* (London, 1936).

Dalton, Charles, *With the Dublin Brigade: 1917–1921* (London, 1929).

D'Arcy, William, *The Fenian Movement in the United States* (Washington, 1947). A dissertation, Catholic University of America.

de Burca, Padraig, and Boyle, J. F., *Free State or Republic?* (Dublin, 1922).

Denieffe, Joseph, *A Personal Narrative of the Irish Republican Brotherhood* (New York, 1906).

de Valera, Eamon, *A National Policy Outlined* (Chicago, 1926).

de Valera, Eamon, *India and Ireland* (New York, 1920).

de Valera, Eamon, *Ireland's Case Against Conscription* (Dublin, 1918).

de Valera, Eamon, *Ireland's Request to the Government of the United States for Recognition as a Sovereign Independent State* (Washington, 1920).

de Valera, Eamon, *Ireland's Stand, Being a Selection of the Speeches of Eamon de Valera during the War (1939–1945)* (Dublin, 1946).

de Valera, Eamon, *Letters from Ireland and from Lincoln Jail, England, by Professor Eamon de Valera* (Philadelphia, undated). Issued by the *Irish Leader*.

de Valera, Eamon, *Recent Speeches and Broadcasts* (Dublin, 1933).

de Valera, Eamon, *The Foundation of the Republic in the Vote of the People. Results of the General Election, December, 1918* (New York, 1919).

de Valera, Eamon, *The Moral Basis of the Claim of the Republic of Ireland for Official Recognition* (New York, 1920).

de Valera, Eamon, *The Unity of Ireland* (Dublin, 1939).

Devoy, John, *Recollections of an Irish Rebel. The Fenian Movement.* (New York, 1929).

Douglas, J. G., *President de Valera and the Senate* (Dublin, 1936).

Dwane, D. T., *Early Life of Eamon de Valera* (Dublin, 1922).

Ewart, Wilfrid, *A Journey in Ireland, 1921* (London, 1922).

Figgis, M. D., *A Chronicle of Jails* (Dublin, 1917).

Figgis, M. D., *A Second Chronicle of Jails* (Dublin, 1919).

Figgis, M. D., *A Short Plot. A Sidelight on Political Expediency* (Dublin, 1918).

Figgis, M. D., *Recollections of the Irish War* (London, 1927).

Fox, R. M., *Green Banners* (London, 1930).

Fox, R. M., *James Connolly. The Forerunner* (Tralee, Ireland, 1946).

Gaffney, St. John, *Breaking the Silence* (New York, 1930).

Gibbons, John, *Ireland the New Ally* (London, 1938).

Ginnell, Laurence, *The Irish Republic. Why?* (New York, 1919).

Gonne, Maud, *Servant of the Queen* (Dublin, 1950). Author is Mme. Maud Gonne MacBride.

Gregory, A. P., *Lady Gregory's Journals 1916–1930* (New York, 1947). Edited by Lennox Robinson.

Griffith, Arthur, *Arguments for the Treaty* (Dublin, undated).

Griffith, Arthur, *The Resurrection of Hungary. A Parallel for Ireland* (Dublin, 1904).

Gunther, John, *Inside Europe* (New York, 1936).

Gwynn, D. R., *De Valera* (New York, 1933).

Gwynn, D. R., *Life of John Redmond* (London, 1932).

Gwynn, D. R., *The History of Partition: 1912–1925* (Dublin, 1950).

Gwynn, D. R., *The Irish Free State 1922–1927* (London, 1928).

Gwynn, Stephen, *John Redmond's Last Years* (London, 1919).

Gwynn, Stephen, *The History of Ireland* (London, 1924).

Hammond, J. L., *C. P. Scott* (New York, 1934).

Harrison, Henry, *Ireland and the British Empire 1937* (London, 1937).

Harrison, Henry, *Ulster and the British Empire* (London, 1939).

Healy, T. M., *Letters and Leaders of My Day* (New York, 1929), 2 vols.

Hendrick, B. J., *Life and Letters of Walter H. Page* (New York, 1926), 3 vols.

Henry, R. M., *Evolution of Sinn Fein* (Dublin, 1920).

Hobson, Bulmer, *A Short History of the Irish Volunteers* (Dublin, 1918)

Hogan, David, *Four Glorious Years* (Dublin, 1953).

Hone, J. M., *Ireland Since 1922* (London, 1932).

Hone, J. M., *W. B. Yeats* (New York, 1943).

Horgan, J. J., *Parnell to Pearse* (Dublin, 1948).

Hull, Cordell, *Memoirs of Cordell Hull* (New York, 1948).

Hyde, Douglas, *A Literary History of Ireland* (London, 1899).

Inman and International Steamship Co., Ltd., *The Inman Line* (New York, 1889).

Jones, F. P., *History of the Sinn Fein Movement and Rebellion of 1916* (New York, 1920).

Joy, Maurice, *The Irish Rebellion of 1916 and Its Martyrs, 1916* (New York, 1916).

Keith, A. B., *Governments of the British Empire* (London, 1935).

Kelly, R. S., *Ireland's Bloodless Revolution (1932–1936)* (Chicago, 1936).

Kohn, Leo, *Constitution of the Irish Free State* (London, 1932).

Lehane, Cornelius, *The Irish Republic* (Dublin, 1916).

LeRoux, L. N., *Patrick H. Pearse* (Dublin, 1932). Translated by Desmond Ryan.

Lewis, Samuel, *A Topographical Dictionary of Ireland* (London, 1837).

Lloyd George, David, *Memoirs of the Peace Conference* (New Haven, Conn., 1939), 6 vols.

Lloyd George, David, *War Memoirs* (Boston, 1933–1937), 7 vols.

Lloyd George, David, *Where Are We Going?* (New York, 1923).

Lynd, Robert, *Ireland, A Nation* (New York, 1920).

Lyons, F. S. L., *The Irish Parliamentary Party* (London, 1951).

Lyons, G. A., *Some Recollections of Griffith and His Times* (Dublin, 1923).

Macardle, Dorothy, *The Irish Republic* (Dublin, 1937).

McCartan, Patrick, *With de Valera in America* (Dublin, 1932).

MacDonagh, Michael, *Life of William O'Brien—The Irish Nationalist* (London, 1928).

MacDonald, Fergus, *The Catholic Church and the Secret Societies in the United States* (Washington, 1946).

McKenzie, F. A., *The Irish Rebellion. What Happened and Why* (London, 1916).

McManus, M. J., *Eamon de Valera* (Dublin, 1944).

McPhail, Andrew, *Three Persons* (London, 1929).

Macready, C. F. N., *Annals of an Active Life* (London, 1924), 2 vols.

Mahony, T. H., *The Monroe Doctrine. The Vital Necessity of Its Continued Maintenance* (Knights of Columbus Historical Commission, no place given, 1921).

Mansergh, Nicholas, *The Government of Northern Ireland* (London, 1936).

Mansergh, Nicholas, *The Irish Free State. Its Government and Politics* (London, 1934).

Martin, Hugh, *Insurrection in Ireland. An Englishman's Record of Fact* (London, 1921).

Midleton, W. St. J. F. B., *Records and Reactions, 1936–1939* (New York, 1939).

Mitchel, John, *Jail Journal* (London, 1913).

Moss, Warner, *Political Parties in the Irish Free State* (London, 1933).

Mulloy, Patrick, *Jackets Green* (London, 1930).

Norway, M. L., *The Sinn Fein Rebellion as I Saw It* (London, 1916).

O'Brien, Conor, *From Three Yachts* (London, 1928).

O'Brien, George, *The Four Green Fields* (Dublin, 1936).

O'Brien, William, *Evening Memories* (Dublin, 1920).

O'Brien, William, *The Irish Revolution and How It Came About* (London, 1923).

O'Connor, Batt, *With Michael Collins in the Fight for Irish Independence* (London, 1929).

O'Connor, Frank, *Death in Dublin. Michael Collins and the Irish Revolution* (New York, 1937).

O'Donoghue, Florence, *No Other Law* (Dublin, 1954).

O'Faolain, Sean, *De Valera* (Dublin, 1933).

O'Hegarty, P. S., *The Victory of Sinn Fein* (Dublin, 1924).

O'Higgins, Kevin, *Civil War and the Events which Led to It* (Dublin, 1922).

O'Malley, Earnan, *On Another Man's Wound* (Boston, 1937).

O'Rahilly, The, *The Secret History of the Irish Volunteers* (Dublin, 1915).

Pakenham, Frank, *Peace by Ordeal: the Negotiation and Signature of the Anglo-Irish Treaty, 1921* (London, 1935).

Parmiter, G. de C., *Roger Casement* (London, 1936).

Pearse, P. H., *Collected Works of Padraic H. Pearse* (Dublin, 1924), 5 vols.

Pechell, G. M., *How They Did It. Life Stories* (London, 1938).

Phillipps, Alison, *Revolution in Ireland, 1906–1923* (London, 1923).

Redmond-Howard, L. G., *Six Days of the Irish Republic, 1916* (Dublin, 1916).

Riddell, G. A., *Intimate Diary of the Peace Conference and After* (New York, 1934).

Riddell, G. A., *More Pages from My Diary 1908–1914* (London, 1934).

Riddell, G. A., *War Diary, 1914–1918* (London, 1933).

Roper, Esther, *Prison Letters of Countess Markievicz* (London, 1934). Edited by Esther Roper, preface by Eamon de Valera.

Ryan, Desmond, *Phoenix Flame* (London, 1937).

Ryan, Desmond, *Remembering Sion* (London, 1934).

Ryan, Desmond, *Unique Dictator* (London, 1936).

Salvidge, Stanley, *Salvidge of Liverpool—Behind the Political Scene, 1890–1928* (London, 1934).

Sinn Fein Scheme of Organization (to be proposed by de Valera) (Dublin, undated).

Soward, F. H., *Moulders of National Destinies* (London, 1940).

Splain, J. J., *Under Which King?* (Manchester, England, 1924).

Stephens, James, *The Insurrection in Dublin* (Dublin, 1916).

Street, C. J. C. ("I.O."), *Administration of Ireland* (London, 1921).

Street, C. J. C. ("I.O."), *Ireland in 1921* (London, 1922).

Stuart, Francis, *Men of Turmoil* (New York, 1935).

Talbot, Hayden, *Michael Collins' Own Story* (London, undated).

Walsh, P. J., *William J. Walsh, Archbishop of Dublin* (Dublin, 1928).

Wells, W. B., *The Irish Convention and Sinn Fein* (Dublin, 1918).

Wheeler, C. N., *The Irish Republic: An Analytical History of Ireland: 1914–1918* (Chicago, 1919).

White, J. R., *Misfit. An Autobiography* (London, 1930).

White, T. de V., *Kevin O'Higgins* (London, 1948).

Yeats, J. B., *Letters to His Son W. B. Yeats and Others* (London, 1944).

DOCUMENTS, ETC.

Where dates are not specified, serial publications were consulted for periods covered in text.

American Commission on Conditions in Ireland, *Evidence on Conditions in Ireland* (Washington, 1921).

Bunreacht na hEireann (Dublin, 1937).

Carty, James, *Bibliography of Irish History 1870–1911* (Dublin, 1940).

Carty, James, *Bibliography of Irish History 1912–1921* (Dublin, 1936).

Dail Eireann, *Address to the Representatives of Foreign Nations Adopted at the January Session of Dail Eireann, 1921* (London, 1921).

Dail Eireann, *Correspondence of Mr. Eamon de Valera and Others* (Dublin, 1922).

Dail Eireann, *Minutes of the Proceedings of the First Parliament of the Republic of Ireland: 1919–1921. Official Record* (Dublin, undated).

Dail Eireann, *Official Report: Debate on the Treaty between Great Britain and Ireland: December, 1921–January, 1922* (Dublin, undated).

Dail Eireann, *Parliamentary Debates: Official Report* (Dublin, Sept. 9, 1922), vol. 1 ff.

Dail Eireann, *Two Documents A and B Found by the Police on the 10th April, 1928: Proceedings of the Council of Deputies, 1926 and 1927* (Dublin, 1930).

Eire, *The Republic of Ireland Act* (Dublin, 1948).

Great Britain Parliament, *Arrangements Governing the Cessation of Active Operations in Ireland* (London, 1921), Cmd. 1534.

Great Britain Parliament, *Articles of Agreement for a Treaty between Great Britain and Ireland* (London, 1921), Cmd. 1560.

Great Britain Parliament, *Correspondence between His Majesty's Government and the Prime Minister of Northern Ireland Relating to the Proposals for an Irish Settlement* (London, 1921), Cmd. 1561.

Great Britain Parliament, *Correspondence Relating to the Land Purchase Annuties in the Irish Free State* (London, 1932), Cmd. 4116.

Great Britain Parliament, *Correspondence Relating to the Proposals of His Majesty's Government for an Irish Settlement* (London, 1921), Cmd. 1470.

Great Britain Parliament, *Correspondence Relating to the Proposals of His

Majesty's Government for an Irish Settlement (London, 1921), Cmd. 1502.

Great Britain Parliament, *Documents Relative to the Sinn Fein Movement* (London, 1921), Cmd. 1108.

Great Britain Parliament, *Evidence Taken before the Royal Commission on the Rebellion in Ireland and Appendix of Documents* (London, 1916), Cmd. 8311.

Great Britain Parliament, *Further Correspondence Relating to the Proposals of His Majesty's Government for an Irish Settlement* (London, 1921), Cmd. 1539.

Great Britain Parliament, *Papers Relating to the Intercourse between Bolshevism and Sinn Fein* (London, 1921), Cmd. 1326.

Great Britain Parliament, *Papers Relating to the Parliamentary Oath of Allegiance in the Irish Free State and the Land Purchase Annuities* (London, 1932), Cmd. 4056.

Great Britain Parliament, *Report of the Committee Appointed to Review the Provisions of the Restoration of Order in Ireland Act* (London, 1920), Cmd. 2278.

Great Britain Parliament, *Reports from Commissioners, Inspectors and Others; Education (Ireland). Royal Commission on University Education in Ireland* (London, 1902), Cmd. 1228.

Great Britain Statutes, *An Act to Recognize and Declare the Constitutional Position as to the Part of Ireland heretofore Known as Eire* (London, 1949), 12 & 13 George 6, Part II.

Great Britain Statutes, *Government of Ireland Act* (London, 1920), 10 & 11 George 5, Ch. 67.

Great Britain, War Office, *Notes on Procedure, etc., in Connection with Trials by Court-martial* (London, 1936).

Hitzen, E. J., *Scrapbooks* (Leamington Spa, England, unpublished, undated). Clippings, letters, photos based on Easter Week, 1916.

House of Commons, *Parliamentary Debates: Official Report* (London, sessional volumes).

House of Lords, *Parliamentary Debates: Official Report* (London, sessional volumes).

House of Representatives, *Hearings before the Committee on Foregin Affairs* (Washington, 1920), 66th Cong., 2nd Sess., H.R. 3404, Dec. 12–13, 1919.

Irish Year Book (Dublin, annual volumes).

National Library of Ireland, *A Chart to the Newspapers in the National Library* (Dublin, undated).

National University of Ireland, *Calendar* (Dublin, 1911).

National University of Ireland, *Handbook* (Dublin, 1932).

Pictorial Review of 1916 (Dublin, undated).

Saorstat Eireann, *Constitution of the Irish Free State, October, 1922* (Dublin, 1922).

Seanad Eireann, *Parliamentary Debates: Official Report* (Dublin, December 11, 1922), vol. 1 ff.

Sinn Fein Rebellion Handbook—Easter: 1916 (Dublin, 1917). Published by *Weekly Irish Times*.

Souvenir of Public Funeral of O'Donovan Rossa to Glasnevin Cemetery (Dublin, August 1st, 1915).

The Truth about the Army Crisis: Official (Dublin, 1923). Foreword by Liam Tobin.

Thom's Irish Who's Who (Dublin, annual volumes).

United States Congress, *Congressional Record* (Washington, sessional volumes).

NEWSPAPERS AND PERIODICALS

Where dates are not specified, publications were consulted throughout periods covered in text.

An Poblacht (Dublin, 1925–1929).

An tOglach. Official Organ of the Irish Volunteers (Dublin, 1918–1922).

Atlantic Monthly (Boston, Feb., 1923), vol. 123, no. 2. Ollivant, Alfred, "The Shears of Destiny—a Memory of Erskine Childers."

Banba (Dublin, 1921–1922).

Boston Sunday Post (Boston, Aug. 18, 1946). Article on the de Valera family.

Christian Science Monitor (Boston, May 15, 1918). Interview with de Valera.

Clare Champion (Clare, Ireland, Aug. 18, 1923). Article on de Valera's arrest.

Commonweal (New York, Feb. 18, 1938), vol. 27, pp. 455–457. Millson, E. C., "My Cousin Eamon de Valera."

Cork Examiner (Cork, Ireland, Aug. 1, 1922). Aiken's letter on civil war.

Daily Telegraph (London, Nov. 23, 1922). Lloyd George, David, "The Irish Treaty— How It Was Signed."

Daily Telegraph (London, March 29, 1932). Article by Austen Chamberlain on how the Treaty was negotiated.

Detroit News (Detroit, Oct. 28, 1928). Jones, E. de W., Article on interview with de Valera.

Dublin Magazine (Dublin, April, July, October, 1936). O'Hegarty, P. S., "Bibliographies of 1916 and the Irish Revolution."

Eire (Place of publication not given, 1923–1924).

Enniscorthy Echo (Enniscorthy, Ireland, Jan. 4, 1930). Recollections about Griffith.

Evening Herald (Dublin, Dec. 10, 1936). De Valera's interview with Sean Russell.

Freeman's Journal (Dublin, July 13, 1917). Article on de Valera's election.

Freeman's Journal (Dublin, Jan. 2 and 5, 1922). Articles on de Valera's position.

Freeman's Journal (Dublin, March 23, 1922). De Valera's correspondence.

Freeman's Journal (Dublin, Feb. 17, 1923). Article on de Valera's peace proposal.

Gaelic American (New York, Feb. 14, 21; March 13, 20, 27, 1920). De Valera's Cuban proposal.

Gaelic American (New York, Jan. 2, 1915). Ua Rathghaille (The O'Rahilly), "The History of the Irish Volunteer Organization Told by Its Treasurer."

Irish Bulletin (Dublin, 1919–1921).

Irish Independent (Dublin).

Irish Independent (Dublin, April 24, 1916). MacNeill's cancellation order.

Irish Independent (Dublin, Aug. 15, 1922). Report on private session of Dail Eireann held on Dec. 16, 1921.

Irish Independent (Dublin, April 9, 1923). Captured documents.

Irish Press (Dublin).

Irish Press (Dublin, Jan 28, 1932). Brennan, Robert, "Irish Memories of Dartmoor."

Irish Press (Dublin, Dec. 14, 1936). De Valera, Sinead, "Give the Children a Chance."

Irish Press (Dublin, May 3, 1932). Doyle, Seumas, Article on Pearse's death.

Irish Press (Dublin, June 27, 1953–July 18, 1953). Williams, Desmond, A series of articles on Irish neutrality in World War II.

Irish Press (Dublin, Nov. 27 and Dec. 6, 1922). Childers' last statement.

Irish Times (Dublin, Dec. 6, 1941). Milroy, Sean, Article on Treaty in retrospect.

Irish Volunteer (Dublin, 1914–1916).

Limerick Chronicle (Limerick, Ireland, May 25, 1915). Whitsunday Volunteers' parade.

Limerick Chronicle (Limerick, Ireland, June–July, 1917). Election campaign in Clare.

London Gazette (London, July 21, 1916). Despatches from field on Easter rebellion.

Manchester Evening News (Manchester, England, Sept. 11, 1922). Exclusive interview with de Valera.

Manchester Guardian (Manchester, England).

Nash's Magazine (London, Feb., 1924), vol. 72, pp. 12–14, 96. Churchill, W. S., "The Irish Treaty."

Nation (New York, June 7, 1919), vol. 108, no. 2814, p. 90. De Valera, Eamon, "Ireland's Right to Independence."

New York American (New York, Feb.–April, 1922). Series of articles by Collins on underground war.

New York Herald (New York, Jan. 19, 1884). Article reporting arrival in United States of Juan de Valera.

New York Times (New York).

New York Times (New York, May 24, 1931). Papal encyclical, *Quadragesimo Anno*.

News Letter of the National Bureau (Washington, 1919–1921). Issued by Friends of Irish Freedom.

Parish Weekly (Church of the Blessed Sacrament, Rochester, N.Y., Oct. 11, 18, 1942), vol. 9, nos. 24, 25. Articles on Mrs. Wheelwright by her priest.

Poblacht na hEireann—War News (Place of publication not given, June 29, 1922–Feb. 2, 1923).

Rochester Democrat and Chronicle (Rochester, N.Y., March 9, 1948). Article on Mrs. Wheelwright.

Rochester Journal American (Rochester, N.Y., April 22, 1932). Interview with Mrs. Wheelwright.

Rochester Journal American (Rochester, N.Y., June 15, 1932). Article about Mrs. Wheelwright.

Rochester Times Union (Rochester, N.Y., June 13, 1932). Article on Mrs. Wheelwright.

Rochester Times Union (Rochester, N.Y., June 29, 1932). Article on Mrs. Wheelwright.

Sinn Fein (Dublin, 1923–1925).

Sinn Feiner (New York, 1920–1921).

Tablet (Brooklyn, N.Y., June 6, 1891), vol. 77, pp. 897–905. Papal encyclical, *Rerum Novarum*.

The Times (London, Aug. 15, 1921). Smuts' correspondence.

The Times (London, April 5, 1948). Statement of E. J. Hitzen on 1916 rebellion.

Times Pictorial (Dublin, May 3, 1952–July 19, 1952). Fox, R. M., "Jim Larkin—Tornado of the Tenements."

Weekly Irish Times (Dublin).

Weekly Summary (Dublin, Sept. 17, 1920; Dec. 17, 1920; Jan. 17, 1921; Jan. 20, 1921; Feb. 4, 1921). Articles on de Valera.

Westminster Gazette (London, Feb. 7, 1920). Exclusive interview with de Valera on Cuban analogy.

INDEX

De Valera, Sinead—contd.
upon, 57; at Greystones, 80, 81, 86, 97; rumours concerning, 99; in U.S., 99; interrogated by Press, 106; rearing of children, 107; home searched, 178; inquiries about husband, 205; letter of, 208; visits prison, 209; Irish language, 210; gift for, 212; home life, 227, 241; interest in language, 251; sacrifice of, 259; writes Irish stories, 280; at "Teach Cuilinn", 288
De Valera, Terry, 174, 210, 227, 251, 280, 288
De Valera, Vivion (father of Eamon), 15–17, 32, 35
De Valera, Vivion (son of Eamon), 32, 65, 86, 178, 180, 182, 204–6, 209, 227, 251, 252, 266, 274, 279, 288, 289
Devolution: mentioned by de Valera, 113; as alternative to partition, 129; proposal for completed, 132; solution for partition, 262
Devonshire, 60
Devoy, John, 43, 44, 85, 90, 92, 93, 99, 100–2, 104
Dictatorship, 135, 190, 216, 246, 248, 257, 258
Dillon, James M., 257, 275, 277, 284, 286, 289, 293, 299
Dillon, John, 59, 74, 79, 82, 257
Document Number 1, 151, 152
Document Number 2, 151, 152, 155
Dominic, Father, 178
Dominican Convent, 27
Dominion status, for Ireland, 117, 121, 122, 124, 131, 138, 141, 147, 148, 255
Donamore Castle, 243
Donegal, 39, 217
Douglas, James, 200, 237
Dowling, Joseph, 76
Down, 39, 82, 112, 137, 212, 213
Downpatrick, Co. Down, 39
Doyle, Paddy, 53
Draft Treaty A, 129, 131–3, 137, 139, 151
Dublin, locations in: Adelaide Road, 201; Ailesbury Road, 191, 231; Bachelor's Walk, 37; Blackhall Place, 47; Blackhall Street, 34; Bolton Street, 28; Camden Row, 47; Church Street, 57; Claremont Road, 188; College Green, 205, 234, 271, 274; Coombe, the, 33; Croke Park, 104; Cross Avenue, 228, 251, 279, 288; Dawson Street, 45, 74; Donnybrook, 31, 36, 40, 41, 47, 269; Earlsfort Terrace, 51, 155; Fitzwilliam Square, 86, 288; Gardener Place, 64; Grafton Street, 146, 175; Great Brunswick Street, 49–51; Harcourt Street,

Dublin, locations in—contd.
73, 77; Herbert Park, 115; Kenilworth Square, 118, 140; Kildare Street, 35, 43, 193, 221; Kimmage Road, 47; Lower Mount Street, 52, 54; Mercer's Street, 175; Merrion Square, 53, 160, 226; Morehampton Terrace, 31, 35, 56; Mount Street, 108; Mount Street Bridge, 52, 53; Nassau Street, 64; North Wall, 52; O'Connell Bridge, 107, 162; O'Connell Street, 34, 50, 176, 177, 219, 272; Parkgate Street, 206; Parnell Square, 29, 251; Pearse Street, 226; Pembroke (district), 44; Phoenix Park, 19, 47, 242, 252, 273; St. Stephen's Green, 27, 52, 73, 195; Sandymount, 188, 195, 205, 209, 221; Serpentine Avenue, 221; Shelbourne Hotel, 117, 218; Smithfield, 167; Suffolk Street, 165, 174, 186, 188, 191, 192, 211, 219; Westland Row, 51, 53, 64; Westmoreland Street, 66
Dublin Bay, 23
Dublin Brigade, 38, 42–4, 49, 50, 66, 136, 159, 175–7, 187
Dublin Castle, 21, 56, 76, 77, 111, 266, 276, 285, 286
Duffy, George Gavan, 127, 129, 131, 136, 137, 147, 148, 160, 193, 199, 273
Duggan, Eamon J., 127, 129, 141, 144, 193
Duke, Henry E., 61, 69, 77
Dun Laoghaire, Co. Dublin, 202, 228. (See also Kingstown)
Dunboden House, 215
Dunne, Reginald, 173
Dwane, David, 111, 174, 178

Early Life of Eamon de Valera, The, 174
Easter (1916) rising: decided on by I.R.B., 43; date set, 46; instructions to Volunteers, 48; takes place in Dublin, 50 ff.; surrender, 54; public censure, 57; de Valera's doubts about, 65; Proclamation pointed to, 67; Ashe's part in, 83; Childers on, 112; de Valera's binoculars, 264
Easter Week. (See Easter rising)
Economic Co-operation Administration, 295, 296
Economic war: onset of, 240; opposition to, 241; de Valera on, 242; results from, 244; problem of, 247; not settled, 250, 260, 262; settled, 264, 265, 281
Edward VIII, King, 254, 255
Eire, 257, 260, 261, 263, 265, 272, 276, 277, 280, 283, 286
Electoral register, Irish, 82

Galway, 30, 31, 76, 143, 280
General elections: (1918), 81, 82; (1921), 113; (1922), 160, 164, 169, 194; (1923), 201; (1927), 219–21, 224; (1932), 234, 235; (1933), 236, 244, 247; (1937), 260; (1938), 265, 266; (1943), 281; (1944), 281; (1948), 290, 291; (1951), 295, 296
General Post Office, Dublin, 52, 53, 219, 279
Geneva, Switzerland, 244, 252, 261, 274
George V, King, 117, 118, 121, 193, 223, 254
George VI, King, 255, 256, 271, 297
George, David Lloyd. (*See* Lloyd George, David)
German aircraft, 275
German air raid, 278
German arms, 76, 233
German captain, of the *Aud*, 49
German diplomatic personnel, 275
German Foreign Office, 48
German hands, 277
German help, 49, 274
German High Command, 275
German intrigues, 76, 276
German invasion, 275, 279
German Legation, 275
German Minister, 273
German offensive, 79
German officer, 275
German parachutist, 275
German "plot", 77, 79, 87
German representatives, 283
German submarine, 76, 276
German-Irish: treaty, 48; collaboration, 76, 77; collusion, 82
Germans, 55, 76, 277, 278, 283, 285
Germany, 36, 37, 43, 48, 49, 73, 75, 76, 78, 79, 81, 93, 94, 243, 272, 275, 277, 283, 300
Gilmore (brothers), 233, 236, 243
Glasnevin Cemetery, 44, 45, 183, 188, 222, 252, 278
"Glenvar", 108, 117
Gloucester Jail, 79, 84
Goertz, Hermann, 275, 285
Gogarty, Oliver St. J., 237, 240, 241
Goraghwood, Co. Armagh, 230
Government, the Irish. (*See* Cabinet, Irish)
Government of Ireland Act, 111, 112, 132, 140, 232
Government Buildings, 238, 247, 249, 269, 275, 279, 296
Governor-General of Ireland, 151, 193, 235, 242, 244, 255, 258
Granard, Earl of, 237
Granville Hotel, Dublin, 177
Gray, David, 273, 281, 283

Greenwood, Hamar, 111, 113, 131, 149
Gresham Hotel, Dublin, 176
Grey, Earl, 249
Greystones, 61, 65, 77, 79, 86, 89, 97, 130, 154, 174, 178, 188
Griffith, Arthur: nationalist author, 25; de Valera on, 28; Sinn Fein president, 33; leaves I.R.B., 38; favours de Valera as Sinn Fein head, 71, 72; at conscription conference, 74, 75; interned, 78, 79; on de Valera, 86; out of I.R.B., 87; Minister for Home Affairs, 88; de Valera on, 92; as deputy-President, 93, 100; imprisoned, 103, 105; on arms surrender, 108; letter from Collins, 109; elected, 114; set free; 118, at truce conference, 119; to London, 120; on reply to Lloyd George, 123; as Vice-President and Minister of Foreign Affairs, 124; London assignment, 126, 127, 129; statement, 130; estimate of, in London, 131; corresponds with de Valera, 132; on Crown as head of association, 133; meets privately with British, 136; final phases, negotiations, 137; presents British proposals to Irish Cabinet, 140 ff.; to seek adjustments, 143; summoned home, 147; favours Irish adoption of terms, 148; Churchill on, 149; at Treaty debates, 150 ff.; de Valera on, 152, 157; elected as President, 158; promises new Constitution, 159; at Sinn Fein *Ard Fheis*, 160; on women's franchise, 164; in Dail, statements, 168; election panel, 171; on Wilson's death, 174; on Republicans' laying down arms, 177; illness and death, 180, 183; de Valera on, 182, 186, 194; letters of, 212; anniversary of death, 245; position of, in 1921, 262
Guinness family, 237

HACKETSTOWN, Co. Carlow, 186
Halifax, Lord, 263, 270, 271
Hamilton, William Rowan, 62
Hamman Hotel, Dublin, 177
Harbours, Irish. (*See* Ports)
Harding, W. G., 101, 105
Harold's Grange, Co. Dublin, 46
Healy, Timothy M., 74, 75, 80, 83, 127, 165, 166, 193
Hebrides, 292
Helga, 52, 57
Hempel, Edward, 273–5, 284
Hermitage, the, 29, 45
Hewart, Gordon, 131
Hibernians. (*See* Ancient Order of)
High Court, Irish, 273